BRITANNIA MILL

MA

UNIVERSITY OF DERBY
Discarded
LEARNING CENTRE

DL 3018772 9

FOCUS ON SCIENCE

THE FOCUS ON SCIENCE SERIES:

Exploring the Natural World
Exploring the Physical World
(Elementary titles in preparation)

UNIVERSITY OF DERBY
Discarded
LEARNING CENTRE

507

FOCUS ON SCIENCE

UNIVERSITY OF DERBY
Discarded
LEARNING CENTRE

Exploring the Natural World

by

Douglas Gough and Frank J. Flanagan

D.C. HEATH CANADA LTD.

1980

£5.50

DERBYSHIRE COLLEGE
OF HIGHER EDUCATION
LIBRARY
UNIVERSITY OF DERBY
Acc. N Discarded
LEARNING CENTRE
500   Gou

© Copyright 1980 D.C. Heath Canada Ltd.

All rights reserved. No part of this publication may
be reproduced or transmitted in any form or by any
means, electronic or mechanical, including photocopy,
recording, or any information storage or retrieval
system, without permission in writing from the publisher.

The metric usage in this text has been reviewed by
the Metric Screening Office of the Canadian Government
Specifications Board.

ISBN 0669-00843-5   Printed in Canada   2 3 4 5 6 7 8 9 10

The publisher wishes to thank Al Teliatnik for his
assistance in the preparation of the manuscript.

Authors' acknowledgements: The authors wish to thank everyone who
helped with the development of this text, including: Tom Fairley and Bob
Grundy, the editors, for their attention to detail; Helen Wasilishin, for her
careful typing; Peter Van Gulik for his clear drawings; Bob Macnaughton
for his photographs; students Joanne Armeni, Michael Keenan, Anne
Massie, Charmaine Peterson, Gerry Schnur, and Deborah Yezerinac of St.
Aidan School, who appear in some of the photographs; Rachel Atlas, Susan
Crowdy, and Steve Mills of D. C. Heath, who pushed the project along;
John Zehethofer, the designer of the book; and the many reviewers for their
helpful comments. Doug Gough would especially like to thank his wife
Louise and his son Steven for their constant encouragement and patience
during the preparation of the text. Frank Flanagan expresses the same
thanks to his wife Ann and children Lynne and Paul.

Photographs and other illustrations, on the pages indicated, were supplied by: Atmospheric
Environment Services (337, 347, 348, 349); Abitibi Paper Company (87); Allyn and Bacon,
Inc. (195, re-illustrated with permission, from EXPLORING EARTH SCIENCE by Walter A.
Thurber, Robert E. Kilburn, & Peter S. Howell — © Copyright 1976 by Allyn and Bacon,
Inc.); Arcana Productions, R. Burch (cover, 26(l), 39(l), 66, 178(botttom)); Dougal Bichan
(4(bottom l), 26(r), 106, 131, 135, 173, 179); California Institute of Technology (275); Dr. W.A.
Crich (2, 4(top l), 53(top & bottom l), 90, 146, 154, 155, 180); Federation of Ontario
Naturalists (58(top), 64(top & bottom l), 67(r), 88, 96, 119, 122, 128, 169, 191, 295, 325); GAF
Corporation (153); Doug Gough (168, 170, 184); Jimages, Jim Ford (49, 178(top), 200, 286,
290, 311, 314, 316(bottom), 327, 331); Lund Observatory (235); Bob Macnaughton (5, 6, 9, 16,
31, 72, 101, 102, 109, 115, 116, 125, 126, 127, 166, 194, 324, 339, 340, 343, 344); Bob Macnaughton — courtesy Royal Ontario Museum, Department of Minerology (188, 192(e), 196,
198(a & c), 207 (r), 218, 221 (bottom), 225(a,b,c)); Larry Miller (30, 39(r), 64(bottom r));
NASA (240, 247, 253, 255, 257, 259, 260); Miller Services (352); National Museums of Canada
(67(l), 157); Jack Newton (230); Ontario Hydro (209, 354); Ontario Ministry of Energy
(208(bottom)); Ontario Ministry of Environment (89); Ontario Ministry of Industry & Tourism
(3(bottom), 62); Ontario Ministry of Natural Resources, Ontario Geological Survey (192(a),
208(top), 215(l)); Ottawa River Solar Observatory, Herzberg Institute of Astrophysics,
National Research Council of Canada(265); Andy Phillips (53(bottom r), 64(top r), 74(bottom), 171, 293, 316(top), 320); Photo Trends (3(top), 138, 163); Melvyn Rosengarden (70,
177); Royal Ontario Museum(207(l), 211(d,e,f,g,h,i)); Science Museum, London (7); Smithsonian Institution Photo #1115 (4); Paul Sterling (64(centre), 74(top)); University of Toronto,
Department of Astronomy(245, 268, 269, 277, 280, 281); Ward's Natural Science Establish-
ment (58(bottom), 186, 192(b,c,d,f,g), 198(b), 205, 206, 211(a,b,c), 213, 215(r), 221(a,b,c),
222, 223, 225(d), 227.

Contents

Exploring the Natural World

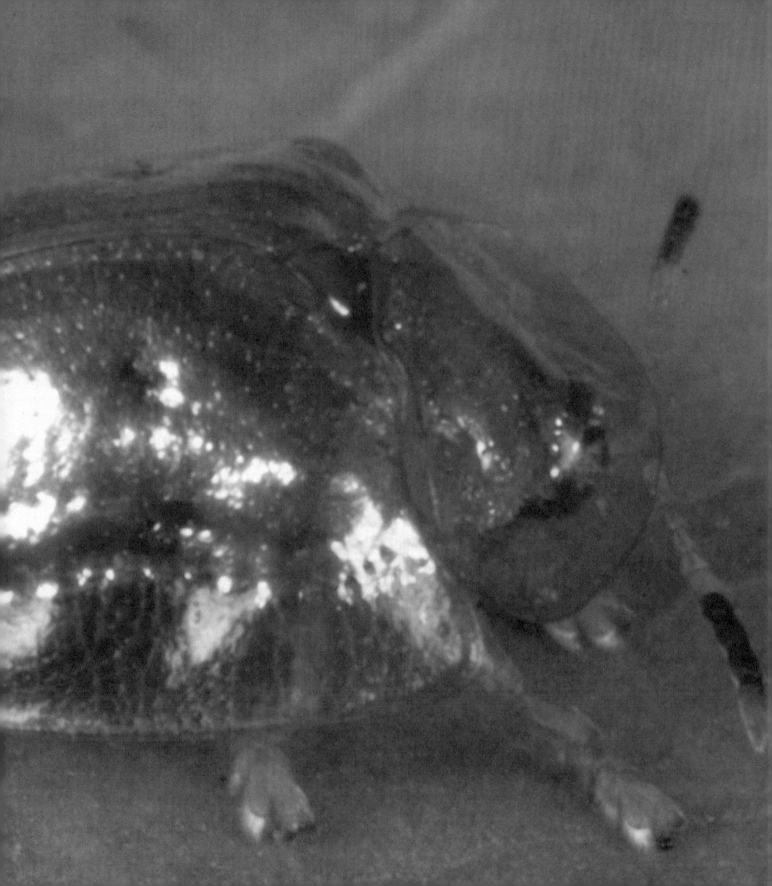

MATLOCK COLLEGE LIBRARY

THE CHARACTERISTICS OF LIVING THINGS

Living things are called organisms. Organisms may differ in shape, colour, and size, but they are all able to perform characteristic activities, or functions. Their ability to do these things is proof that they are alive. If a frog does not perform its characteristic life functions, it is dead.

A rock does not perform functions of any kind. Rocks consist of non-living, or inorganic, material. Some rocks contain fossils, which are traces of long-dead organisms. Fossils are described as organic material, because they are derived from organisms.

A frog, whether living or dead, is considered an organism. It is able, or at one time was able, to perform the functions of life. These functions include metabolism, growth, reproduction, adaptation, irritability, movement, and locomotion.

Variety in living things

Each different kind of living thing forms a species. There are more than 1 300 000 species of organisms on Earth. Of these, about 1 000 000 are animals and nearly 300 000 are plants. There are some 20 000 others that are called protists.

These frogs are alive.

Rocks are non-living.

A tortoise beetle

Douglas fir trees (top), a young killer whale (bottom), and a model of a blue whale at the Smithsonian Institution (right)

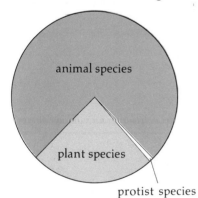

Proportions of animal, plant, and protist species

As for size, organisms range all the way from protists, which can only be seen with the help of a microscope, to certain animals and plants that are so big they cannot be taken in at a glance unless they are far away. The Douglas fir tree, found in British Columbia, can reach a height of 100 m. The blue whale sometimes grows to a length of 30 m and a mass of more than 125 000 kg.

Organisms that live in water are called aquatic. Organisms that inhabit land are called terrestrial. There are many living things such as frogs and ducks, that may be found in both of these environments. A walk through a garden will quickly demonstrate that organisms occur in almost every imaginable colour. Organisms are found in a great variety of shapes and sizes. The overall appearance of an organism suggests its structure, or form.

MATERIALS

pen or pencil
paper

PROCEDURE

1. Look around you in the classroom for specimens of different kinds of living things.
2. Use pictures and books to help you find more examples of living things.
3. Record the names of 10 kinds of living things, as widely varied as possible.
4. For each living thing, write three observations, describing its size, its colour, and its shape.

OBSERVATIONS

1. Complete the work called for in steps 3 and 4 of the procedure. Share your selections with your classmates.
2. (a) Divide the organisms you noted in step 3 into two groups.
   (b) Give each of these groups its appropriate name.

QUESTIONS

1. What characteristics are shared by all the organisms you observed?
2. What organism was most often chosen by your classmates?

INVESTIGATION: To find living things in the school yard
and observe how they differ from each other

MATERIALS

pen or pencil
paper
clipboard (if available)

1. Go to the school yard and look for living things.
2. Record the names of the different kinds of living things that you see there.
3. For each type of organism, record the colour, shape, and approximate size.

OBSERVATIONS

1. Complete the work described in steps 2 and 3.
2. Compile a table classifying the organisms you saw into two groups. Give each group its proper title.

QUESTIONS

1. (a) What colour did you observe most often in the organisms you saw?
   (b) Suggest a reason for the variety of colour displayed by living things.
2. What was the most plentiful organism you saw?
3. What was the largest organism you saw? The smallest?
4. What was the most unexpected organism you saw?

Hooke's "cells"

Organisms can be very different from each other, but they all have one thing in common. The basic similarity of all living creatures is that they are all made of one or more small building blocks called cells.

It was in 1665 that an Englishman, Robert Hooke (1635-1703), first used the word cell – to describe little box-like shapes that he observed when looking at thin slices of cork through his primitive microscope. The first living cells were seen by Anton van Leeuwenhoek (1632-1723), a Dutchman, as he looked at some one-celled organisms called protozoans.

In 1838 and 1839, two German scientists, M.J. Schleiden (1804-1881) and Theodor Schwann (1810-1882), proposed a theory of cells. They described cells as both the simplest form of life and the building blocks of all living things. They also suggested that all cells come from previously existing cells.

The microscope

Cells are so small that they can only be viewed with a microscope. Microscopes came into use at the beginning of the

17th century. Leeuwenhoek made his observations with an instrument he designed himself. It had one lens and was essentially the same as a magnifying glass.

Hooke used a microscope with a lens at each end of a tube – a compound microscope much like those still in use.

In the 1930s, scientists in Germany and Canada assembled electron microscopes which permitted much greater magnification. Electron microscopes have 10 000 times the strength of microscopes that use light.

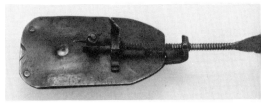

Leeuwenhoek's microscope

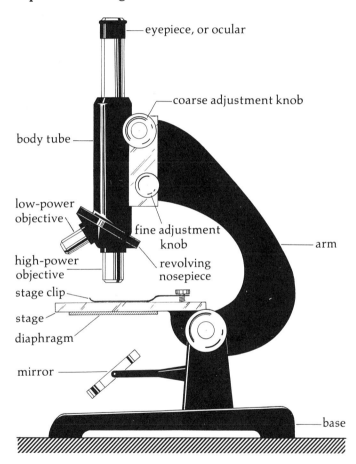

Robert Hooke's compound microscope

An electron microscope

The care of the microscope

The microscope is an important tool of science. It should always be used with care and patience. Some points to remember:

1. Always keep the microscope in an upright position.

2. To carry it, use both hands – one grasping the arm, the other supporting the base.
3. Always cover it with a dust cover when it is not in use.
4. Always leave the low-power objective in position when the microscope is not in use.
5. The lenses are made of optical glass, which is soft and scratches easily. Clean them by blowing away any dust or dirt, and then by breathing on them and wiping them carefully. For wiping, use only lens paper, and rub lightly in one direction only – not back and forth.

INVESTIGATION: To learn how a microscope is used

MATERIALS

compound microscope
prepared slide

PROCEDURE

1. Place the microscope directly in front of you.
2. Make sure that the low-power (shortest) objective lens is in line with the tube. If it is not in place, turn the revolving nosepiece until it clicks into place.
3. Lower the objective by turning the coarse adjustment knob until the lens is about 0.5 cm (the thickness of a pencil) above the stage.
4. Look into the eyepiece and adjust the mirror, or diaphragm, until the field of view appears bright.
5. Place a slide on the stage and centre the part of it that is to be examined under the objective.
6. Looking through the eyepiece, slowly raise the tube (using the coarse adjustment knob) until you see the object.
7. Use the fine adjustment knob to obtain the clearest possible image of the object.
8. Adjust the diaphragm to get the greatest amount of light.
9. Slowly move the slide on the stage, noting what happens to the image when you do so.
10. Search the slide for an interesting part and move that part to the exact centre of the field of view.
11. Adjust the focus, to make the image clear.

12. Swing the next higher-power objective into position and obtain a sharp focus with the fine adjustment knob. If you are not successful immediately, return to the lower-power objective and repeat the procedure.
13. Adjust the diaphragm to get the greatest amount of light.

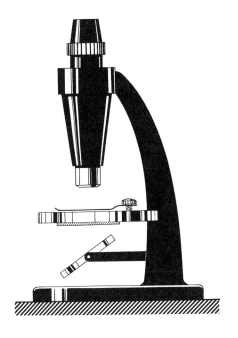

OBSERVATIONS

For good results with a microscope, the light, the focus, and the positioning of the object are important. Make brief notes covering what controls the amount of light, how to control the focus, and where to place the specimen.

QUESTIONS

1. Why must a microscope be carried in an upright position, with two hands?
2. Why must it be stored in its dust cover?
3. How is a microscope cleaned?
4. Why must special lens paper be used?
5. How can you tell whether the objective is in the correct position?
6. How close to the stage should the objective be before you look in the eyepiece?
7. Where is the slide placed?

Some microscopes have only one objective, fixed in position at the bottom of the body tube. This type of microscope is focused by turning the body tube slowly. This raises or lowers the tube. The procedure for adjusting the light and placing the slide is similar to the procedure for the compound microscope.

Some schools have binocular microscopes. These are compound microscopes with two eyepieces. The procedure for using them is the same as for an ordinary compound microscope.

Cells

All organisms are composed of cells. Protists, such as protozoans, are organisms that have only one cell. Organisms that are multicellular may be either plants or animals. Cells vary considerably, but they all have similar internal parts,

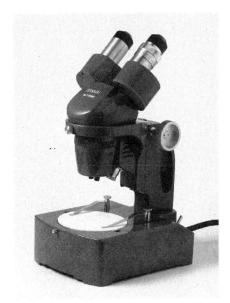

A binocular microscope

A typical animal cell

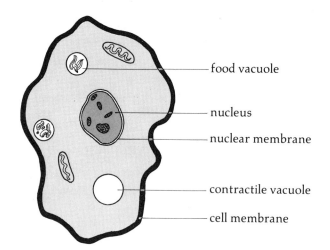

food vacuole

nucleus

nuclear membrane

contractile vacuole

cell membrane

called organelles. All cells are surrounded by a membrane that encloses a cytoplasm and a nucleus.

Examine the diagrams of typical cells. The nucleus is the organelle that appears dark. It is the control centre of the cell and is surrounded by a nuclear membrane. The nucleus contains genetic information that determines the characteristics of the living organism.

A typical plant cell

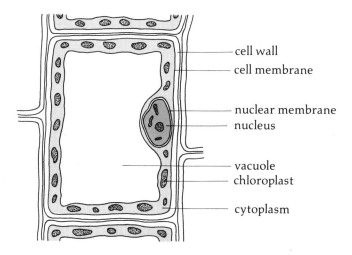

cell wall

cell membrane

nuclear membrane

nucleus

vacuole

chloroplast

cytoplasm

The internal parts of a cell, apart from the nucleus, are called the cytoplasm. It carries out the functions of the cell as instructed by the nucleus. It differs physically, chemically, and structurally from cell to cell, depending on the function of the cell. Nerve cells whose function it is to carry messages differ from muscle cells whose function it is to contract.

In the cytoplasm, microscopic examination reveals organelles that resemble bubbles. These are vacuoles, and there are two kinds of them. Food vacuoles contain food particles and are used to digest, or break up, food. Contractile vacuoles may appear to be empty, but they are used to collect and get rid of excess water and gases.

Another important organelle is the chloroplast, which is found only in certain plant cells. It contains chlorophyll, the green chemical pigment that is necessary for photosynthesis (the process by which plants make their own food) and provides the colour in green plants.

The membrane is an important part of the cell. It keeps the contents of the cell (cytoplasm and nucleus) together and controls the flow of materials in and out of the cell. It is selective: it will allow only certain amounts of certain dissolved substances, such as simple sugars, to enter the cell, and keeps all others out.

Plant cells have not only a cell membrane but also a cell wall outside the membrane. Unlike animal cells, plant cells have a double border. The cell wall has no control over the passage of materials in and out. Its function is to provide stiffness and so give strength and support to the plant cell, and to the plant.

INVESTIGATION: To examine some plant cells

MATERIALS

microscope
slide and cover-slip
tweezers
piece of elodea or onion
eye-dropper

PROCEDURE

1. With the tweezers, carefully remove the epidermis (thin transparent skin) of the elodea, or the inner epidermal skin of a section of onion.
2. Unroll the epidermis so that it is flat, and place it in the middle of a clean slide.
3. Add a drop of water to the tissue on the slide.

4. Using the tweezers, place one edge of the cover-slip on the slide and slowly lower the rest of it. This method will lessen the chance of air bubbles between the slide and the cover-slip.
5. Observe the specimen with the microscope. Use the low-power objective first. Be sure to keep the stage of the microscope level, because what you are viewing is a wet-mount slide.

OBSERVATIONS

1. Write a description of what you saw in step 5, mentioning the shape of the cells, whether they were all the same size, the location of the cytoplasm, and the appearance of the nucleus and chloroplast.
2. Find a good example of a plant cell and make a sketch of it. Label the parts that you can identify.

QUESTIONS

1. How many nuclei are there in a cell?
2. What is the space in the centre of the cell called?
3. What is the function of the cell wall?
4. How is a cell arranged in relation to its neighbours?

Now that you have examined a plant cell, it will be interesting to examine one of your own cells, and then compare the two. This will, of course, be an example of an animal cell.

INVESTIGATION: To examine a cell from your cheek

MATERIALS
microscope
slide
cover-slip
tweezers
methylene blue stain

PROCEDURE

1. Using the blunt end of the tweezers or the flat end of a toothpick, scrape the inside of your cheek lightly.

2. Mix the scraping with a drop of water in the centre of a clean slide.
3. Place a cover-slip on the sample.
4. Place a small drop of methylene blue stain on one edge of the cover-slip. If you put a blotter at the opposite edge of the cover-slip, the stain will be pulled towards the sample.
5. Observe the slide with the low-power objective; then look for organelles with the high-power objective.

OBSERVATIONS
1. Note the shape of the cells, and the part of them that is most darkly stained.
2. Draw and label a diagram of a single cell.

QUESTIONS
1. Did you see a cell wall? Explain your answer.
2. Did you see any chloroplasts? Explain .
3. Describe how the cytoplasm was arranged.

Protists

You have used a microscope to observe and compare plant and animal cells. Now you will observe some examples of protists. Observation of these one-celled organisms may present a problem, because most of them are highly mobile.

INVESTIGATION: To find protists in pond water

MATERIALS
microscope
slides
cover-slip
tweezers
eye-dropper
pond water

PROCEDURE
1. With the eye-dropper, place a drop of pond water on a clean slide and apply a cover-slip.

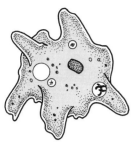

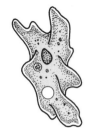

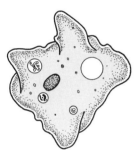

The amoeba can exist in a great variety of shapes.

2. Observe the slide, and be sure to keep the stage of the microscope level.
3. If you fail to find protists anywhere on the slide, prepare a new slide with another sample of pond water, and look again.

OBSERVATIONS

1. Draw sketches of three different protists that you observed.
2. Describe the shapes and sizes of the protists you observed, and any unusual structures that were attached to the cell membrane.
3. Note whether the protists you saw had any characteristics of plant cells or animal cells.

QUESTION

Why do you think scientists classify the protists in a group separate from plants and animals?

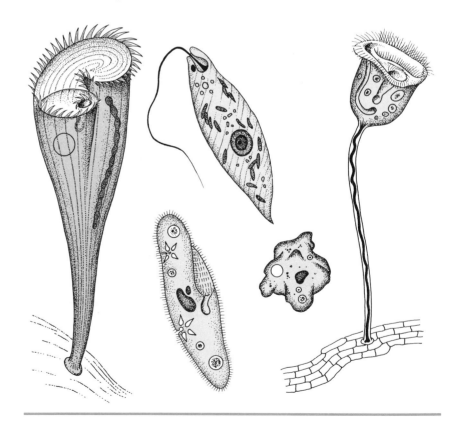

Some common types of protists

The functions of life

You will recall that all living things carry out functions that distinguish them from non-living matter. These functions include metabolism, growth, reproduction, adaptation, irritability, movement, and locomotion.

Metabolism

"Metabolism" is used to describe physical and chemical processes that are concerned with obtaining energy, storing it, and supplying it to the cells of an organism. The metabolic processes include respiration, ingestion, digestion, and excretion.

Respiration is the process of taking in oxygen for the cells. Organisms have various mechanisms for extracting oxygen from air or water. These mechanisms include:

(a) the cell membranes of protists
(b) the external and internal gills of tadpoles and fish
(c) the book lungs of crustaceans
(d) the tracheae of insects
(e) the lungs of terrestrial animals

Once oxygen has been obtained by an organism and transported to the cells, the process of respiration can occur. It involves the combining of oxygen with food to release energy. The energy comes from the chemical energy stored in food.

The process of respiration not only releases energy but also produces carbon dioxide and water. The organism must remove these products from the cells. It does so by a process called excretion, which will be described later.

Thus, when respiration occurs in an organism, the cells release energy from food and carry out an exchange of gases, using oxygen and releasing carbon dioxide.

INVESTIGATION: To observe how strenuous exercise affects your rate of respiration

---

MATERIALS

clock or watch with a second hand

1. Measure the number of times you breathe in 1 min while sitting at your desk.
2. Run quickly on the spot beside your desk, or do sit-ups, for 1 min.
3. Measure your breathing rate again.
4. Sit quietly at your desk for 5 min and then measure your breathing rate again.

OBSERVATIONS

Record and compare your breathing rates from steps 1, 3, 4.

QUESTIONS

1. Why was the rate increased by the exercise?
2. What was your body trying to do, by increasing your breathing rate?
3. Why did your breathing rate go back to normal when you had rested for a time?
4. How did the changes in your rate of breathing compare with those of other students in the class?

The rate of breathing of an organism is controlled by the amount of carbon dioxide gas in the system. As the level of carbon dioxide increases, the rate of breathing increases, to bring the amount of carbon dioxide down to the normal level. A person who is doing strenuous exercise needs more energy, and to supply it the respiration process speeds up. The person then breathes more rapidly in order to get rid of the extra carbon dioxide in the system.

Food

Neither metabolism nor respiration can occur unless food is present. So it is a continuous task of each living organism to supply its cells with food.

Plants that have chloroplasts are able to make their own food (sugar). They use the energy of the sun to combine water and carbon dioxide. This process is called photosynthesis, and it produces sugar and oxygen. The oxygen that is released is essential for the respiration of organisms.

Organisms that are able to make their own food are called autotrophs. Organisms that do not have chloroplasts and are not able to make their own food must obtain it from their environment. They are called heterotrophs, and they have the ability to obtain their food from their surroundings.

Once an organism has found some food, it must transfer the food into its body, and eventually to its cells. The initial taking in of food is called ingestion. Most multicellular organisms have a cavity or passageway through which the food is directed. In this passageway, the process of breaking up the food starts. This process is called digestion. The food particles are then transferred to the cells, where the final stages of digestion occur.

In one-celled organisms, the process of ingestion is different. The paramecium, for example, has a special structure called an oral groove. Food is directed by the movement of the organism into the opening of this groove. Upon entering the cytoplasm, the food becomes enclosed in a food vacuole in which digestion occurs.

Heat is a form of energy, and the release of heat by a living organism indicates that metabolism is occurring. Your metabolism produces enough heat to keep your body temperature at about 37°C all the time you are in good health.

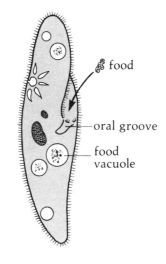

This is how a paramecium eats.

Excretion

The metabolic processes of an organism produce waste products, such as carbon dioxide and water. The carbon dioxide will poison and kill an organism if it is not removed. Water is important to the cells, and a certain amount of it must be retained. If too much water is lost, dehydration occurs, and the organism may die. The process of removing the waste products is called excretion.

Protists collect their waste products in vacuoles, which move to the membrane of the cell and release the wastes through it. Plants have openings called stomata on the lower surfaces of their leaves, to release excess moisture. Insects release excess carbon dioxide and water through their spiracles, which are small holes in the sides of their bodies. Animals remove carbon dioxide by exhaling. Excess water and mineral salts are removed by perspiration and urination. Some water is also released in exhaled breath, as may be shown by blowing on a mirror.

INVESTIGATION: To demonstrate the excretion of carbon dioxide

MATERIALS

yeast in sugar water
test tube
beaker

yeast in sugar water

PROCEDURE

1. Completely fill a test tube with the yeast and sugar water.
2. Put some water in the beaker and invert the test tube in it, so that the opening of the test tube is submerged (see illustration).
3. Observe what forms in the test tube and collects at the top of it.
4. Remove the test tube to allow the remaining liquid to flow out, and quickly insert a flaming splint.
5. Feel the test tube and note any change in temperature.

OBSERVATIONS

Record everything you observed in steps 3, 4, and 5.

QUESTIONS

1. What metabolic process was occurring in the test tube?
2. What product was collected by the test tube?
3. What other product must have been produced?

Growth

The energy that is produced by metabolism in the cells of an organism may be used for growth. Growth may occur in two ways: the cell may increase in size, or more cells may be produced. A cell may make proteins to add to its membrane and other proteins for its other organelles. This results in more cytoplasm and an increase in the size of the cell.

When cells grow by producing more cells, one cell divides

and produces two cells. This cell division, or cell reproduction, is called mitosis. After mitosis, the new cells are just like the ones they came from. That is, blood cells produce blood cells and nerve cells produce nerve cells. Cell reproduction is a continuing process. It enables an organism to repair damaged cells, replace worn out cells, and produce new cells for growth.

INVESTIGATION: To determine how growth occurs

Growth is usually a slow process, and this investigation requires observation over a period of days.

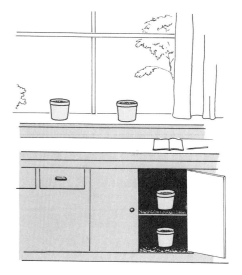

MATERIALS

4 flower pots
36 bean seeds

PROCEDURE

1. Soak half the seeds in water for a couple of hours.
2. Plant half of the soaked seeds in one pot and the other half in another pot. Use just enough earth to cover the seeds.
3. Plant half of the remaining seeds in each of the remaining pots.
4. Water the four pots equally, until the soil is thoroughly dampened.
5. Place one pot containing pre-soaked seeds and one containing unsoaked seeds on a window ledge. Place the other pots in a dark cupboard.

OBSERVATIONS

1. Observe the pots once a day. Measure and record the growth of the seedlings.
2. Note which seeds grow best.

QUESTIONS

1. Why did some of the seeds not grow?
2. Why were you told to plant four pots?
3. What is happening when a seedling is growing?

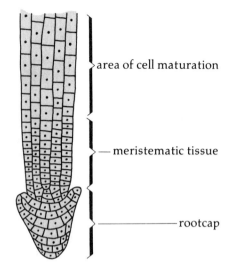

The areas of growth in a root tip

The growth of plant roots makes an interesting study. Examine an onion root tip and note that there are definite areas where growth occurs. The root cap is a region of protective cells. Next to it is the "meristematic" tissue. (Tissue is a collection of similar cells.) The meristematic cells are cells in a state of mitosis: they are dividing to produce more cells. Farther up the root is the area of cell maturation, where individual cells are growing, becoming larger and longer. Thus, both types of cell growth occur in an onion root tip.

Reproduction

Reproduction is an essential function of life, because each organism lives for only a certain length of time. Some organisms have very short life spans. Certain insects live for only a few hours and others live for just a few days. Some organisms live for hundreds of years – for example, the redwood, sequoia, and Douglas fir trees.

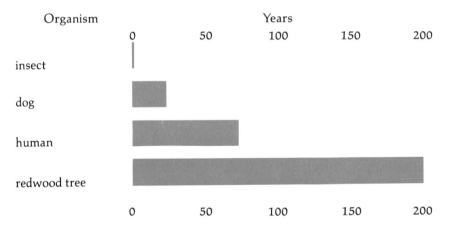

At some time during its life, each organism produces new organisms. This ensures that the species will continue. If organisms of a species do not succeed in reproducing, that species will become extinct.

There are two types of reproduction – asexual and sexual. When a new organism develops from a part of another organism, what has occurred is asexual reproduction. This happens when a piece of a geranium stem or an African violet leaf is placed in water or damp soil. Roots appear and a new plant starts to grow. A new organism has been produced from

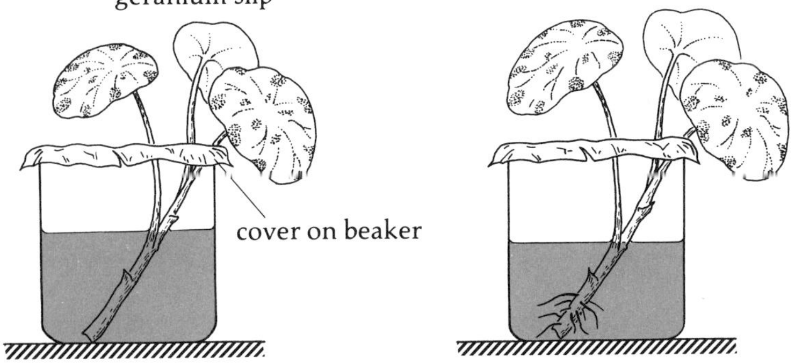

geranium slip

cover on beaker

Vegetative reproduction by a geranium stem

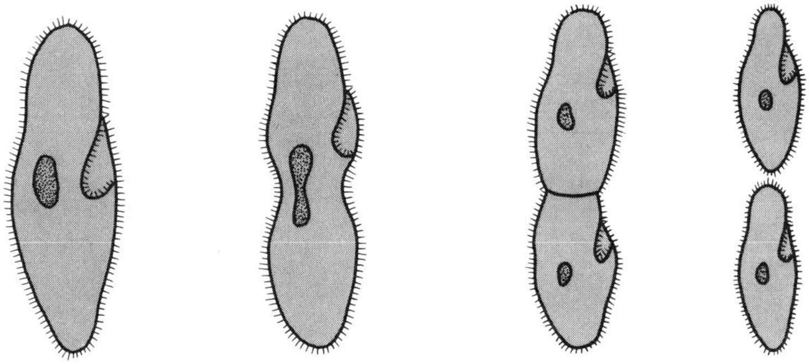

Kinds of asexual reproduction in protists

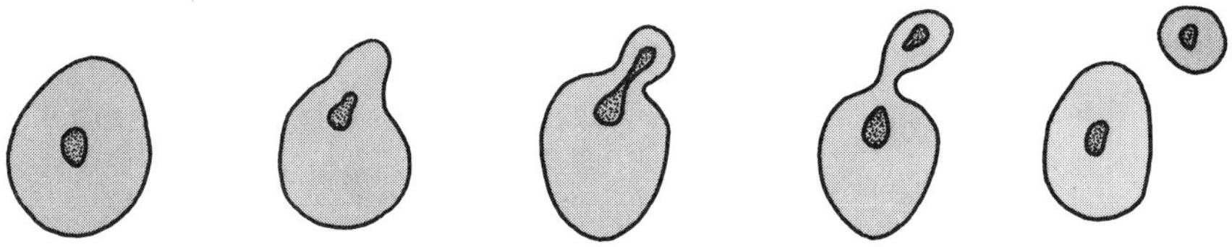

a part of another organism, by what is called vegetative reproduction.

There are other kinds of asexual reproduction. There is fission, which is what occurs when an organism divides itself into two new organisms, and budding, which is the reproductive process used by yeast.

INVESTIGATION: To observe how yeast reproduces

Yeast is a one-celled organism that reproduces rather quickly under ideal conditions.

microscope
slide
cover-slip
yeast culture in sugar water
eye-dropper

1. Prepare a slide of the culture and place it on the stage of the microscope for viewing.
2. Locate a number of cells with the low-power objective and then switch to the high-power objective.
3. Observe the cells for 20 to 30 min.

Keep a record of what you observe in step 3, noting the size of the individual cells and the activity on the outer boundary of each cell.

In sexual reproduction, two parent organisms produce off-spring. Each parent supplies half of the genetic material for the offspring, so that some of the characteristics of each parent are passed on to the offspring. Sexual reproduction occurs with seed-producing plants, worms, arthropods, and vertebrates.

Some simple organisms are able to reproduce both sexually and asexually, but most kinds of organisms use only one method. There is more information on this topic in the section dealing with life cycles.

Movement and locomotion

Another characteristic of living organisms is their ability to exhibit movement and/or locomotion. "Movement", as the word is used here, means a change in the shape of an organism or a motion within an organism. "Locomotion" implies a change in the position of an organism. When a dog stands still and wags its tail, it is exhibiting movement; when it runs after a ball, it is exhibiting locomotion. Both of these activities require energy.

Individual cells exhibit movement for the simple reason that the liquid-like cytoplasm is never at rest. This is called cytoplasmic streaming and it may be observed in protists, such as the amoeba, the paramecium, and the euglena, with a microscope with 400 × magnification. A plant turning its leaves and flowers towards the sun is another example of movement.

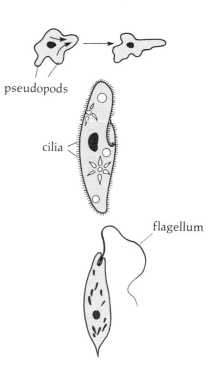

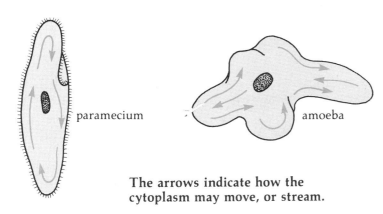

The arrows indicate how the cytoplasm may move, or stream.

Special structures for locomotion in protists

Locomotion occurs when an organism moves from one place to another. Most plants are firmly rooted in one place and therefore do not exhibit locomotion. But they are autotrophs and are able to produce their own food. It is the heterotrophs that must search for food and thus need to be able to move around.

Protists demonstrate various methods of locomotion. The amoeba has the finger-like projections called pseudopods. When it extends these projections, the cytoplasm flows into them. The paramecium has hair-like projections on its body, called cilia. These are extensions of the cytoplasm, and they are able to vibrate and cause the organism to move. Another group of protists, including the euglena, have one or more long whip-like projections called flagella – again, extensions of the cytoplasm that permit locomotion.

Most animals have special cells called muscle cells whose job it is to produce locomotion. In worms and snakes, muscle contraction enables the organism to move. Other animals have special body parts designed for movement. These parts are controlled by muscles and can cause different types of locomotion depending on the environment in which the animal lives.

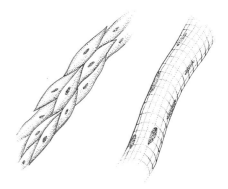

Types of muscle cells

Copy the chart into your notebook and complete it.

ANIMAL	ENVIRONMENT	SPECIAL BODY PART FOR MOVEMENT	TYPE OF LOCOMOTION
Fish	Water	Fins	Swimming
Bird			
Grasshopper			
Frog			
Horse			
Monkey			
Caterpillar			
Human			

External factors may also result in movement and locomotion by organisms. Wind is capable of producing movement in plants, and water may carry insects downstream, thus causing locomotion.

Irritability

The ability of organisms to respond to stimuli from the environment is called irritability. This is another characteristic of living things. It is more common with animals than with plants because of animals' ability to exhibit locomotion. But response to stimuli may be demonstrated with protists and plants as well.

INVESTIGATION: To determine how a paramecium responds to table salt and vinegar

---

grain of salt

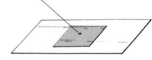

thread with vinegar

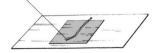

MATERIALS

microscope	vinegar
slides and cover-slip	thread
table salt	paramecium

PROCEDURE

Part A
1. Prepare a slide with a drop of paramecium culture.
2. Add a grain of table salt to the culture.
3. Add a cover-slip and observe.

Part B

1. Prepare another slide with culture.
2. Dip a short piece of thread in the vinegar and place it across the drop of culture.
3. Add a cover-slip and observe.

OBSERVATIONS

Record what the paramecium did in each part of the investigation.

QUESTIONS

1. What was the stimulus in Part A? In Part B?
2. What evidence was there that the paramecium could sense the stimulus?
3. Why did the paramecium respond the way it did?
4. Is a paramecium able to display irritability?

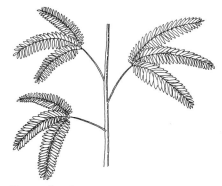

Normal mimosa

Plants are able to respond to the stimulus of light by turning their leaves and flowers towards the sunlight. Why do you suppose plants do this? In the absence of sunlight, many flowers will close their petals. The mimosa plant reacts to being touched by closing its leaves and drooping.

Living things are continually receiving stimuli from their environment. They react favourably to some stimuli. A source of food is a common positive stimulus. But many stimuli are in some way unpleasant and organisms react by avoiding them. An organism tends to continue to respond in the same way to a repeated stimulus. Once a response has been learned, it becomes part of the organism's behaviour. This is explained more fully in the section dealing with adaptation and behaviour. An ability to be sensitive to changes in the environment helps organisms to survive.

Adaptation

Why is the polar bear found only in the arctic regions? Why do kangaroos live only in Australia? Why are house flies found in most parts of the world? In each case, it is a matter of an organism being adapted to a certain kind of environment.

What factors determine the adaptability of living things?

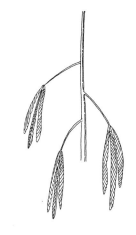

Mimosa after being touched

Polar bears live naturally in the arctic regions.

Kangaroos live naturally in Australia.

Probably the most important factor is the availability of food. If an organism finds suitable food in sufficient quantities in a certain region, it is more likely to be able to survive there. When two or more types of living things that need the same food inhabit the same region, competition will occur. Then, the fastest, or strongest, or smartest will survive. Predation is another factor. It occurs when one organism is the prey of another organism.

The availability of water and light and the temperature range also affect an organism's ability to survive in a certain region. Plants require a certain amount of water and light, and temperatures within a certain range, in order to survive. If the conditions are not suitable, they become dormant. They commonly go through dormant stages as seeds or spores and resume an active life when the proper conditions return. Grain seeds still capable of growing were found in the pyramids of Egypt, where they had been placed thousands of years before.

When animals are faced with intolerable factors in the region where they are living, they may either hibernate or migrate. Hibernation is a state of dormancy that some reptiles, amphibians, and mammals enter in the winter time. Hibernation occurs when food is not abundant. The animal's metabolism is greatly reduced and the body temperature drops. The need for food decreases because of the animal's inactivity. The animal remains alive by using food stored in its body.

Migration is the seasonal movement of living things away from undesirable conditions to areas where the conditions are more favourable. Migration occurs when the food supply diminishes, when water becomes scarce, or when the temperature becomes too hot or too cold.

Each spring, the caribou migrate northwards into the tundra because they can find an abundance of ground vegetation there. But every autumn they return to forests at the southern edge of the tundra, seeking protection from the weather. The annual migration of birds such as the Canada goose and the snowy owl have been observed and studied for many years.

So the presence or absence of a certain organism in a certain region depends on its ability to adapt itself to conditions in that region. The important factors include food, water, light, and temperature. The adaptation of living things is described more fully in the sections on the interdependence of living things and on adaptation and behaviour.

REVIEW QUESTIONS

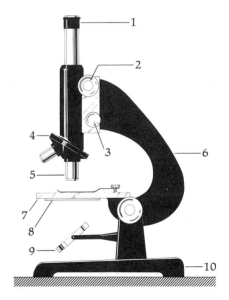

1. Explain how organisms differ from non-living matter.
2. Is a bean seed a living thing? Explain your answer.
3. Name the three groups into which scientists divide all living things.
4. Explain the difference between a simple microscope and a compound microscope.
5. Examine the diagram of a microscope and answer these questions.
   (a) What type of microscope is it?
   (b) Name each numbered part.
   (c) What are the functions of the parts numbered 2, 3, 4, 8, and 9?
6. Explain how to clean a microscope.
7. Explain the difference between animal cells and plant cells.
8. Mushrooms are plants. Why are they not green?
9. What are the purposes of metabolism?
10. (a) How do autotrophs get energy?
    (b) Where do heterotrophs get energy?
11. How do cells exhibit growth?
12. Why is reproduction necessary?
13. Name the two types of reproduction and explain the difference between them.

14. (a) Do all organisms exhibit movement?
    (b) Are all organisms capable of locomotion? Explain your answers.
15. Is movement essential to life?
16. What special structures do protists have for locomotion?
17. (a) What causes a living thing to exhibit irritability?
    (b) Describe some ways in which organisms show irritability.
18. List the environmental factors that determine the distribution of organisms.
19. What might happen to an organism that is insensitive to its environment?
20. Describe the processes by which plants and animals adapt to environmental change.
21. Choose one plant or animal, and describe how it has adapted itself to its environment.

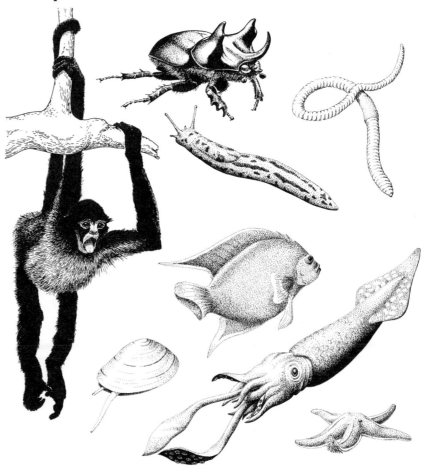

IMPORTANT TERMS

organism—a living thing

species—all the members of each well defined group of organisms that differ only in small ways and are capable of breeding with each other

cell—the simplest form of life and the building material of all living things

nucleus—the control centre inside a cell

cytoplasm—the internal parts of a cell, apart from the nucleus

organelles—the various internal parts of a cell. The nucleus is one kind of organelle

chloroplast—a type of organelle found in plant cells, containing the green chemical called chlorophyll

respiration—the process of combining oxygen with food to produce energy

excretion—the process of removing the waste products from an organism

photosynthesis—the food-making process that takes place in the chloroplasts of plant cells

mitosis—the process of cell division, or cell reproduction

tissue—a collection of similar cells

asexual reproduction—the production of a new organism by a single parent organism

sexual reproduction—the production of a new organism by two parent organisms

movement—activity that causes a change in the shape of an organism

locomotion—activity that causes a change in the position of an organism

irritability—the ability of an organism to respond to changes in its environment

hibernation—a resting stage that occurs annually with certain organisms

migration—movement of an organism, usually seasonal, to a more favourable region or climate

THE CLASSIFICATION OF LIVING THINGS

When you go to the library for a book on a certain subject – trees, say – you can find out from the card catalogue where to look, among the thousands of books that are there. Or you can look for a sign that says "Science" or "Plants" and steer yourself to the right section. Imagine what it would be like if the books were jumbled and you had to look through them all to find the one you want! Librarians arrange books in groups, by subjects. They do this to make each book easy to find. Whenever objects are grouped in a planned way, they are said to be classified.

Examine the picture carefully. "A collection of buttons" describes accurately what you see. But if you do some sorting you will be able to give a better description. You can arrange the buttons in groups according to size. When you do that, you are classifying them in a certain way. Then you are on the way to a fuller description. Apart from their size, the buttons have other characteristics by which they can be grouped. For example, they are of various colours and they have varying numbers of holes. You can make an even better description of the collection by using that information, too.

A collection of buttons

MATERIALS

collection of coloured cardboard pieces like the ones illustrated

PROCEDURE

1. Choose a method of sorting the pieces.
2. Write an accurate description of the collection, using your
   chosen method of sorting the pieces.

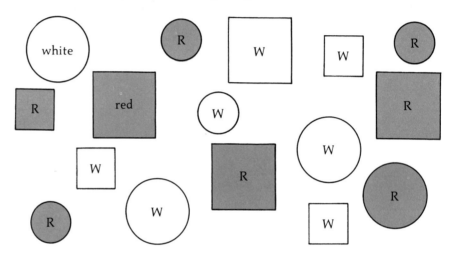

QUESTIONS

1. Name one other method of sorting, apart from the one you
   chose.
2. (a) How many circles are there in the collection?
   (b) How many squares are there?
3. (a) How many of the pieces are white?
   (b) How many are red?
4. (a) How many of the pieces are large?
   (b) How many are small?
5. List all the characteristics by which the pieces can be
   classified.

Classification is a process of sorting to permit easier understanding. You can see this, from the examples of books, buttons, and cardboard pieces. Classification is a process of arranging related objects or facts in logical groups. Objects are related to one another when they share one characteristic or more. From the examples that have been used, you can see that there are often several different ways in which collections of objects can be classified.

Two ways of classifying

After studying the collection of cardboard pieces, you had three kinds of information about the pieces. You had information about their size (large or small), their shape (round or square), and their colour (red or white). Each piece had one or the other of each of these three pairs of characteristics. All of this information can be put down in the form of a tree diagram.

In this example, each of the 16 objects (pieces of cardboard) has the same three distinguishing characteristics: colour, shape,

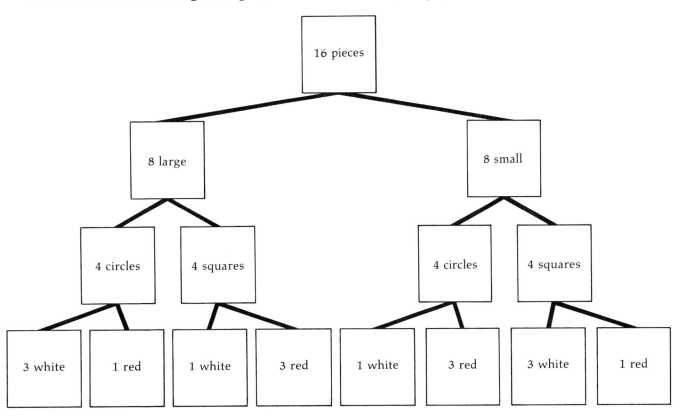

and size. So the 16 pieces can be sorted into groups in three different ways – according to colour, shape, or size. Whenever all the objects being studied display all of the kinds of characteristics that are being considered, it is possible to summarize the information in what is called a cross-classification table. Here is such a table for the 16 cardboard pieces.

		WHITE	RED
Circles	Large	3	1
	Small	1	3
Squares	Large	1	3
	Small	3	1

Now, examine the following list.

baseball
bowling
fishing
gymnastics
hockey
jogging
volleyball
wrestling

A tree diagram can be used to classify these eight activities. The first box, at the top of the diagram, will include all the activities. Below that, the activities may be subdivided into smaller and smaller groups according to their most obvious characteristics. Each group at every level must be clearly defined, so that anyone using the same system would group the activities in the same way. One way of classifying the eight activities in a tree diagram is illustrated.

Notice that the eight activities do not all exhibit all the characteristics that are being considered. For example, none of the sports listed is a "recreational team sport". Therefore, a cross-classification table is not a suitable way of classifying the activities.

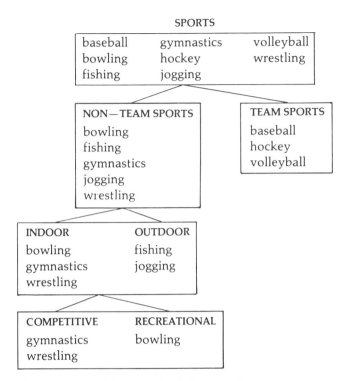

SPORTS

baseball	gymnastics	volleyball
bowling	hockey	wrestling
fishing	jogging	

NON—TEAM SPORTS

bowling
fishing
gymnastics
jogging
wrestling

TEAM SPORTS

baseball
hockey
volleyball

INDOOR

bowling
gymnastics
wrestling

OUTDOOR

fishing
jogging

COMPETITIVE

gymnastics
wrestling

RECREATIONAL

bowling

(Suggest a possible way of subdividing the team sports.)

INVESTIGATION: To make a cross-classification table for a collection of cardboard pieces

MATERIALS

green and blue cardboard pieces of these shapes and sizes

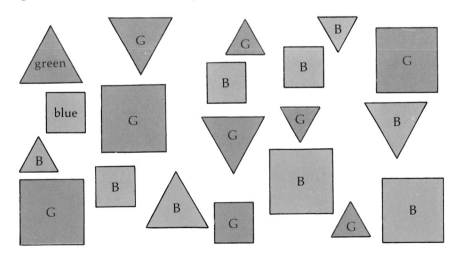

1. Examine the collection and count the pieces.
2. Decide what are the distinguishing characteristics of all the pieces.
3. Draw a tree diagram for the pieces.
4. Devise a cross-classification table for the pieces.

OBSERVATIONS
1. Write down the information from steps 1 and 2 of the procedure.
2. Complete the tree diagram and the cross-classification table.
3. Compare your results with those of others in the class.

QUESTIONS
1. Why is it that your tree diagram may differ from another student's tree diagram?
2. (a) What would be the effect of adding a third colour to the collection?
   (b) How could you deal with the problem this would present?

Classifying familiar things

It is necessary to examine thoroughly the objects and organisms in the next investigation. Look for similarities that may help you to arrange them in meaningful groups, and to divide the main groups into smaller groups, the way you did with sports activities.

MATERIALS

common objects and organisms, such as those illustrated

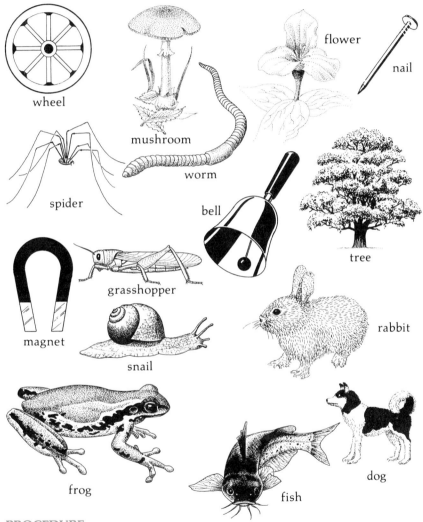

wheel

mushroom

flower

nail

worm

spider

bell

tree

magnet

grasshopper

snail

rabbit

frog

fish

dog

PROCEDURE

1. Examine carefully each item in the collection.
2. Classify the items as living or non-living.
3. Divide the living group between plants and animals.
4. Subdivide the plants between green ones and non-green ones.

5. Subdivide the animals between those with appendages (arms, legs, fins, etc.) and those without appendages.
6. Subdivide the animals with appendages between those with four appendages or fewer, and those with more than four.

OBSERVATIONS

1. Write down the lists called for by steps 2, 3, 4, 5, and 6.
2. Using the lists, make a tree diagram.

QUESTIONS

1. Suggest a possible way to subdivide the non-living group.
2. Explain why a cross-classification table cannot be made for this collection.

Man's first classifications of plants and animals probably grouped them according to their usefulness as a source of food or clothing, or both. Aristotle (384-322 B.C.), a Greek philosopher and scientist, divided organisms between plants and animals. He divided plants into three groups: trees, shrubs, and herbs. Animals he subdivided according to where they lived: on land, in the sea, or in the air.

It was an English botanist, John Ray (1627-1705), who decided that organisms should be named as well as classified. He referred to organisms with the same characteristics and the same kind of parents as belonging to the same species. In the last part of the 17th century, Ray described and named over 18 000 species of plants.

Classifying living things

The name taxonomy has been given to the scientific classification of living things. The greatest contribution to taxonomy came from a Swedish botanist, Carolus Linnaeus (1707-78). He decided that organisms should be grouped according to similarities in bodily structure. He also gave each species of living thing a name – in Latin, so that it would be equally acceptable to scientists of all languages.

Linnaeus divided all species of living things into two categories, which he called kingdoms. The plant kingdom and animal kingdom were the two categories. He subdivided each kingdom into groups of species according to similarities in bodily structure. Each subdivision of each kingdom he called a phylum. Linnaeus continued to subdivide every new group, sorting species first by general characteristics and then by more specific ones. Each time a group was subdivided, a new taxonomic level was created and given a name. There are seven taxonomic levels, called kingdom, phylum, class, order, family, genus, and species.

Each species is made up of all the organisms in the world that are fundamentally similar to one another (though not identical in detail) and can breed with each other and produce offspring which, in turn, can breed.

Consider the common house cat *(Felis domesticus)*. All house cats, whatever their colour and size, belong to the species *domesticus* of the genus *Felis*. The genus is a broader group of organisms, made up usually of two or more species. Members of species of the same genus are alike in structure, but only in certain ways. The lion *(Felis leo)* is much larger than the house cat, but otherwise similar. You can tell from its name that it belongs to the same genus as the house cat but forms a distinct species. Your library will have information about other members of the genus *Felis*.

Since the time of Linnaeus, scientists have continued to use his methods to classify organisms. However, his system has

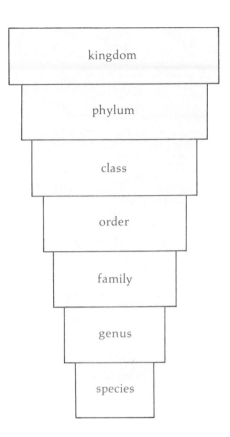

Felis domesticus — a cat

Felis leo — a lion

had to be altered from time to time in the light of new discoveries. For example, instead of his two kingdoms, three are now recognized: the plant kingdom, the animal kingdom, and the protist kingdom of one-celled organisms. Approximately 1 500 000 species of living things have been classified and each year a few thousand more are added, mainly plants, protists, and insects.

Animal classification

Members of the kingdom Animalia are all multicellular organisms composed of animal cells, as opposed to plant cells. There are over 1 000 000 species of animals. When you set out to classify an animal, examine its characteristics carefully, looking for answers to each of the following questions.

1. Does it have a backbone?
2. Does it have a skeleton? If so, is the skeleton internal or external?
3. Is its body segmented?
4. Does it have legs? If so, how many?
5. Does it have wings? If so, how many?
6. What type of body covering does it have?

INVESTIGATION: To classify an assortment of animals

MATERIALS

magnifying glass
specimens (living or preserved) of the animals shown on page 42

PROCEDURE

1. Divide the organisms into two groups — those with backbones and those without backbones. (*Hint:* Five of the organisms have backbones.)
2. Divide the non-backboned group into two sub-groups – organisms with legs and organisms without legs. Note that some of the organisms have very small legs.
3. Subdivide the non-backboned, no-legs sub-group further, using such characteristics as the presence or absence of segmentation or a shell.

4. Divide the non-backboned, with-legs sub-group into smaller groups according to the number of legs present.

1. Write down the lists called for by steps 1, 2, 3, and 4.
2. Copy this tree diagram into your notebook. Fill in the names, using the information you gathered in the investigation.

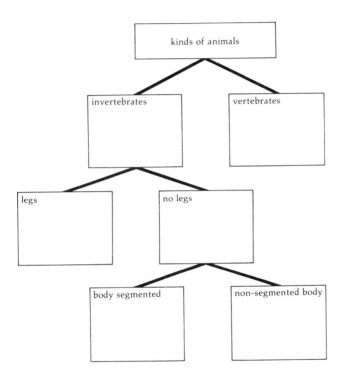

QUESTIONS

1. Describe the main differences between the five species that have backbones.
2. (a) How many of the specimens you viewed had no backbone?
   (b) Did those non-backboned specimens have legs?
3. (a) Name one other organism that uses each of the four methods of locomotion you observed in this investigation.
   (b) Name the organism that uses each of those four methods.

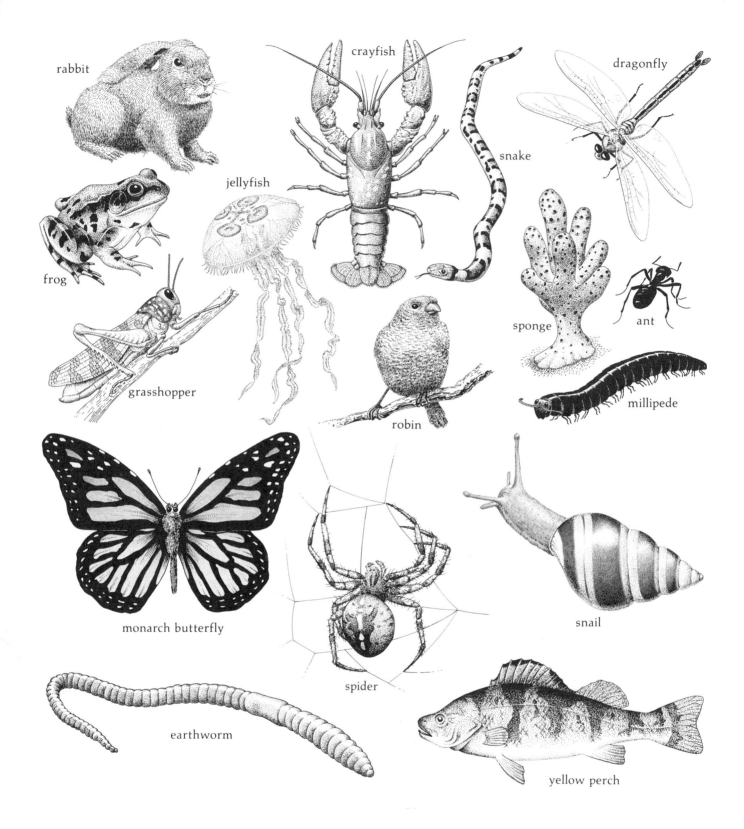

rabbit

crayfish

snake

dragonfly

frog

jellyfish

grasshopper

robin

sponge

ant

millipede

monarch butterfly

spider

snail

earthworm

yellow perch

Invertebrates

Invertebrates are animals that lack an internal skeleton and thus have no backbone. Invertebrates are of many different kinds. They are found in most parts of the world and in most types of environment. Some of the common groups of invertebrates are described in this section.

Protozoans. Protozoans are microscopic one-celled organisms that belong to the kingdom Protista. They sometimes live in colonies but each organism consists of just one cell. There are many different kinds of them. They live in water and are so small that they can only be observed with a microscope.

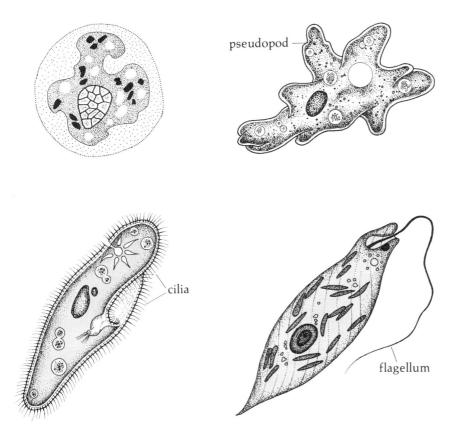

Plasmodium (top left), paramecium (bottom left), amoeba (top right), and euglena (bottom right)

Sponges. Sponges are classified in the phylum Porifera. They have external openings, or pores, that are connected to internal channels. Most species take in water through the channels and remove food such as plankton from the water by a filter-feeding method. There are about 5000 species of sponges.

A jellyfish (top), a sea anemone
(centre), and a bath sponge
(bottom)

Jellyfish. Jellyfish, coral, and sea anemones are members of the phylum Coelenterata, which has about 9600 species. These organisms have a sac-like digestive cavity with an opening that acts as a mouth. Most of them live in the ocean, but some species are found in fresh water.

Worms. The 30 000 species of worms are grouped into three phyla: Platyhelminthes, Aschelminthes, and Annelids. Platyhelminthes are often called flatworms because all of the worms in this phylum have flat bodies. Many, like the tapeworm, are parasitic and depend on other creatures for shelter and nourishment.

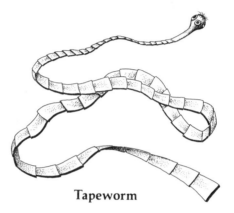

Tapeworm

Aschelminthes, or roundworms, have long, tube-shaped bodies that are usually smooth. They may be found in the ocean, in fresh water, and on land. Many are parasites living on various types of organisms, including humans.

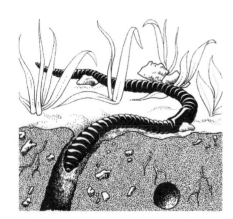

Earthworm

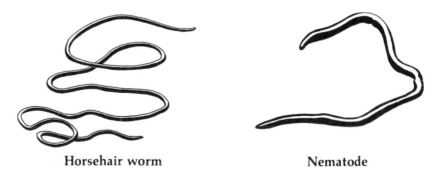

Horsehair worm   Nematode

Annelids are sometimes called segmented worms because their bodies are divided into segments. Earthworms and leeches are the most familiar members of this phylum.

Mollusks. Mollusks are soft-bodied animals that belong to the phylum Mollusca. About 100 000 species have been identified. There are many ocean species of mollusks, but also many that live in fresh water or on land. Most mollusks have shells. Snails have one coiled shell and are called univalves. Clams have two hinged shells and are called bivalves. Mollusks such as the octopus and squid appear to have no shell but actually do have one, in the form of plates within the body.

Arthropods. The phylum Arthropoda has about 1 000 000 species. They include such animals as the spider, the millipede, the centipede, the lobster, the crayfish, the shrimp, and all the insects. Arthropods inhabit all regions of the earth, and they comprise approximately 80% of the species of the animal kingdom.

Although they vary widely in appearance, all arthropods share certain characteristics. All have a tough outside skeleton, or exoskeleton, made of a material called chitin. All species have bodies divided into distinct sections, and all have legs with definite joints.

The phylum Arthropoda is divided into a number of classes. Four major ones are the crustaceans, myriapods, arachnids, and insects. Crustaceans, such as the lobster and crab, live in water and have hard exoskeletons. Myriapods, such as centipedes and millipedes, have many legs. Arachnids, such as

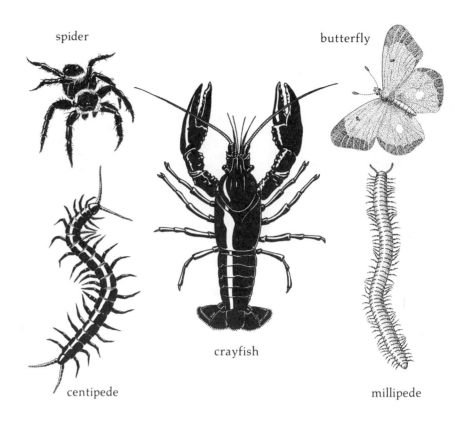

spider

butterfly

crayfish

centipede

millipede

spiders, usually have eight legs and often spin webs. The insects all have six legs and three-part bodies.

Many of the arthropods, particularly the insects, have interesting life cycles. Some of these are described in another part of this book.

INVESTIGATION: **To examine some common arthropods**

MATERIALS

magnifying glass
tweezers
live or preserved specimens of
a spider, a crayfish, and a
grasshopper

PROCEDURE

1. Using the magnifying glass, carefully examine each specimen, in turn.

2. As you examine each specimen, look for:
   (a) body sections (how many?)
   (b) legs (how many?)
   (c) eyes (how many?)
   (d) antennae (how many?)
   (e) special features

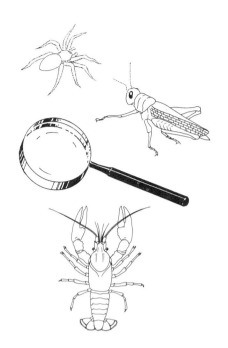

OBSERVATIONS

Copy this chart into your notebook and fill in the spaces.

CHARACTERISTIC	GRASSHOPPER	CRAYFISH	SPIDER
Number of body sections			
Number of legs			
Are there eyes? If so, how many?			
Are there antennae? If so, how many?			
Method of locomotion			
Special features			

QUESTIONS

1. How do you know that the three specimens are arthropods?
2. In what important ways do the three specimens differ from each other?

Vertebrates

The vertebrates are much less numerous than the invertebrates, but they are much more familiar to us. Many species of vertebrates have been domesticated or are used as pets. All vertebrates belong to the phylum Chordata, which has about 46 000 species. All members of this phylum have backbones, and nearly all have two pairs of limbs, or appendages. Enclosed in the backbone of these animals is a spinal cord. The cord is part of a complex nervous system controlled by a well-developed brain, which makes the members of this phylum the most advanced in the animal kingdom. The main classes of vertebrates are fish, amphibians, reptiles, birds, and mammals.

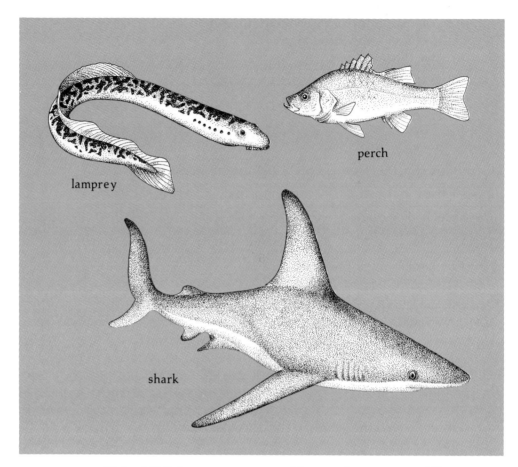

lamprey

perch

shark

Fish. All fish are aquatic and live only in water. Their internal skeleton is made of bone or a tough material called cartilage. All fish breathe through gills and move through the water by using appendages called fins. Their motion is aided by their streamlined bodies. The body of a fish is covered with small, overlapping plates called scales. The scales are covered with a slime that protects the fish and makes it slippery. This makes it easier for the fish to move through the water. Many fish are coloured dark on top and light underneath as camouflage to protect them from their natural enemies.

Amphibians. Amphibians are vertebrates that have a double life. When young they live in water and breathe with gills, but as adults they live mainly on land and breathe with lungs. The young look quite different from the adults. Striking changes in their form and appearance occur during their development. The change in form is called metamorphosis. Young amphibians are noticeably fish-like in appearance.

The amphibians include the frog, the toad, and the salamander. Their bodies are covered with a thin, loose skin that is normally moist. The skin is coloured and usually spotted, to camouflage the animal. Amphibians have two pairs of legs, and the feet are often webbed. Movement is accomplished by walking, hopping, or swimming.

Reptiles. In the days of the dinosaurs, the reptiles were very numerous and provided the Earth with its largest animals. Today, the reptiles are less common and much smaller. Included in the reptile class are turtles, lizards, snakes, and crocodiles.

All reptiles have a scaly skin that is tough, and often rough and dry. They may be found in water, but they are land animals. They breathe air by using lungs and lay eggs on land, usually burying them in sand. Except for snakes, reptiles have feet with clawed toes. They move by walking, creeping, or swimming.

Many reptiles are brightly coloured, sometimes with stripes or spots. Some lizards, such as the chameleon, are able to change their colour to match the environment.

Birds. Birds are vertebrates that are adapted for flight, although some species do not fly. The front appendages are adapted as wings while the hind legs enable them to stand or perch. The bones are usually hollow and therefore very light. A bird's body is covered with feathers, which help to keep its body temperature up to about 39°C.

toad

salamander

frog

turtle

lizard

alligator

Birds develop from eggs that have a protective shell. The eggs are often laid in nests where they are incubated by the parent sitting on them. Young birds are usually cared for by one or both parents during the early stages of development.

Birds, generally, have good eyesight, and most species have a voice. They are very active and require large amounts of food. Most of them eat insects or seeds. They vary greatly in size, from the hummingbird (5 cm long) to the ostrich, which may grow to a height of 2 m.

Many species of birds migrate in the spring and fall, sometimes travelling thousands of kilometres.

Mammals. Mammals are vertebrates that have hair or fur on their skin. They all breathe by means of lungs. Most mammals are born alive and fed milk from the mammary glands of the mother. Mammals, like the birds, are warm-blooded creatures and maintain a constant body temperature. The appendages of mammals may be legs, arms, wings, or fins, depending on the animal and where it lives.

Ostrich

Hummingbird

The classification of plants

Like all organisms, plants must be examined closely when they are being classified. A simple classification may be made by answering these questions about each specimen:

1. Is it green?
2. Does it have roots, a stem, and leaves?
3. Does it have tubes inside it, for transporting water?
4. Does it produce flowers or cones?

Seed plants. Seed-producing plants are the world's most abundant plants. They are found in forests, farms, grasslands, parks, and gardens. Seed plants have roots, a stem, and leaves, and a system of internal channels, or tubes, for transporting water. Each seed contains an embryo that is capable of developing into a new plant. Seed plants are classified into two groups: gymnosperms, of which 725 species are known, and angiosperms, with about 250 000 species. Each group produces a distinct type of seed.

Gymnosperms. These seed plants are all woody plants, and most species are evergreen. "Gymnosperm" means "naked seed", and plants of this type produce seeds that are not enclosed in a fruit.

Some of the different kinds of seeds

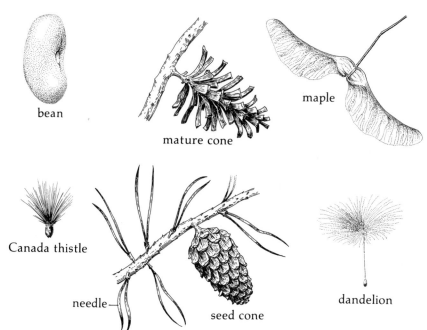

bean

mature cone

maple

Canada thistle

needle

seed cone

dandelion

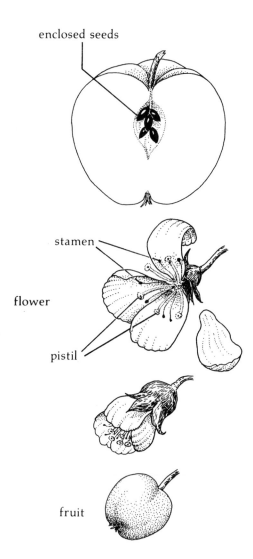

enclosed seeds

stamen

flower

pistil

fruit

The production of an apple — a type of fruit

Most gymnosperms are conifers, which means that they produce cones. Cones are special structures in which the seeds develop. Pine trees produce cones of two types. Pollen cones, which are soft and small, produce pollen grains. Pollen is transferred by the wind to the seed cones. Fertilization occurs about a year after pollination, and seeds develop under the scales of the seed cones, which are harder and larger than the pollen cones. As the seed cone matures, the scales open and the winged seeds fall out. The wind carries the seeds away, and some of them land in suitable spots and produce new trees. Pine, spruce, and fir are some of the trees that produce seeds in cones.

Angiosperms. More than half of all known plant species are angiosperms. These plants produce flowers, and their seeds are enclosed within fruits. "Angiosperm" means "covered seed". The angiosperms include grasses, flowering plants, vegetables, and all non-cone-producing trees, such as the maples and the oaks. Angiosperm plants produce flowers or blossoms. Within each blossom, the most important parts are the pistil and the stamens. The stamens produce pollen, which is transferred to the pistil. Fertilization produces a zygote, which develops into a seed.

The plant stores food around the seed, and a seed coat, or

What do maple trees, tomato plants, and grasses have in common?

covering, develops. The enclosed seed is called a fruit. The stored food that surrounds the seed supplies nourishment for the germinating seed until it can produce its own food. The structure of flowers and the production of fruits and seeds are dealt with more fully in another part of this book.

Fungi. More than 50 000 species of fungi have been identified. Unlike the more complex members of the plant kingdom, fungi have no roots, stems, leaves, or flowers. They are either one-celled or thread-like. Yeast is an example of a one-celled fungus. Moulds are of the thread-like type. The thread-like mass is called a mycelium, and the single threads or filaments are called hyphae. The umbrella-shaped part of a mushroom is the spore-producing structure. The spore is a tiny

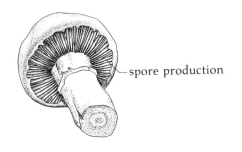

spore production

yeast

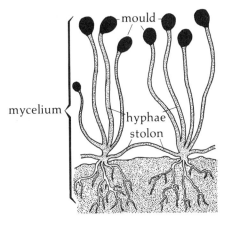

mould

mycelium

hyphae
stolon

Types and parts of certain fungi

VIN R

R

**The manufacture of these
products depends on fungi.**

seed-like structure that is able to produce a new plant. If a piece of the mycelium of a mould is transferred to a new source of nourishment, it will produce a new plant. This process is known as fragmentation.

Fungi such as mushrooms are non-green because they do not contain the material called chlorophyll. This pigment, or chemical, which is found in all green plants, enables them to produce their own food. Fungi have two ways of obtaining nourishment in order to survive. Some, called saprophytes, feed on dead animal or plant matter. Others, called parasites, live in, or attach themselves to, living organisms. Bracket fungus is an example of the parasite type. It is commonly found on trees. Parasitic fungi are important because they help to change dead plant and animal matter into fertile soil.

Because of their parasitic nature, fungi are often responsible for food spoilage and crop destruction. Black mould is often found on stale bread and blue moulds develop readily on over-ripe citrus fruits. Rust and smut are plant diseases that are caused by fungi. They damage field crops such as wheat and corn. Some fungi attack fabrics in certain conditions of temperature and humidity. An example of this type of fungus is mildew. A human affliction called athlete's foot is caused by a fungus.

Some fungi are beneficial to man. Many antibiotics and drugs are obtained from them. An example is penicillin, which is extracted from the fungus *Penicillium notatum*. Fungi are also essential for industrial processes that involve fermentation. Beer, wine, bread, and some kinds of cheese require fungi for their production. Many fungi, such as mushrooms and puffballs, make tasty food.

Some mushrooms and fungi are deadly poisonous, however. Never eat a mushroom or fungus unless you are certain that it is non-poisonous.

MATERIALS

piece of mouldy bread
magnifying glass
tweezers
water
three pieces of stale bread
containers to hold bread slices
   (plates and covers will do)

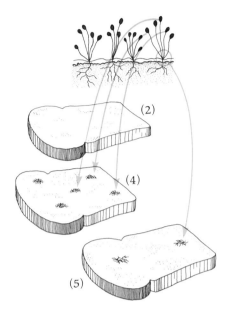

PROCEDURE

1. Sprinkle water on the pieces of stale bread. The bread should be damp but not wet.
2. Cover one of the three dampened slices immediately.
3. Examine the mouldy bread.
4. Find the dark spore cases at the ends of the hyphae. Transfer five of them to another of the pieces of stale bread and cover it.
5. Find the mycelium and transfer a few pieces of it with the tweezers to the third piece of stale bread. Cover it.
6. Use masking tape to identify the three covered slices. Place all three on a shelf that gets no sunlight.

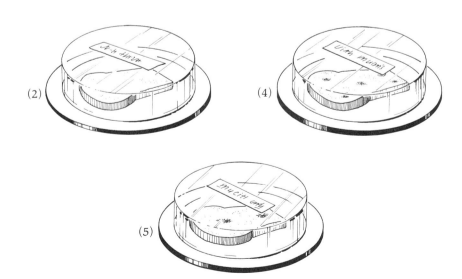

1. Examine each of the three slices daily for several days, and record in your notebook what you observe from day to day.
2. Draw a labelled diagram of the bread mould, as you observed it in step 3.

QUESTIONS

1. Explain why each of the three slices was used the way it was in this experiment, namely:
   (a) slice alone
   (b) slice with spores
   (c) slice with pieces of mycelium
2. Why were the slices covered?
3. Explain the difference between "saprophyte" and "parasite".
4. Are spores capable of producing a new plant? Explain your answer.
5. What name is given to the type of reproduction in which a new plant develops from a piece of mycelium?
6. Why are fungi non-green?

Mosses

Mosses are small green plants that are found in moist places. They are closely related to a group of plants called liverworts. About 14 000 species of moss and 8500 species of liverworts have been identified. Mosses require moist and shady habitats. They grow on damp soil, on rocks, and on tree bark in almost every region of Earth. They may grow in dense, carpet-like mats, which in damp northern forests and bogs often cover many square metres.

Moss plants seldom grow higher, or longer, than 20 cm. They have structures that resemble leaves, stem, and roots, but these structures have no channels, or tubes, for carrying liquids. This results in poor movement of water and minerals within the plant, and explains why it does not grow larger.

The roots of moss are called rhizoids. These are hair-like structures that anchor the plant to the ground and absorb water and minerals. The long slender stalk is called a seta. It

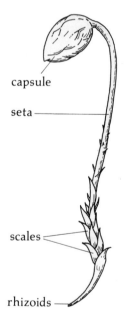

capsule

seta

scales

rhizoids

MATLOCK COLLEGE LIBRARY

supports the spore-producing capsule. Attached to the seta are small, green, leaf-like scales.

Reproduction in most plants of this type is carried out by means of spores. The capsule opens, releasing spores that are carried away by the wind. A spore that lands in a moist area may germinate to produce rhizoids and a bud. The bud develops into a new plant. Some species of moss use the method of reproduction called fragmentation, in which pieces break away from a plant and take root, becoming new plants.

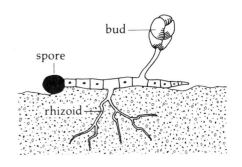

All mosses contain chlorophyll and so are able to produce their own nourishment.

Mosses are often the first plants to gain a foothold in barren places, and they can grow even on rocky surfaces. The rhizoids of this type of plant are able to release chemicals that break up the rock into small particles. By doing this, the mosses help to create conditions that will enable other types of plants to grow. Mosses that inhabit aquatic environments tend to fill in pools and ponds and thus to build new soil. Mosses can absorb and retain large quantities of water. This is particularly true of the genus *Sphagnum*, which are commonly called peat mosses. Even when these mosses are dead they can retain water, and they are used in gardens to hold water for other plants. In nature, the water-retaining property of mosses helps to reduce soil erosion.

QUESTIONS

1. Why do mosses never grow to be very large?
2. Name the parts of a moss plant that correspond to the following parts of other plants.
   (a) roots
   (b) stem
   (c) leaves
3. What method of reproduction do most mosses use?
4. Moss is often found growing at the base of a tree trunk, usually on the north side. Explain this statement.

Ferns

Ferns are larger than mosses and liverworts and are commonly seen as green leafy structures on the forest floor. About 9300 species grow in forests, swamps, and gardens. Ferns require

Canadian ferns grow wild in forests.

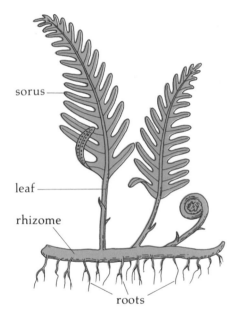

sorus

leaf

rhizome

roots

The parts of a fern

rather large amounts of water and grow where the moisture content of the air and the soil is high. Because of the drying effect of direct sunlight, ferns prefer shady habitats. They are widely distributed throughout the world, wherever favourable conditions exist. Some species that grow in tropical regions are tree-like and reach heights of 3 m or 4 m, but the maximum heights of species found on forest floors in Canada is usually less than 1 m.

A fossil of a tree fern

Ferns are green plants with roots, stem, and leaves. They have underground stems (rhizomes) to which thread-like roots are attached. These roots anchor the plant and absorb water and minerals from the soil. Large green leaves with long stalks emerge directly from the soil. The roots, the stems, and the leaves have tubes to conduct liquids. On their undersides, the leaves have what look like small dots. Each dot is a sorus, which produces spores.

Approximately 300 000 000 years ago, large tree-like ferns dominated the Earth's vegetation. The conditions on Earth changed about 100 000 000 years ago. The sea level rose and the large ferns were drowned and became extinct. The fern forests became buried under layers of sediment, which had eroded from the land and been carried into the oceans by the rivers. As the sediment deepened, its enormous mass created pressure on the buried plants and changed them into coal. Today this coal is mined and used as fuel.

Wild animals eat some species of ferns. Other species are used as ornamental plants in gardens.

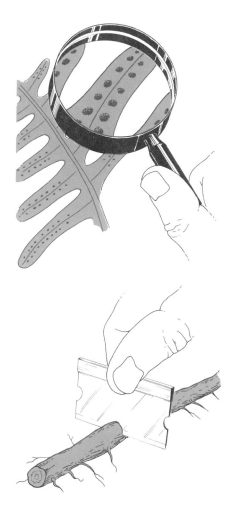

INVESTIGATION: To examine a fern

MATERIALS
magnifying glass
razor-blade cutter
shovel
fern plant (preferably in its natural habitat)

PROCEDURE
1. Examine a fern leaf. Using the magnifying glass, find the soruses.
2. Using the shovel, carefully dig the soil away from the roots and rhizomes.
3. Cut across a rhizome and a leaf stalk, and examine the cross sections.

OBSERVATIONS
Draw and label a diagram of the fern you examined.

QUESTIONS

1. Exactly where did you find the soruses and what did they look like?
2. What did you see that indicated the presence of tubes to transport water in the fern?
3. Ferns are autotrophs, that is, organisms capable of producing their own food. Explain this statement.
4. Why is a rhizome considered to be an underground stem and not a root?
5. Large tree ferns are extinct, but they are still important today. Explain why.

REVIEW QUESTIONS

1. What is meant by classification?
2. What is the point of classifying objects and organisms?
3. Describe two methods of classification.
4. What is taxonomy?
5. What is a species?
6. What contribution did Linnaeus make to taxonomy?
7. Name the seven levels of classification that are used in taxonomy.
8. What is the difference between a vertebrate and an invertebrate?
9. Name three kinds of legless invertebrates.
10. What is a parasite?
11. Complete this chart of vertebrates.

	FISH	AMPHIBIANS	REPTILES	BIRDS	MAMMALS
Where do they live?					
What does their body covering consist of?					
What appendages do they have?					
What is their method of locomotion?					
Do they lay eggs? If so, describe them.					
What are their normal body temperatures?					

12. What does "arthropod" mean?
13. What is an exoskeleton?
14. Insects are an example of an arthropod. Name four other examples of arthropods.
15. List three kinds of mollusks that provide food for humans.
16. (a) List the four main groups of plants.
    (b) Explain how they differ from one another.
17. Explain how each group of plants is important to man.
18. Explain how coal was formed.
19. Describe three ways in which plants differ from animals.

IMPORTANT TERMS

classification—a process of sorting to permit easier understanding
taxonomy—the scientific classification of living things
invertebrate—an animal that has no backbone
vertebrate—an animal that has a backbone
seed—a structure produced by certain types of plants, capable of developing into a new plant
fruit—an enclosed seed

THE INTERDEPENDENCE OF LIVING THINGS

If you examine a pond, or a woodlot, or a field, you will see that many different kinds of living things, or organisms, exist there. In a pond, plants, frogs, fish, insects, worms, and small animals all live together in the same area. They not only live together but depend on each other for survival. The most obvious way in which living things depend on each other is for food. Fish feed on plant life, insects, and smaller fish. Insects eat plant life or other insects. And so on. But organisms depend on each other in other ways as well, and in this chapter we will examine some of these ways.

Natural communities

All the organisms of one kind that live in a certain area form a population of that organism. An area such as a pond will have a number of populations, such as a frog population, a minnow population, and a water lily population. Taken all together, the populations that make their home in the area of the pond make up the pond community.

There are many kinds of natural communities, such as stream communities, field communities, forest communities,

Can you name the types of communities pictured here?

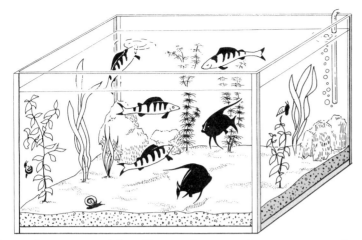

An aquarium

and marsh communities. For each type of community there are populations of plants and animals that make their homes there.

The aquarium illustrated is also an example of a community. It has a fish population, a snail population, and a plant population. What kind of natural community does this aquarium resemble?

This terrarium is another example of a community made to resemble a natural community.

A terrarium

INVESTIGATION: To examine a natural community such as a small park or garden

MATERIALS

magnifying glass   small trowel

1. Decide on the limits of the area you will examine. Try to choose obvious boundaries such as fences or sidewalks.
2. Explore the area carefully, taking note of all the different living things that you see.
3. With the trowel, dig up a small patch of earth. Choose a place where your digging will not be noticeable, such as the edge of a flower bed. Examine the soil with the magnifying glass, and find as many different organisms as you can.

OBSERVATIONS

Under the headings "Plant Populations" and "Animal Populations", list the organisms you found.

QUESTIONS

1. Suggest headings that could be used to subdivide each of your lists into smaller groupings.
2. Use an identification guide to identify the organisms you found.

Relationships in natural communities

There are two major types of relationships in natural communities: dependence and competition. Dependence occurs in various ways, but, in every case, the organism relies on other organisms to continue to live the way it does.

A brown bear

All animals use other living things for food. Most of them eat a variety of other organisms. The sparrows that are found throughout Ontario, for example, eat the seeds of many different kinds of plants. Brown bears will eat insects, berries, fish and other small animals, and even the garbage from human communities. Using more than one source of food increases an animal's chances of survival. A disease or a change of climate might at any time remove one or two species of plants or animals from the terrain of a community. Then any animals that depended entirely on those species could not survive.

There are other types of dependence, as well. Many birds build their nests in trees. They depend on trees for protection as

Robins build their nests in trees (above left) — bees and plants depend on each other (above).

well as for some of the materials they need for their nests. The young of birds and mammals need one or both parents to supply food, shelter, and warmth until they are old enough to look after themselves. Bees use the pollen and nectar of flowering plants for food. Plants depend on bees to transfer pollen from one flower to another, and this transfer is a necessary part of the reproductive process of plants. These are just some of the ways in which organisms depend on each other. As you continue to study nature, you will find many others.

Competition in natural communities takes many forms. Organisms are constantly competing for food and for living space, since there is only a limited amount of each in any community. Competition does not always take the form of a physical struggle or fight, however.

Plants require moisture, and other materials from the soil, and sunlight in order to live. Those plants that are best able to obtain these things are the most likely to survive. In a lawn community, for example, weeds are competing against the grass, and if man did not interfere the weeds would soon replace much of the grass. This is because most weeds grow faster than grasses and thus reproduce more often and use up the nutrients in the soil.

Competition among animals sometimes takes the form of an actual struggle. Many animals will defend their territory against others of their species. The male robin, for example, stakes out a territory each spring for himself and his mate.

Much of his day is spent announcing the limits of his territory, by means of a song, so that other male robins will be duly warned to stay away. If another robin happens to come near, it will be attacked and scared away.

Much of the competition among the animals in a community is over food. Competition may be among members of the same species or between different species. Animals that are best at finding or catching food are the most likely to survive.

INVESTIGATION: To examine some of the relationships that occur in an aquarium community

---

MATERIALS

well-established aquarium with a variety of organisms
magnifying glass

PROCEDURE

1. Examine the aquarium and identify as many kinds of animals as you can. Look carefully in all areas, especially among the plants.
2. With the magnifying glass, examine the area near the bottom of the aquarium. Look closely, because some of the organisms you are looking for are very small.
3. Examine the different plants in the aquarium. Note how they are growing and where they are most abundant.
4. With the magnifying glass, examine a snail that is on the glass wall of the aquarium. Note what happens as the snail moves.
5. Sprinkle a small amount of fish food on the surface of the water. Watch the actions of the fish.

OBSERVATIONS

1. List the animal populations you found in step 1. Describe where in the aquarium you found each population.
2. Describe what you saw in step 2. Add to your list any additional animals that you found.
3. List the plant populations you found in step 3. Describe how they were growing and where they were most abundant.

4. Describe the actions of the snail you observed in step 4.
5. Describe the actions of the fish when you added food.

QUESTIONS
1. Some of the smaller fish were among the leaves of the plants. Suggest a reason for this.
2. When you examined the bottom of the aquarium, you probably found a number of very small organisms. These creatures eat all the debris that falls to the bottom. What would happen if they were not present?
3. Discuss what might happen if all the snails were removed from the aquarium.
4. Do the plants use the gravel in the aquarium? If so, what do they use it for?
5. The two principal types of relationships that occur in a natural community are competition and dependence. List as many examples of each kind of relationship as you can from your observation of an aquarium community.

In the last investigation, you found a number of different ways in which dependence can occur. The smaller fish depend on the plants, which enable them to hide from the larger fish that might eat them. The snails depend on the dead plants and algae growing on the glass, for food. Sometimes, the dependence is not so obvious. The fish and the plants would soon die if both the snails and the small organisms that live at the bottom were removed. Both of these populations remove dead and decaying materials by eating them. These materials, if left to build up, would greatly increase the growth of the algae, which would then compete with the other plants and the fish for the oxygen in the water.

Ecology

So far, in examining communities, we did not consider any of the non-living parts, such as air, water, soil, and light. All of these things are part of the community's environment, and they are vital to its populations of organisms. The study of the relationships between the populations in a community and the environment is called ecology. When we study a community and its environment we are studying an ecological system, or ecosystem. In this section we will examine some of the elements of an environment that affect the organisms living in it.

The air that surrounds the Earth is a mixture of several gases, two of which are essential for life. These are oxygen, which is used by almost every living organism to obtain energy from food, and carbon dioxide, which green plants use, along with water and light energy, to make food for themselves. Organisms that live in water can also use the same two gases, since they are both soluble in water.

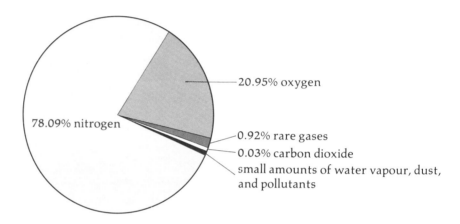

78.09% nitrogen

20.95% oxygen

0.92% rare gases
0.03% carbon dioxide
small amounts of water vapour, dust, and pollutants

Soil contains materials called nutrients that plants need for growth. As plants grow they absorb nutrients from the soil, so that after a while these nutrients are used up. In an ecosystem, the nutrients in the soil are replaced as organisms die and decay. Nutrients can also be replaced by the additon of fertilizer to the soil. Commercial fertilizers contain nutrients that dissolve in the moisture in the soil and are then taken up by the plants.

A plant, to produce food for itself, requires carbon dioxide, light energy, and water. It absorbs water from the soil through its roots, and it absorbs light energy through all its green-coloured parts.

In the next two investigations you will see how two elements of the environment affect plant growth, and you will have an opportunity to create a simple ecosystem.

INVESTIGATION: To see how light and water affect
plant growth

MATERIALS

3 potted plants of the same size and species (such as coleus, geranium, bean)
box large enough to cover one plant completely
camera (optional)

PROCEDURE

1. Number the plants 1, 2, and 3, using a piece of masking tape on each pot.
2. Put the plants on a sunny window ledge.
3. Cover plant 3 with the box.
4. Water plants 1 and 3 every other day.
5. Examine the plants every other day and note any changes. If you have a camera, take a picture of the plants each time you examine them.

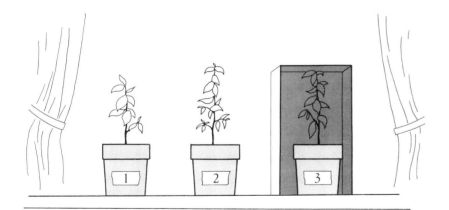

OBSERVATIONS

Draw a table like the one on page 72, in your notebook, and record your observations in it. (If you took photographs, an enlarged table including them would make an excellent display.)

CHANGES OBSERVED ON	PLANT 1	PLANT 2	PLANT 3
Day 1			
Day 2			
Day 3			

QUESTIONS

1. What non-living thing was missing from the environment of plant 2? What effect did this have on the plant?
2. What was missing from the environment of plant 3? What effect did this have?
3. Suggest what you might do in order to help plants 2 and 3 return to a healthy condition.

INVESTIGATION: To create an ecosystem by assembling a simple aquarium

---

MATERIALS

large jar with lid (4 or 5 L)
   or rectangular glass aquarium
   with cover
aquarium gravel
plants (such as duckweed and
   elodea)
animals – 2 or 3 snails and
   fish such as guppies (one male
   and one female)
tropical fish food
camera (optional)

PROCEDURE

1. Wash the jar with warm water. Do not use soap.
2. Rinse the gravel two or three times in running water to remove dirt.

3. Put the gravel in the jar so that there is an upward slope from the front to the back.

4. Place a piece of paper on the gravel and slowly pour water onto the paper. Add water until it is about 3 cm from the top of the jar.

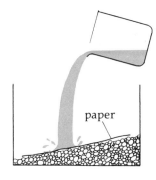

5. Remove the piece of paper and let the jar stand for a day with the lid off.

6. Set the plants in the gravel, using a finger to make holes for the roots. If a plant floats to the surface, put a pebble on the roots to hold it down. Place the smaller plants around the outer edge with the taller plants behind them. Leave an open space in the middle, so that it will be easy to observe the fish.

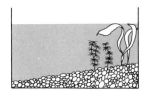

7. From a pet store obtain one male and one female guppy, and two or three snails.

8. Put the pet shop bag containing the fish and snails into the jar so that the bag floats on the surface. Leave it there for about an hour before untying the bag to let the fish and snails swim or crawl into the aquarium. When all organisms have entered the aquarium, remove the bag.

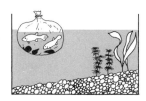

9. Feed the fish once a day. Sprinkle only enough food on the surface to provide a two-minute meal. Be sure the jar is near some source of light so that the plants will be able to grow. Keep the lid on the jar except during feedings. Do not make holes in the lid.

10. Examine the aquarium closely at least once a week. If after one week the fish and the plants appear to be healthy, the lid may be applied firmly and no more food need be added. Look for any changes in the populations of organisms and in the environment.

OBSERVATIONS

1. Write a brief description of the changes you observe each week. If you have access to a camera, take one or two pictures of the ecosystem each week.

2. You may want to record your descriptions on a large chart mounted beside the aquarium. The pictures could also be included in the chart.

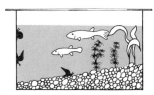

A terrestrial community

1. Why were the animals left in the bag for a time, when they were first put into the aquarium?
2. Draw a table in your notebook similar to the one on page 72 and complete it, to show the possible effects of changes.

Types of communities

The natural communities we have considered so far are of two types. Some of them consist mostly of land, such as forest, field, soil, or desert, and these are called terrestrial communities. The others include bodies of water, such as a pond, a stream, a lake, a marsh, or an ocean, and these are called aquatic communities.

You have already examined a few natural terrestrial communities. The next investigation will give you a chance to examine a natural aquatic community. Depending on what is available in your area, choose one of the following to study: a pond community, a stream community, or a marsh community.

An aquatic community

MATERIALS

magnifying glass
collecting jars with lids
microscope and slides
plastic pail or tub

kitchen strainer
muffin tin
clipboard
identification key for pond life

PROCEDURE

1. When you arrive at the area you will be studying, sit down for at least 10 min and quietly observe the plants and animals there. Make use of your identification key. Also, look for any evidence of animal life, such as tracks and droppings.
2. Move quietly to another location in the area and take note of any new organisms you see.
3. Repeat step 2.
4. Put a little water in your pail and in the muffin tin.
5. Using the strainer, scoop up material from the water and examine it carefully. If you find any organisms, put them in the pail. Repeat this step in several different places.
6. Transfer specimens you want to examine more closely from the pail into the muffin tin.
7. Examine each specimen carefully.
8. Use the identification key and try to identify each organism you find.
9. If you are working in a rocky stream, examine the rocks along the bottom carefully. Add any new organism you find to your muffin tin.
10. Scoop up some mud from the bottom and examine it for new organisms. Put some of the mud in a collecting jar for further study back at school.
11. Examine the plants growing in the water.
12. Collect some plant material and put it in a collecting jar with some water.
13. After you have completed all of your observations of the specimens you collected, return them carefully to the water (except for what is in the two collecting jars).
14. When you return to school, examine the materials that

you collected under a microscope. Use one drop of material at a time. You will have to add one or two drops of clear water to the mud.

OBSERVATIONS

1. Make a list of all the animals you saw. Indicate where each organism was found (on the surface of the water, in mud, on the bottom, etc.). Make another list of all the plants.
2. Choose four of the organisms you have listed and sketch each of them on separate pieces of paper.
3. Make sketches of any tracks you found.
4. Make rough sketches and try to identify any organisms you find in examining the mud and plant material, in step 14.

QUESTIONS

1. Which animal populations were most abundant?
2. Name the plant population that was the most common.
3. In what ways does this aquatic community differ from the terrestrial communities you have looked at?
4. Identify some of the relationships between the populations in this aquatic community.
5. If you found animal tracks, try to identify the animals that made them.

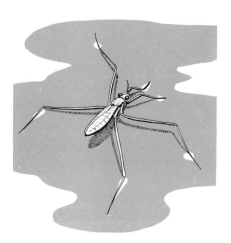

A water strider

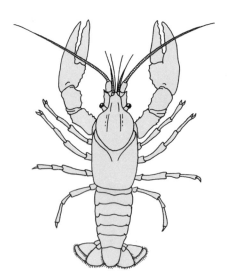

Crayfish are common in Canadian aquatic communities.

In your examination of an aquatic community, you found many different organisms. You also found that each organism has its favourite kind of place. For example, if you found water striders, you found them on the surface of the water and if you found crayfish, you found them on the bottom of a stream or pond. The place where an organism usually lives is called its habitat. Sometimes habitats are very limited. Crayfish, for example, can live only along the beds of shallow ponds, streams, rivers, or lakes. The habitat of man, on the other hand, can be almost anywhere in the world.

Why do organisms choose specific habitats to live in? Usually it is because of the availability of things they need to sustain themselves, such as certain foods, warmth, protection from predators, oxygen, water, nutrients, and light. But as you study organisms and their habitats more closely, you will find that the reasons can be more complex.

Squirrels live in habitats that have many trees that produce seeds and fruit. They depend on these for food. Often, they will bury some of the seeds they collect, in preparation for winter. They depend on their sense of smell to find the buried food later, and some of it never does get dug up again. What the squirrels have done, in effect, is to plant seeds that will grow into more trees, and these new trees will eventually provide the squirrels with more food.

This type of relationship is called interdependence. The squirrels depend on the trees for food and the trees depend on the squirrels to help disperse their seeds. Bees and flowering plants are another example of interdependent organisms.

The next investigation will give you an opportunity to look for other examples of interdependence in a community.

INVESTIGATION: To examine soil samples from different areas

MATERIALS

plastic bags with ties
microscope and slides
magnifying glass
popsicle stick or fork
large piece of white paper
trowel

PROCEDURE

1. Collect soil samples from the following types of areas: a sandy area with little vegetation; an area at the edge of a flower bed; a grassy area; an area near a swamp; and a forest or woodlot. Make sure you mark each bag, so that you will know where each sample came from.
2. Place a large piece of white paper on a desk. Gently pour one of your soil samples onto the paper.
3. Use the popsicle stick or fork to separate the soil. Look for any animals that may be present. Use the magnifying glass to help you find tiny organisms.
4. Look for evidence of plant life.
5. Place some specimens of interesting organisms on slides, and examine them with the microscope.
6. Repeat steps 2 to 5 for the other soil samples.

1. Describe the colour, texture, and feel of each soil sample.
2. Identify and list all the organisms you found in the soil.
3. Explain how you were able to tell the difference between plant and animal organisms in your soil samples.

QUESTION

Each soil sample may be thought of as a small community. Explain with examples how interdependence between plants and animals occurs in the soil.

Food chains

Every organism in a community requires food in order to survive. The food contains nutrients and energy that enable the organism to perform its life functions, such as growth and reproduction. Green plants, because they can make their own food from non-living materials, are called producers. Animals obtain their food by eating other organisms and are called consumers.

Some animals, such as grasshoppers, rabbits, and deer, eat only plants. These animals are called herbivores. Such animals as owls, hawks, foxes, and wolves eat other animals, usually herbivores, and are called carnivores. There are also a number of animals that normally eat both plants and animals. Raccoons, bears, and humans are examples of this type of consumer. They are called omnivores.

If you examine the relationships between the producers and the consumers that live in a community, you will find that you can arrange the organisms into "food chains". Green plants, the producers, are the first step in every food chain. The second step comprises herbivores that eat only green plants. The next step consists of the carnivores that get most of their food by eating herbivores. Then there are the larger carnivores that eat the smaller carnivores.

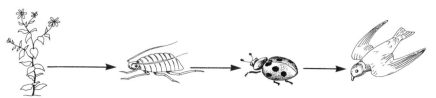

A food chain

There are a great many food chains in every community. Typical food chains in a meadow community are:

GRASS ⟶ RABBITS ⟶ FOXES
GRASS ⟶ RABBITS ⟶ HAWKS

Each of those examples has three stages, but a food chain may have only two stages or as many as five or more.

CARROTS ⟶ HUMANS
HAY ⟶ CATTLE ⟶ HUMANS
GREEN PLANTS ⟶ INSECTS ⟶ FROGS ⟶ RACCOONS
GREEN PLANTS ⟶ INSECTS ⟶ FROGS ⟶ FISH ⟶ HUMANS

As you can see from the examples, an organism may be part of more than one food chain. In fact, there are only a few organisms that belong to only one food chain.

QUESTIONS

1. Examine your list of plants and animals from the investigations of communities. Write at least three food chains that could exist in each of the communities you studied.
2. Are people producers or consumers? Explain.
3. (a) Copy the following names of organisms into your notebook. Underline all the producers and circle all the consumers.
   (b) Arrange the organisms into as many different probable food chains as you can.

grass	frogs	hawk
insects	humans	pond plants
fox	fish	rabbits
weeds	vegetables	snakes
cows	grains	chickens

4. Make a list of the herbivores mentioned in question 3(b).
5. Suggest why most organisms are part of more than one food chain.

You have seen that food chains consist of a number of steps, beginning with a producer and followed by one or more consumers. Since the producers are constantly taking nutrients

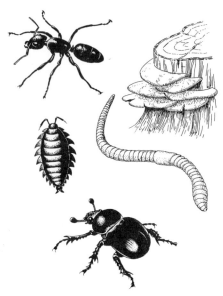

Some examples of decomposers

from the soil, after a time there would be none left unless they were somehow replaced. On farms and in gardens, man replaces the nutrients by adding fertilizers, but how does nature take care of the problem?

In every food chain there are organisms whose role it is to consume dead and decaying material wherever it appears in the chain. These organisms, called decomposers, eat up the remains of any organism that dies at any point along the food chain. The decomposers are microscopic bacteria that live in the soil and also non-green plants such as fungi. Insects and small animals that live in the soil, such as earthworms, are also considered to be decomposers because they break decaying material down into smaller bits.

When an organism dies and falls to the ground, the nutrients that are a part of it cannot be used by plants until the decomposers in the soil have broken down the material. The decomposers use only part of the nutrients, for their own life processes, and the rest becomes available to the green plants growing in the soil. In this way the nutrients are recycled.

A food chain looks like this:

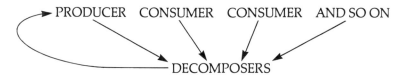

The bacteria are microscopic and difficult to observe, but it is possible to examine the work of the other decomposers, and that is the purpose of the next investigation.

INVESTIGATION: **To examine the work of decomposers**

MATERIALS
magnifying glass
tweezers
several baby food jars with lids

PROCEDURE
1. Locate a piece of rotted log in a forest or woodlot.
2. Examine the ground near the log and note what you see.
3. If possible, lift the log and examine the underside for

animals. Pick up any specimens you see with the tweezers, and put them into the jars.
4. Examine the surface of the log for growths.

OBSERVATIONS
1. List any animals you found in step 3.
2. Draw sketches of two of the animals you found.
3. List any plants you found growing on the log.
4. Draw a sketch of one of these plants.

QUESTIONS
1. Which of the animals or plants you listed in your observations could be considered decomposers?
2. What will eventually happen to the log you examined?

Energy

All organisms must have food, to survive. Food gives an organism the energy it needs to grow, to move, and to reproduce. The consumers in a food chain obtain their food by eating other organisms. The producers, the green plants, make their own food. They use the energy of sunlight to combine carbon dioxide gas and water to make simple sugars. This process is called photosynthesis. The sun's energy is stored in the sugars, and the sugars are stored by plants in various ways until they are needed. During photosynthesis, green plants also produce a waste product – oxygen gas.

Animals that consume plants use some of the stored energy they get from the plants and store the rest of it in their bodies. All organisms release the energy stored in sugars by a process called respiration. In this process, oxygen gas is used to release the stored energy from the sugars. At the same time, two waste products are formed – carbon dioxide gas and water.

A food chain, then, may also be considered an energy chain. The producers store the sun's energy and use some of it for themselves. The herbivores use some of the energy stored in what they eat and store the rest, and so on. At each step of the food chain, about 90% of the energy is used up and the rest is stored.

GRASS ⟶ RABBIT ⟶ FOX

Photosynthesis involves these steps.

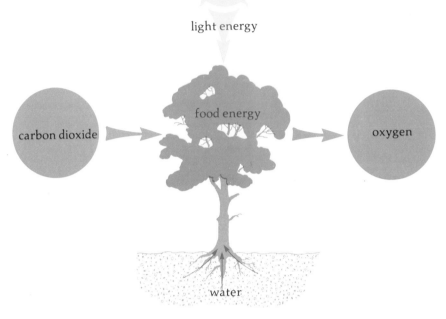

In this food chain, the rabbit uses up all but 10% of the energy stored in the grass it eats. The rabbit uses energy for digging its burrow, escaping its enemies, hunting for food, keeping its heart beating, digesting its food, and generally keeping all the parts of its body working.

Respiration involves these steps.

The processes of photosynthesis and respiration illustrate the interdependence of organisms. Plants depend on carbon dioxide to produce food and oxygen. Both plants and animals depend on oxygen to release the energy stored in food, and at the same time they produce carbon dioxide.

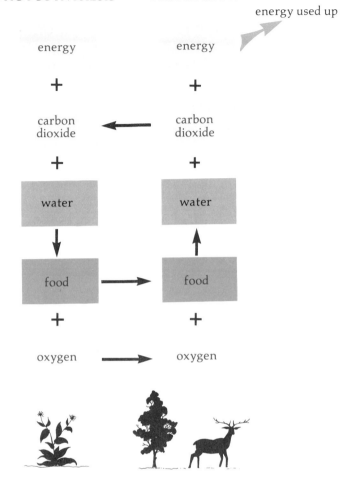

PHOTOSYNTHESIS   RESPIRATION

sun

energy used up

Photosynthesis and respiration are closely related processes.

Changes in nature

Changes in nature usually happen quite slowly. If you revisit one of the natural communities that you have investigated, the changes you see there will depend on how much time has elapsed between your visits. Some of the changes may be seasonal ones, such as the appearance of the leaves in spring, or the fall of leaves in autumn. Others may be the result of the growth of the plants in the community. Since these are changes in the living things in a community, they are called biological changes.

Other biological changes are more difficult to observe because they take place over a period of years rather than days or weeks. The plant material in a pond, for example, gradually builds up until the pond fills in and becomes a marsh. The plant material continues to build up until the marsh becomes a grassy area and, eventually, a forest. This type of change takes hundreds of years, and there are other kinds of biological changes that take thousands and even millions of years.

In the next investigation you will examine some of the short-term changes that occur in a community.

INVESTIGATION: To observe signs of biological change

MATERIALS

A vacant lot or the lawn of an abandoned house
key to common weeds
hoop
well-kept lawn

PROCEDURE

1. Observe an unkept lawn (or vacant lot or abandoned farm).
2. Look for signs of pollution in the form of garbage.
3. Throw the hoop onto the lawn. Count the weeds that are within the hoop. Repeat this in three different parts of the lawn. Identify the common weeds.
4. Repeat step 3 for a well-kept lawn.
5. For comparison, look for signs of pollution on a well-kept lawn.

OBSERVATIONS

1. Make a list of the signs of pollution you found in each of the communities.
2. List the plant populations you found on the unkept lawn and record how many specimens you found of each.
3. List the plant populations you found on the well-kept lawn and record how many specimens you found of each.

QUESTIONS

1. What were the most common plant populations on the two areas?
2. Suggest reasons for the differences in plant populations between the two areas.

3. Describe what the well-kept lawn would probably look like if it were left unattended for a year.
4. Suggest why the weed populations tend to increase.
5. Why are some plants considered weeds?

Communities are usually balanced, so that changes occur very gradually. Just enough food energy is available at each step in a food chain to support a certain number of animals at the next step. This keeps the populations in balance.

In a grassland community, for example, each rabbit needs to graze several square metres daily. Each rabbit grazes a different area each day, so the grass population has a chance to grow again, and it continues to provide enough food for the rabbits. If the population of rabbits were to increase, so that three or four rabbits had to share the same grazing areas, the rabbits would soon eat all the available grass. The grass could not grow fast enough, and the rabbits would move to another community or die off. It is in much the same way that nature maintains a balance between all the populations in a community.

Disturbance in nature

Sometimes a disturbance in the environment, such as a fire, a flood, an epidemic, or a change in climate produces a rapid change in a community.

Forest fires destroy trees and other plant life as well as animals, and often destroy a whole community. After a forest fire, the plant populations must be replaced before the animal populations can return.

Floods also disturb the balance of a community. Many organisms are drowned, and animals that survive must move to new areas to find food. Even if the flooding only lasts a short time, the water may remove the topsoil with all the nutrients it contains, so the plant populations suffer.

Most diseases affect only one of the populations in a community. If that population is destroyed, however, the rest of the community will be affected, because of the population's place in the food chains.

Changes in climate can have dramatic effects on a com-

Changes can occur in natural communities.

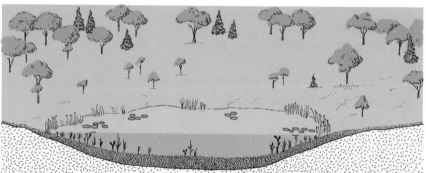

A forest fire destroys the balance in the community.

munity. Each organism can only survive if the temperature and moisture are within certain limits. If an environment becomes too hot or too cold or if it is too wet or too dry, the populations will change. How would the area you live in change if it were summer all year round?

RESEARCH QUESTIONS

1. What are some of the causes of forest fires?
2. Why do forest managers sometimes deliberately set small fires in a forest?
3. What changes occur in an area after the populations have been destroyed by fire?
4. How do humans try to prevent damage from floods,
5. What is Dutch elm disease? How has it affected the natural communities in Canada?
6. What would be the effects of a year-long drought in the area you live in?
7. What is dioxin?

Two other types of disturbances should be noted. One is the effect of a sudden change in the size of one population in a community. In the past few years, for example, the populations of tent caterpillars have multiplied in Ontario. These caterpillars feed on the leaves of deciduous trees. They

Tent caterpillars

have grown so numerous that trees are often stripped of all leaves in the space of a few hours. When that happens to a tree, it dies and many food chains are affected.

Finally we will examine a type of disturbance that has, in the last few hundred years, had a great effect on many natural communities – disturbances caused by people.

The impact of people

Wherever people live, they try to improve their own lives by making changes in the environment. Some of the changes are physical ones, such as filling in marshland for housing projects and airport runways or building sewer systems to collect and dispose of waste. Others are biological changes, such as killing pests that cause diseases or using fertilizer to obtain more food from the soil. Such changes, although beneficial to people, often have a greater impact on nature than was intended.

Since about 1946, in Africa and the Far East, a chemical pesticide called DDT has been sprayed extensively to kill off mosquitos that carry malaria germs. Malaria is often fatal, and the use of DDT has saved approximately 10 million lives, according to United Nations statistics. DDT has also been used in other parts of the world to control other insect pests.

However, DDT, like a number of other chemicals, does not break down and disappear in the environment. It is stored in the body of any organism that is exposed to it and it remains there until the organism dies or is eaten. If the organism is eaten, the DDT is absorbed by the consumer. If it dies, the DDT is absorbed by plants. Thus, once DDT enters a food chain, it is passed to each succeeding step. Not only is DDT passed on, but the amount of it in each individual creature increases as it is passed along the food chain. One herbivore will consume a large number of plants, each of which may only contain a small amount of DDT. Many herbivores will then be the food supply for the carnivores in the next step of a food chain. The animals at the ends of the food chains, then, will contain the largest amounts of DDT.

Today, traces of DDT can be found in almost every organism on Earth. Freshwater and saltwater fish, birds, land and sea mammals, and man all contain small amounts of DDT in their bodies. Many predatory bird populations are on the

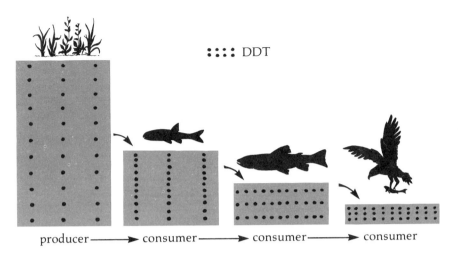

plants   herbivores   small carnivores   larger carnivores

:::: DDT

producer ⟶ consumer ⟶ consumer ⟶ consumer

verge of extinction because of the accumulation of DDT in their bodies. In North America, the osprey and the bald eagle have become endangered species because the presence of high levels of DDT in the body of the female causes the shells of her eggs to be very thin. As the birds nest, the eggs break, and the young die. Scientists do not yet know what will be the effects of high levels of DDT in the bodies of other animals, and other pesticides like DDT are still in use.

The use of pesticides such as DDT has had another serious effect. These pesticides kill most of the insects they are intended for, but a few are resistant and survive. These multiply and soon the insects again become a problem, and stronger pesticides have to be used. Malaria mosquitos that were resistant to DDT survived the sprayings and multiplied, so that the incidence of malaria is once again increasing in tropical countries.

In the Maritimes, a strong chemical pesticide was used to control an insect that was destroying the spruce forests. The spruce budworm population was almost totally eliminated. The few that survived were resistant and now the spruce budworm is again a problem in the Maritimes. In both of these examples, the end result of the large-scale use of a chemical pesticide was to produce a species of insect that is much more difficult to control.

We have become so dependent on chemical pesticides in

A plane spraying DDT

recent years that it would be impossible to stop using them without serious consequences. Most of the crop plants of the world would be destroyed by insects, and many people would die from the resulting famine.

How can the problem be solved? The answer lies in much more careful use of the chemical pesticides and in the development of other ways of controlling pests. A start has been made at using scientific knowledge of food chains to control some insect pests. One way of doing this is to increase the populations of consumers that feed on insect pests, thus keeping their numbers down and limiting the damage they can do.

A few gardeners are now releasing ladybird beetles in their gardens to eat the aphids and other insects that would feed on their plants and vegetables. Scientists are also trying to develop chemical pesticides which will break down into harmless chemicals after they have done their job.

The use of fertilizers by farmers has become widespread. By adding nutrients to the soil, the farmer can greatly increase the amount of food he is able to produce. The nutrients must be dissolved in water in order for the plants to make use of them, and some of them end up in streams and rivers. These empty into lakes, where the nutrients are used by plants in the water, especially the algae. Algae are microscopic floating plants that

A ladybird beetle

often form a scum on the surface of ponds. In the next investigation, you will see how the growth of algae is affected by a type of nutrient that is found in fertilizers – the phosphates.

INVESTIGATION: To examine the effects of phosphates on the growth of algae

MATERIALS

5 small glass jars with lids   sodium phosphate
algae from an aquarium   5 mL graduated cylinder
5 microscope slides   eye-dropper
microscope

PROCEDURE

1. Half-fill each jar with water from an aquarium.
2. Add 5 drops of the algae to each jar.
3. Label the jars 1, 2, 3, 4, and 5.
4. Add 5 mL of the sodium phosphate to jar 1, 3.75 mL to jar 2, 2.5 mL to jar 3, and 1.25 mL to jar 4.
5. Write the quantities added on the jar labels.
6. Gently shake the jars.
7. Place a clean microscope slide in each jar, so that it remains upright.
8. Place the jars side by side in a sunny window and leave them there for two or three weeks.
9. Examine the jars.
10. Remove the slides and examine them under the microscope.

OBSERVATIONS

1. Describe the colour of the water in the five jars, in step 9.
2. Describe what you saw in the microscope, in step 10. Draw a sketch of one of the organisms.

QUESTIONS

1. Which jar appeared to have the most algae?
2. Which jar had the fewest algae?
3. Estimate the relative number of algae in the other three jars.

4. Compare the colour of the solution in each jar with the estimated number of algae it contains.
5. Compare the estimated number of algae in each jar with the amount of sodium phosphate that was added to it.
6. How does sodium phosphate affect the growth of algae?

In the last investigation, you saw how the addition of a nutrient can greatly increase the growth of algae. In a lake or pond, the algae also grow very quickly when extra nutrients are introduced. Once the extra nutrients have been used up, the algae die and sink to the bottom where the decomposers begin their work of consuming them. Because of the large amount of decaying material from the algae, the decomposers also increase in numbers. The larger population of decomposers then uses up more oxygen than the smaller one did. The decrease in the amount of oxygen in the water then kills off fish that require high levels of oxygen, such as trout, pickerel, and bass, and other fish such as carp and perch begin to increase in numbers.

As you can see, the effects of adding chemicals to the environment can be far-reaching and they may not appear until long after.

We have examined some of the indirect effects on nature of man's activities. People can also upset the balance in a natural community directly – by disrupting a food chain as they sometimes do by hunting and fishing.

SHRUBS ⟶ DEER ⟶ WOLVES

In this food chain, the wolves are the natural predators of the deer. The populations in the food chain are balanced, in such a way that the deer will support a certain number of wolves, and the populations of both stay about the same from year to year. If hunters kill off substantial numbers of deer, the food chain will look like this:

Now there are two predators of the deer – humans and wolves. But while man has other food sources, the wolf does not. Deer killed by humans are no longer available as food for the wolf population. Some of the wolves, then, will die because less food is available.

It has long been recognized that hunting and fishing can have detrimental effects on animal populations, and much work has gone into laws and regulations designed to ensure that that does not happen.

Man also affects the natural environment by his waste products and the manner in which he disposes of them. As the world's human population increases, so does the amount of sewage and garbage it produces. What do we do with it all? Most of the garbage is buried or burned. A large part of the sewage is simply dumped into rivers or lakes. The sewage acts like fertilizer in the rivers and lakes. The garbage that is dumped includes industrial chemicals that do not decompose and have a way of reappearing where they are not wanted, sometimes with damaging effects.

Man has been on the Earth for only a short time, but his impact on nature has already been greater than that of any other creature. He has the ability to change the environment drastically – for worse as well as for better – and may even be in danger of destroying himself.

RESEARCH QUESTIONS

1. Encephalitis, or sleeping sickness, is a disease that is carried by mosquitos. It occurs in many parts of North America. How do the authorities in your area deal with this problem?
2. What are the laws governing the use of DDT in your area?
3. Describe various ways in which sewage can be disposed of safely.
4. How do industries in your area dispose of their chemical wastes?

REVIEW QUESTIONS

1. Explain the difference between a community and a population.

2. What is the difference between a human community and a natural community?
3. Explain what competition is and give two examples of it in an aquarium.
4. What is the ecological relationship of dependence?
5. Ecology is a special field of science. Describe it briefly.
6. How does an ecosystem differ from a community?
7. (a) Explain the difference between terrestrial and aquatic communities.
   (b) Name three examples of each type.
8. What does "habitat" mean?
9. Explain the meaning of interdependence.
10. Explain the differences among herbivores, carnivores, and omnivores.
11. Explain the following food chain:
    grass ⟶ cricket ⟶ frog ⟶ snake ⟶ hawk
    (a) Name the producer.
    (b) Name a consumer.
    (c) Name a herbivore.
    (d) Name a carnivore
12. (a) What are decomposers?
    (b) What is their role in food chains?
13. Why is it necessary for a person to eat?
14. What is the name of the process that organisms use to get energy from food?
15. (a) Name three disturbances that can occur in the environment.
    (b) Describe how a disturbance can be beneficial.
16. Each of the following statements describes a change humans have made in the environment that was beneficial to them. In each case, suggest one or more possible harmful results of the change.
    (a) To dispose of radioactive wastes and excess pesticides, people bury them in the ground.
    (b) To create a recreational lake for swimming and boating, people construct a large dam across a river.
    (c) To eliminate rats from the local dump, people spread poison on the garbage.
    (d) To eliminate the smell from the chimney of a local factory, people make the chimney taller.

(e) To create space for a new housing development, people fill in a marsh with earth.

(f) To transport more oil to countries where it is needed, people build larger tankers.

17. (a) Describe a change in the environment that was carried out in your community.

(b) Explain why this change was necessary.

(c) Suggest any possible harmful results of the change.

IMPORTANT TERMS

population—all the organisms of one kind in a certain area

community—a group of populations that inhabit the same area

interdependence—refers to the ways in which organisms of certain species assist organisms of other species

dependence—refers to the ways in which organisms of certain species depend on organisms of other species

competition—refers to the ways in which certain organisms compete with one another for food or space

ecology—the study of the relationships between the populations in a community and their environment

food chain—a number of species of organisms related to one another by their eating habits

herbivore—a plant-eater

carnivore—a meat-eater

omnivore—an eater of both plant and animal matter

decomposer—a small organism that eats up the remains of dead plants and animals

PLANTS

Plants are found throughout the world. Different types grow in water, on the surface of water, in soil, and even on rocks. Plants may have four main structures: roots, stems, leaves, and flowers. Not all types of plants have all four structures.

As you complete the following investigations, you will become more aware of plant structures and their functions.

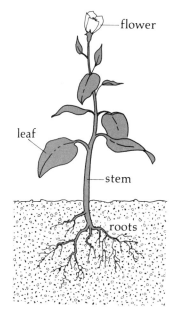

The main parts of plants

INVESTIGATION: To observe some roots and their growth

MATERIALS

radish seeds	saucer with clear cover
beaker	magnifying glass
blotter (dark colour)	

PROCEDURE

1. Soak some radish seeds overnight in water.
2. Soak the blotter in water and place it in the saucer.
3. Put a few seeds on the blotter and cover the saucer.
4. Put the saucer in a dark place. Add water from time to time, if necessary, to keep the blotter moist.

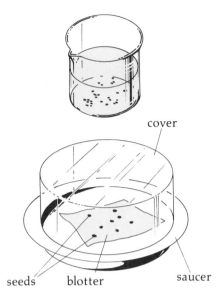

cover

seeds blotter saucer

5. Observe the seeds daily and note the formation of roots.
6. Using the magnifying glass, examine the roots for small, fuzzy growths on the sides.

OBSERVATIONS

1. Describe the changes that occurred in the seeds when they were soaked in water.
2. Record your observations from steps 5 and 6.

QUESTIONS

1. When seeds start to grow, what is happening is called germination. What conditions are required for the germination of seeds?
2. Why was a blotter used in this investigation?
3. (a) Did all the seeds germinate?
   (b) If some did not, give a probable explanation.

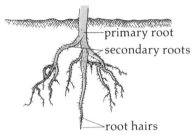

primary root
secondary roots

root hairs

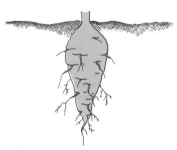

A tap root (top), a fibrous root (centre) and a fleshy tap root (bottom)

Roots

The roots differ from one type of plant to another. They may vary in size, in shape, and in the number of their parts. The main part of a root is called the primary root, and the roots that grow out of the primary root are called secondary roots. Small root hairs grow at the tips and on the outer surfaces of many of the roots.

Roots that have all three parts (primary root, secondary roots, and root hairs) are called tap roots. Some plants have roots that are highly branched but do not seem to have a primary root. Such roots are called fibrous roots.

Some plants in the vegetable group have very large primary roots and are called fleshy tap roots. An example is the carrot.

Roots perform specific functions for the rest of the plant. The roots hold the plant in the ground and keep the soil in place, preventing erosion that might wash the soil away. The roots absorb from the soil water and minerals that are needed, for the plant to grow. Some plants use their roots to store food they have made. This function is easily observed in fleshy tap roots. Thus, the roots of a plant may have three functions: to anchor the plant, to absorb water and minerals, and to store food.

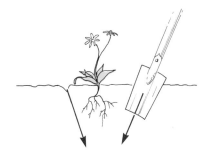

INVESTIGATION: To collect plants and examine their roots

MATERIALS

shovel or hand trowel
ruler

PROCEDURE

1. Select an area of the school yard or a vacant lot in which to collect some plant specimens.
2. Dig down and around the roots with the trowel. Try to remove the whole plant without damaging the roots.
3. Carefully shake the plant to remove the soil from the roots. Caked soil may be removed by putting the roots in a pail of water.
4. Be sure that your specimens include a weed, such as a dandelion, and a small clump of grass.

OBSERVATIONS

1. Examine the roots of all the plants you collected and record information about their size.
2. Write a description of the root system of the dandelion.
3. Write a description of the roots of the grass.
4. Group your specimens according to the type of roots they have. What type is the most common?

QUESTIONS

1. Name the three parts that may be found in a root.
2. Which of the three parts is missing in the roots of grass?
3. From your observations of the roots of the dandelion, explain why it and other weeds tend to be hardy plants.

Stem

The roots of a plant are connected to the plant's stem. There are basically two types of stems: herbaceous stems and woody stems. The stem of a herbaceous plant consists of three main parts. The outer layer, called the epidermis, stays soft throughout the life of the plant. The spongy inner part is called the pith. In the pith there are a number of hollow tubes, called vascular bundles. In plants with woody stems, the epidermis forms a hard, dark-coloured bark; and, as the plant grows, the inner part becomes hard and forms wood.

INVESTIGATION: To examine a herbaceous stem

MATERIALS

tulip plant (or lily, iris, corn, or sugar cane)
magnifying glass
sharp knife or razor blade
food colouring

PROCEDURE

1. Soak some stems overnight in a mixture of food colouring and water.
2. Cut a stem across to give a cross-section view.
3. With the magnifying glass, examine the cross section.
4. Locate the epidermis and the pith.
5. Locate the vascular bundles.

OBSERVATIONS

1. Write a description of the stem, mentioning its external features, its texture, and whether it is rigid or flexible.
2. Draw and label a diagram of the cross-section view.

QUESTIONS

1. Why were you told to soak the stems in food colouring mixed with water?
2. (a) Where were the vascular bundles located in the stem?
   (b) Were they all the same size?
3. Suggest a use for the vascular bundles.
4. Suggest a use for the pith.

INVESTIGATION: To examine a woody stem

MATERIALS

slice of a good-sized log	shellac or varnish
sandpaper	paint brush

PROCEDURE

1. Examine the outside surface of the log and note its colour, texture, and toughness.
2. Examine the bark and note that it is made up of two layers.
3. Examine the cross-section view.
4. With sandpaper, smooth one surface of the wood. If you want to preserve the surface, cover it with two or three coats of shellac or varnish.

OBSERVATIONS

1. Describe the external features of the log.
2. The centre of this type of stem is called the heartwood. Surrounding the heartwood is the sapwood. Observe the difference between the two, and look for the boundary between them.
3. Draw and label a diagram of the cross-section view.
4. There is a thin layer between the bark and the wood, called the cambium. Look for it in your specimen.

QUESTION

It is possible to determine the age of a woody stem by counting the rings. (a) Find out how this is done. (b) How old is your specimen?

Side view

Cross-section view

The stem of a plant connects the roots to the leaves and flowers. It supports the plant and holds the leaves and flowers up in the air towards the sun. The stem carries water and dissolved minerals from the roots to the leaves, as well as carrying food from the leaves to the roots. Stems usually store some of the plant's food. Green herbaceous stems are also able to make food for the plant. So the stem of a plant may have as many as three functions: support of the plant, transportation of materials, and storage of food.

Stems sometimes divide to produce branches, as in many common trees. The branches continue to divide as the tree grows, becoming smaller and smaller. The ends of branches are called twigs.

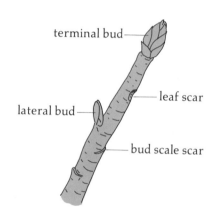

terminal bud

leaf scar

lateral bud

bud scale scar

INVESTIGATION: To examine twigs

(This activity should be conducted in late fall or early winter.)

MATERIALS

pencil   sketching paper   razor blade or sharp knife

PROCEDURE

1. Find a tree with some twigs you can observe without climbing it.
2. Find the terminal bud at the end of a twig, and note whether there is one bud or a group of buds.
3. Examine the bark of the twig and note its characteristics.
4. Locate other buds on the same twig. These are lateral buds. Compare them with the terminal bud.
5. Along the twig you will find a series of circles close together. This is the bud-scale scar, marking the position of the terminal bud of the previous year.
6. Use the razor blade to remove one bud from the tree. Bisect this bud and examine it.
7. Find a tree of a different type and repeat steps 2 to 6.

OBSERVATIONS

1. Write a description of the external features of the twig (colour, texture, location, and number of buds).
2. Draw and label a diagram of the twig you examined from each of the two trees.
3. Draw sketches of the buds of both trees, taking care to show any differences.
4. Your twigs may have had leaf scars, indicating where leaves have fallen off. If they did, record a description of them.
5. Determine the age of one of the twigs by counting its bud-scale scars.

QUESTIONS

1. The distances between bud-scale scars vary considerably. Explain why this is so.
2. What is the function of the bud?

Leaves

Attached to the stem or twigs of many plants you will find leaves. Leaves occur in many different shapes and sizes. They usually have two main parts: a blade and a petiole.

The petiole is the stem that attaches the leaf to the plant. In some leaves, the petiole may be very short or even missing entirely. The part of the blade that appears to be a continuation of the petiole is called the mid-rib. Branching out from the mid-rib is a network of veins.

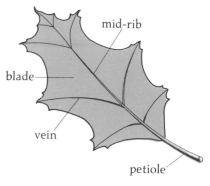

The main parts of a leaf

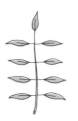

A simple leaf, a deeply cut leaf, and two compound leaves (left to right)

Leaves are sometimes grouped according to whether they are "simple" or "compound" in shape. A simple leaf has its blade in one piece. It may be deeply cut the way maple and oak leaves are. If a leaf's blade is divided into separate parts, the leaf is a compound one, and the parts are called leaflets.

entire (or smooth)   lobed   serrated

The outer margins of leaves have a wide variety of shapes. The pattern formed by the veins also varies considerably. In one pattern, many large veins spread out from the tip of the petiole, like the fingers of a hand. This pattern of veins in a leaf

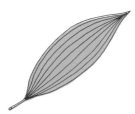

is called palmate. Some leaves have smaller veins branching out on either side of the mid-rib. This pattern is called pinnate. In another type of vein pattern, usually found in herbaceous plants, there are many veins running parallel to each other from the petiole to the tip of the leaf. This pattern is called parallel.

In some plants, the leaves do not look like leaves as we ordinarily think of them. In evergreen trees, the leaves are long and slender and are commonly called needles. The cedars have leaves that look like overlapping scales.

The leaf is a very important part of a plant. The chlorophyll in the cells of a leaf enables a plant to produce its own food. This process is called photosynthesis. As a living organism, a plant must have food, and it is supplied with food by the leaves. Leaves also release excess water from the plant through tiny openings on their undersides, called stomata. This release of excess water is called transpiration.

INVESTIGATION: To classify an assortment of leaves

MATERIALS
assorted leaves

PROCEDURE

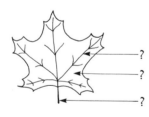

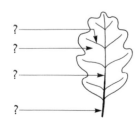

1. Collect leaves from eight or 10 different kinds of trees.
2. Examine your leaves closely. Try to identify the petiole, the blade, the vein, and the mid-rib in each leaf. Some kinds of leaves have no mid-rib.
3. Give each leaf a number.
4. Classify your leaves into three groups: simple leaves, deeply cut simple leaves, and compound leaves.
5. Examine each leaf closely to determine what type of margin it has and the pattern of its veins. In your notebook, draw a chart as explained in the observations, and start filling it in.
6. If time permits, preserve your leaves for future use. Place the leaves individually on blotting paper or newspaper. Put more similar paper on top of the leaves. Add a board and some additional weight (bricks or books). Let the leaves dry out completely before removing them.

7. For more permanent preservation, press the dry leaves with a warm iron between two sheets of waxed paper (see diagram). To keep wax off the iron and the ironing board, be sure to use heavy paper, as illustrated.

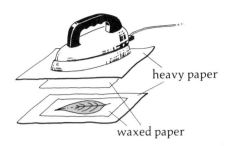

heavy paper

waxed paper

OBSERVATIONS

1. Sketch three different leaves, one from each group. Label your sketches to indicate the parts.
2. This chart is for your numbered leaves. Use a leaf identification chart to help you fill in the last column.

LEAF NO.	LEAF TYPE (simple, deeply cut, or compound)	LEAF MARGIN (entire, lobed, serrate, or other)	VEIN PATTERN (palmate, pinnate, or parallel)	KIND OF PLANT
1.				
2.				
3.				
4.				
5.				

QUESTIONS

Among the leaves you collected, what was the most common (a) leaf type, (b) leaf margin, and (c) vein pattern?

Flowers and fruit

The fourth major part of a plant is the flower. Remember the other three main parts? The function of the flower is to form seeds to produce new plants. To understand this function, you must be familiar with the flower's parts.

INVESTIGATION: To examine the parts of a flower

MATERIALS

simple flower (lily, petunia, tulip,
    buttercup, toadflax, or morning glory)
tweezers
magnifying glass

PROCEDURE

1. Examine the part of the plant that holds up the flower. This is the stalk, or peduncle. Note that the upper region

of the peduncle is enlarged. This swelling is the receptacle.

2. Examine the leaf-like structures, or sepals, that are attached to the base of the receptacle. Count the sepals, remove them carefully with tweezers, and place them on a piece of paper.
3. Examine and count the larger, leaf-like pieces. These are the petals. Remove the petals carefully with the tweezers, and place them on the paper, near the sepals.
4. Now you have a better view of the internal parts of the flower. Surrounding the base you will see a number of similar slender parts with enlarged ends. These are the stamens. Count the stamens in your flower. Examine the end of a stamen with the magnifying glass. Remove all the stamens and place them on the paper.
5. The central part that remains is the pistil. Touch the top of the pistil gently, and note how it feels. Notice that the pistil is enlarged at the base.

OBSERVATIONS

1. Record everything you observed in steps 2-6.
2. Draw and label a diagram of each of the parts you removed from the flower.

QUESTIONS

1. Name the parts that were attached to the receptacle.
2. Why did the stamens appear rather fuzzy?
3. Why are the petals large and colourful?

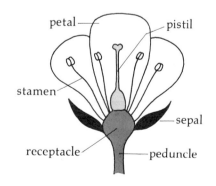

The parts of a typical flower

You have seen that a typical flower has four main kinds of parts – sepals, petals, a pistil, and stamens. These parts are attached to the plant by the peduncle. The peduncle supports the flower and holds it up in the air. The enlarged end of the peduncle is the receptacle, to which all the flower's parts are attached. The sepals, which are usually green, are the small leaf-like structures at the base of the flower. As a group, the sepals of a flower are called the calyx. The calyx protects the flower from wind and rain when it is in the bud stage of growth.

The larger, leaf-like parts of a flower are the petals. As a group, they are called the corolla. The corolla is usually colourful, perhaps to attract insects; it also serves in most flowers to protect the pistil and the stamens.

The stamen has two parts: an anther and a filament. The filament is the long, slender stem that supports the anther. The anther is the fuzzy end of the stamen and is usually yellow. If you touch an anther, a fine powder, called pollen, will probably stick to your finger. The pistil is located in the central part of the flower. It sometimes resembles a small bowling pin. The top of the pistil is the stigma. It is usually sticky. The narrow middle part of a pistil, supporting the stigma, is the style. The enlarged base of a pistil is the ovary. It is within the ovary that the seeds develop.

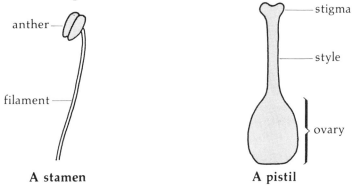

A stamen   A pistil

If a flower has all of the four main parts (calyx, corolla, pistil, and stamens) it is known as a complete flower. If it lacks one or more of the four main parts, it is called an incomplete flower.

For a flower to produce seeds, many things must occur. First, the anthers must produce pollen, and the pollen must then be transferred to a stigma. This transferring process is called pollination. Pollen may be transferred from an anther to a stigma of the same flower. This is called self-pollination. But pollen may also be transferred from an anther of one flower to a stigma of another. This is called cross-pollination. Wind and insects are the chief agents that help in the process of pollination.

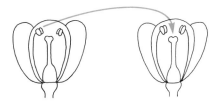

Types of pollination

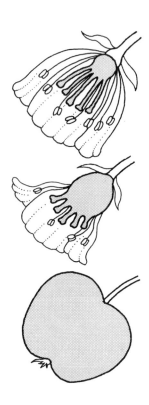

Apple blossoms develop into apples.

After pollination has occurred, another biological process, fertilization, takes place in the ovary. When both pollination and fertilization have occurred, seeds will develop in the flower's ovary. Each of these seeds has the ability to produce a complete new plant, when given suitable conditions.

As a seed develops in an ovary, it grows and ripens. The ripening ovary is called the fruit. It is not only trees such as the apple tree and the orange tree that have fruits. Scientists define a fruit as a ripened ovary of any flowering plant. They think of fruits as including the ripened ovaries of garden flowers, wild flowers, flowering trees, cereal grains (such as wheat, oats, and corn), nut trees, and many vegetables (such as squash, beans, peas, and cucumber). Thus, a very wide range of plants produce fruit.

Apples begin to develop when the flower, or blossom, of an apple tree has been pollinated and fertilization has taken place. These processes cause seeds to form in the ovary of each blossom. The ovary swells as the ripening process occurs, and the other parts of the blossom, such as the rest of the pistil, the stamens, the petals, and the sepals, dry up and fall off. The fully ripened ovary gradually takes on the characteristic size and shape of a ripe apple.

Fruits are vital to their plants. They protect the seeds that they enclose, and help to scatter them. Often, the fruits store nourishment and moisture to help the seeds develop into new plants.

INVESTIGATION: To examine some fruits

MATERIALS

specimens of several fruits (apple, pear, cucumber,
 walnut, pumpkin, acorn, cherry, wheat, bean, corn)
toothpicks
knife

PROCEDURE

1. Examine each fruit and note its shape, size, and colour.
2. Try to puncture each fruit with a toothpick. Whenever you have been able to penetrate the skin, observe carefully as you remove the toothpick.

3. Carefully cut with the knife (or break) each of your fruits, and note what is inside.

4. From your findings in step 3, classify the fruits into two groups – those you were able to cut with a knife, and those you had to break.

OBSERVATIONS

1. Record your observations of each fruit.
2. Write down your two lists of fruits, from step 4. Title one list "fleshy fruits" and the other "dry fruits".

QUESTIONS

1. Describe the difference between fleshy fruits and dry fruits, from your observations.
2. Name three fruits the whole of which may be eaten.
3. Name three fruits of which you may eat just the fleshy part.
4. Name a fruit from which only the seeds are eaten.

Because fruits are an important source of food for man, much research has been done to improve their production. One method that is used is "controlled pollination". Pollen from an anther of one flower is transferred to the stigma of another flower, perhaps of a different species. In this way, a new "hybrid" variety of fruit tree can be developed that gives larger, or hardier, or tastier fruits than either of the original trees.

Seedless oranges are popular. It had been discovered that

some orange trees produce seedless oranges. Branches from such trees were transplanted by grafting to the trunks of ordinary orange trees and in this way whole orchards of trees were created that would yield seedless oranges. The same has been done with grapes and grapefruit.

Seeds

One of the main functions of every living organism is to produce more of its own kind so that the species will continue. Not all plants use the seed method of reproduction, but most of them do. Seeds occur in many sizes and colours, but all have the same three parts. Each seed has a covering, called the seed coat, to protect the inner parts. Inside the seed coat are an embryo and food for the embryo from the time it starts to grow until it has leaves that enable it to produce its own food. The embryo has tiny roots, a stem, and leaves that will develop into a new plant.

Most seeds store their food in seed leaves called cotyledons. "Monocotyledon" plants, such as corn, have a single seed leaf in each seed. "Dicotyledon" plants, such as the bean, have two seed leaves in each seed.

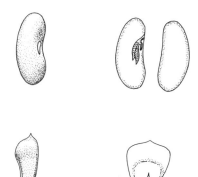

The two types of seeds — bean (top) and corn (bottom)

INVESTIGATION: To examine some typical seeds

MATERIALS
lima bean seeds
corn seeds (kernels)
magnifying glass
razor blade
beaker
Lugol's iodine stain
slice of bread
dish and spoon

PROCEDURE
1. Soak some of the lima bean seeds in water overnight. Leave some seeds unsoaked, for purposes of comparison.
2. Examine one of the soaked seeds. Remove the seed coat and examine it. Carefully separate the two cotyledons and

examine them with the magnifying glass. Find the embryo and note where it is located.

3. Place a few dry lima bean seeds on a dish and mash them up with a spoon. Add some water to the resulting powder. Add a couple of drops of Lugol's iodine stain. Observe what happens. Then add a couple of drops of the stain to the slice of bread. Observe what happens.
4. Repeat steps 1-3, this time with the corn seeds.

OBSERVATIONS

1. Make a sketch of each type of seed and label the seed coat, the cotyledons, and the embryo.
2. Bread contains starch. Describe what happened when you added Lugol's iodine stain to the mashed seeds and to the bread.

QUESTIONS

1. How is the bean seed different from the corn seed? In what ways are the two seeds similar?
2. What are the three parts of a seed?
3. What was the purpose of using Lugol's iodine stain?

Seeds remain dormant until conditions are right for them to develop. In addition to water and air, seeds need a certain amount of warmth. They also need a certain amount of space. That is why they are usually dispersed away from the plant that produced them. Nature helps to disperse seeds in various ways. When a seed settles in the ground and the proper conditions of moisture and temperature occur, it will begin to grow. This process is called germination.

You have observed the germination of seeds (page 19). As seeds absorb water, they begin to swell. The moisture also causes the seed coat to soften, so that the embryo can grow through it. The embryo produces roots, which grow down into the soil, and a stem, which grows up into the air. Then tiny leaves appear on the stem and the new plant starts to produce its own food by photosynthesis. Until the leaves appear, the growing embryo is nourished by the food stored inside the seed.

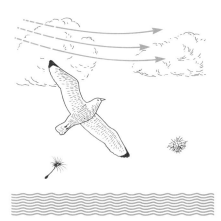

Can you name three things in the diagram that aid seed dispersal?

INVESTIGATION: To observe the germination of a bean seed and a corn seed

MATERIALS

beaker
lima bean and corn seeds
dark blotting paper

absorbent cotton
peat moss (or vermiculite)

PROCEDURE

1. Soak all the seeds in water overnight.
2. Place blotting paper around the inside of the beaker. Stuff the cotton into the centre, to hold the blotting paper against the sides of the beaker.
3. Place the bean seeds and the corn seeds between the blotting paper and the sides of the beaker.
4. Add water to the cotton until the blotting paper is wet. Keep the blotting paper moist throughout the experiment. Place the beaker in a warm place away from direct sunlight.
5. Observe the seeds each day until they have sprouted.

OBSERVATIONS

1. Keep notes on the changes you observe from day to day during the germination of the seeds.
2. Compare what happens to the two types of seeds.

QUESTION

Why is sunlight not necessary for the germination of seeds?

INVESTIGATION: To determine whether seeds give off carbon dioxide during germination

MATERIALS

lima bean seeds
flask with two-hole stopper
thistle tube
tubing (glass, or rubber, or plastic)
beaker
limewater

PROCEDURE

1. Soak about 25 lima bean seeds in water overnight.
2. Put the seeds in the flask and add water until about one-half of them are submerged.
3. Insert the thistle tube into the stopper so that the end of the tube almost touches the bottom of the flask. Put some water in the beaker, and connect the other hole in the stopper to the beaker, as illustrated.
4. Leave the apparatus for a couple of days, then empty the water from the beaker and pour limewater into it. Be sure that the end of the glass tubing is below the surface of the limewater.
5. Pour water into the thistle tube until the flask is about one-half full.
6. Observe the end of the glass tubing that is in the limewater.

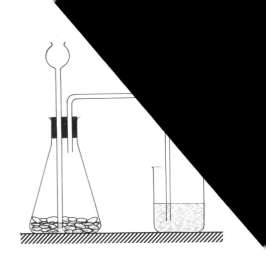

OBSERVATIONS

Describe in detail the signs you observed indicating that the seeds were germinating.

QUESTIONS

1. Explain why bubbles emerged from the glass tubing when water was added to the flask.
2. What changes occurred to the limewater, and what did the changes indicate?

Man has found many uses for seeds and seed products. The seeds of grass plants such as rice, oats, wheat, and corn are his most important source of food. Chocolate, cocoa, and coffee are obtained from different species of bean seeds. Oils from peanut and cotton seeds are used for cooking, and oil from the seeds of plants such as the coconut tree is used to make candles and soap. Oil from the seeds of the flax plant is used to make paints and varnish. Fibres from the seed covering of the cotton plant are used to make cotton cloth.

You would probably have no trouble naming half a dozen seed products that you have eaten or used in the last day or two.

Plant growth

Have you ever wondered why cactus plants do not grow naturally outdoors in most parts of Canada? Why don't Canadian farmers grow coffee, bananas, or pineapples? Why doesn't the Douglas fir tree grow in eastern Canada? The answer is that these plants do not find suitable growth conditions in the areas named.

The conditions that affect plant growth include water, temperature, sunlight, soil, and the chemicals in the soil. Each type of plant has a certain temperature range within which it thrives, and beyond which it will die. Some plants require sandy soil. Others need soil that contains large amounts of clay and humus. Each type of plant has its own optimum daily quota of sunlight, which scientists call its photoperiod.

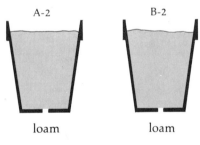

A-1   B-1

sand   sand

A-2   B-2

loam   loam

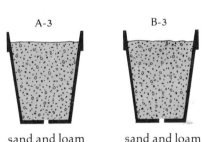

A-3   B-3

sand and loam   sand and loam

INVESTIGATION: To determine the ideal conditions for growth of bean plants

---

MATERIALS

12 healthy young bean plants   100 mL graduated cylinder
6 plant pots of equal size   centimetre ruler

PROCEDURE

1. Put sand in two of the pots and loam in two others. Into the last two pots put equal parts of sand and loam, mixed.
2. Label the pots as shown in the diagram.
3. Plant two bean plants in each of the six pots.
4. Place the six pots on a window sill so that they will all receive the same amount of sunlight and be subjected to the same temperatures.
5. Water the six pots at the same time every two or three days, giving pots A-1, A-2, and A-3 exactly half as much water as pots B-1, B-2, and B-3.
6. Observe the pots and start measuring the tallest sprout in each pot daily. Continue your observations for two weeks.

OBSERVATIONS

Record your measurements in your notebook in a table like this.

HEIGHT OF PLANTS (cm)						
	A-1	A-2	A-3	B-1	B-2	B-3
Day 1						
Day 2						
Day 3						
Day 4						
Day 5						

QUESTIONS

1. On the basis of your observations, what are the preferred conditions for growth of bean plants?
2. Suggest why two plants (instead of just one) were placed in each pot for this investigation.

Plant reproduction

Most new plants grow from seeds, but there are several other ways in which plants can reproduce themselves.

Certain types of plants, such as the sweet potato, the radish, the carrot, and the turnip, are able to produce new plants from roots. If the narrow end of a sweet potato is supported in water by toothpicks, and put in a warm, dark place, it will grow roots and stems. Water should be added from time to time. The new plant may be moved into the sunlight and planted in the ground as soon as the roots and stems appear.

Some plants, such as the iris and the trillium, have long underground stems that grow horizontally, just under the surface of the ground. These are known as rhizomes. As the rhizome grows, it produces new plants along its length. These new plants spring up through the ground. You can observe this by getting an iris from a greenhouse and planting it about 2 cm below the surface of the ground. Water it regularly, and watch how it grows.

In certain plants that grow rhizomes, such as the potato, the ends of the rhizomes become swollen. These swellings, called tubers, contain food stored by the plant. Tubers are able to produce new plants. You can demonstrate this by suspending a potato in water. Follow the same instructions you used for the sweet potato, and the tuber will produce a new plant in about two weeks. It should then be moved into the sunlight.

The African violet and the begonia are plants that can

A sweet potato grows roots and stems.

An African violet clipping

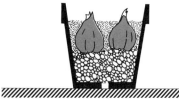

Bulbs are planted in this way in order to produce new plants.

reproduce from their leaves. Fill a flower pot with sand, and water it until the sand is moist. With a clean, sharp instrument, make several cuts across the underside of a leaf of one of these plants, so that the cuts go through the veins. Place the leaf in the pot with the veins touching the surface of the sand, or simply insert the petiole of the leaf into the sand. Cover the pot with clear plastic or glass to reduce the loss of water by evaporation.

After two or three weeks, roots should start to grow from the cuts (or the petiole) and stems should begin to form. Remove the covering and start watering the new plants regularly. When the new plants are growing well, plant them in individual pots, with soil.

Some plants have short and thick underground stems called bulbs, which can grow into new plants. Examples of this type of plant are the tulip, the daffodil, and the narcissus. Bulbs are usually planted in spring or early summer for outdoor growth, but they may be planted during the winter for indoor growth. The growth of bulbs at times other than their normal growing period is known as forcing. Obtain some narcissus bulbs from a florist or greenhouse and place them in a refrigerator for a cooling period of two weeks or more, depending on the type of bulb. (Most bulbs need such a cooling period before growth.) Then place pebbles in the bottom of a shallow flower pot and stand the bulbs (in clumps of three or four) on the pebbles. Sprinkle in sandy soil, loosely, until only the top half of each bulb is showing. Water regularly to keep the soil and the bulbs moist. Keep the pot in a cool, dark place for about six weeks, or until stems begin to grow. Then move the pot into the sun. Beautiful flowers may be grown indoors at any time of year by this method.

There are still more ways of growing new plants, besides those already mentioned. Two other methods involve corms and stem cuttings, or slips. You could find out about these methods in the library, and try them out.

The effect of chemicals on plant growth

Plant growth depends on environmental conditions, such as moisture, temperature, soil conditions, and photoperiod. But it is regulated by chemical substances called hormones, which are produced by the plant itself. Plants produce these hormones in quantities that are minute, but still sufficient to affect their growth and reproduction.

A type of hormone that has been widely studied is the auxins. Their main function is to accelerate growth, particularly by enlarging the cells. Auxins will also act, along with other hormones, to promote the rooting of plants. They have an important role in the production of seedless grapes and oranges, and they help to keep fruits such as apples from falling from the trees.

Plant hormones such as the auxins cause many of the growth effects that may be observed in plants.

RESEARCH QUESTIONS
1. "Roots search for water." Explain this statement.
2. Describe and explain the response of roots to gravity.
3. What part of a root produces new roots when stimulated by an auxin?
4. Why must the tip bud on a branch be removed before the side buds will develop?
5. Explain how a tendril is able to twist around a string as rapidly as it does.
6. Find out what effect it has on a plant to change the photo-period.
7. What does an auxin do to fruit that prevents it from falling ?

The classification of plants

Plants may be arranged into groups and sub-groups according to their characteristics. The external features and the structure of each plant must be examined, and the following questions answered.

(a) Is the plant green?
(b) Does the plant have roots, stems, and leaves?
(c) Does the plant have channels, or tubes, for transporting water?
(d) Does the plant produce flowers or cones?

The answer to these questions will enable you to classify each plant into one of the four main groups. Refer to pages 51-60 for information about the four groups of plants.

In the process of classification, organisms are divided into groups, and these groups are then subdivided a number of times. For each new subdivision there is a distinguishing name. The largest group is called the kingdom, and all plants belong to the kingdom Plantae. The kingdom is subdivided into phyla, which are subdivided into classes and so on down through the levels of order, family, genus, species, and variety. Here is the classification for the red delicious apple.

KINGDOM	Plantae	
PHYLUM	Tracheophyta	has channels, or tubes
CLASS	Angiospermae	is a flowering plant with enclosed seeds
SUB-CLASS	Dichotyledoneae	has seeds with two cotyledons
ORDER	Rosales	is a rose-type plant
FAMILY	Rosaceae	produces flowers that look like roses
GENUS	*Pyrus*	produces apple fruits
SPECIES	*malus*	is a cultivated plant
VARIETY	red delicious	

Often, botanists disagree over the classification of a plant, since it can be a complex matter. Biological keys have been made, and you will find them helpful for classifying plants. But, even with such aids, you must start by examining each specimen's external features and structure. The next investigation will give you some practice in examining plant specimens.

INVESTIGATION: To compare two types of trees – coniferous and deciduous

---

MATERIALS

a coniferous tree and a deciduous tree (specimens should have leaves you can examine without climbing the tree)
magnifying glass
note pad and pencil

PROCEDURE

1. Find suitable specimens in the schoolyard or nearby.

2. Examine the bark of each tree. Note the colour and roughness of the trunks.
3. Note how the trunk branches, and where the branches originate.
4. Examine and compare the leaves of the two trees.
5. Examine each tree carefully for any evidence of how it reproduces.
6. Try to obtain a seed from each tree. Note where the seeds are produced and compare the seeds of the two trees.

OBSERVATIONS

1. Sketch the silhouette of each tree from a short distance away.
2. Sketch a leaf from each tree.
3. List ways in which the two trees differ.
4. List ways in which the trees are similar.

ACTIVITY: To make a permanent record of a tree's bark

MATERIALS

plasticine	borax
plaster of Paris	shellac
vaseline	paint
cardboard strips	brush
paper-clips	

PROCEDURE

1. Use the brush to remove loose debris from the area of bark that is to be recorded.
2. Soften some plasticine in your hands and press it onto the area to be recorded. Shape the outer edge of the mould to make it oval or round.
3. Remove the plasticine carefully, peeling it off slowly so that it remains in one piece.
4. Coat the plasticine with vaseline so that the plaster will not stick to it.
5. Form the strip of cardboard into a collar around the mould.

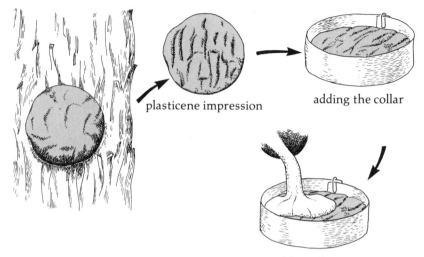

plasticene impression

adding the collar

adding plaster

6. Mix water and plaster of Paris in a disposable container. The mixture should be like glue and should have no lumps.
7. Pour the plaster into the mould. Allow air to escape by tapping the collar. Push a paper-clip into the plaster so that the cast will have a hanger when it is dry.
8. After the plaster has hardened, remove the collar and the plasticine. Clean the vaseline from the cast. To harden the cast, boil it in a mild borax and water solution.
9. Paint the cast to match the bark.

REVIEW QUESTIONS

1. What are the four main parts of a plant?
2. (a) Name three types of roots.
   (b) How do the three types differ?
3. Describe three functions of roots.
4. Why do plants have stems?
5. What is the function of a plant's buds?
6. Copy this diagram of a leaf and label the parts. What type of leaf is pictured? What type of margin does the leaf have? What is the name of the leaf's vein pattern?
7. Name two functions of leaves.
8. What is transpiration?
9. What is the function of a plant's flowers?
10. Explain the difference between a calyx and a corolla.

11. Explain the functions of the following parts of a flower: anther, filament, stigma, ovary, and receptacle.
12. What is pollination?
13. Explain the difference between a complete flower and an incomplete flower.
14. Discuss how a fruit is formed.
15. Name three examples of fleshy fruits and three examples of dry fruits.
16. What is grafting?
17. What is the function of a seed?
18. How does nature help to disperse the seeds of plants?
19. What conditions are necessary for germination?
20. Describe three uses of seeds.
21. Explain how to grow a new plant without starting with a seed.
22. What effects do auxins have on plants?
23. Name four main groups of plants?
24. To what kingdom do all plants belong?
25. Name in descending order, the taxons, or levels, that are used in the classification of plants.

IMPORTANT TERMS

root—a plant structure that usually grows below the surface of the ground

stem—a plant part that connects the roots with the leaves

leaf—a plant structure that grows out of a stem

transpiration—the process of releasing excess water that occurs in leaves

flower—the seed-producing part of a plant

pollination—the process that occurs in flowering plants by which pollen is transferred from an anther to a stigma

germination—the process of growth of a seed

hormone—a chemical substance that regulates growth

LIFE CYCLES

Every species of organism continues to exist for hundreds or even millions of years, but the life span of an individual organism is very short in comparison. Individuals live for a limited period of weeks or years, and must be able to reproduce themselves before they die if their species are to continue. The life span can vary from a few weeks in the case of some insects to a few thousand years, for a few species of trees.

ORGANISM	MAXIMUM LIFE SPAN (APPROXIMATE)
mayfly (some species)	3 weeks
blue jay	14 years
cicada	17 years
bullfrog	30 years
Canada goose	30 years
catfish	60 years
man	103 years
giant tortoise	152 years
oak tree	500 years
sequoia tree	3000 years
bristlecone pine	5000 years

A monarch butterfly will emerge from this chrysalis.

Few organisms achieve the maximum life span of their species, because most of them have shortened life spans due to accidents, diseases, or starvation. Enough individuals of a species must reproduce before dying to ensure that the species will not become extinct. We will examine the methods organisms use to produce new individuals.

Although the actual process of reproduction varies from species to species, there are two basic methods – asexual and sexual. In asexual reproduction one parent organism is able to produce new individuals. In sexual reproduction two parent organisms are usually required.

Asexual reproduction

Many green plants and protozoans, as well as a few animals, are able to reproduce asexually. Most green plants are able to reproduce from a part of a parent plant. Cuttings of coleus, geraniums, or African violets, for example, will grow roots and eventually develop into new plants if they are kept in suitable conditions. This form of asexual reproduction is called vegetative reproduction. The new individuals that develop are identical to the parent organism. In the next investigation you will examine vegetative reproduction in two different plants.

INVESTIGATION: To compare vegetative reproduction in two different plants

MATERIALS

coleus or geranium plant
African violet plant
two 250 mL flasks
small tray about 5 cm deep
vermiculite (enough to fill the tray)
aquarium (large enough to cover the tray)
scalpel or razor blade

PROCEDURE

1. Cut two branches about 10 cm long, each with several leaves, from the coleus plant. Make each cut just below a leaf, and then cut off that leaf.

MATLOCK COLLEGE LIBRARY

2. Fill the two flasks with water, and insert one cutting into each flask.
3. Put the flasks in a sunny place.
4. Add water when necessary, so that the flasks remain full.
5. Cut three or four leaves from the African violet plant. Make the cut close to the stem.
6. Fill the tray with vermiculite and add water until it overflows. After a few minutes, drain off the excess water.
7. With a pencil, poke holes in the damp vermiculite, and place one cutting in each hole. Press the vermiculite firmly around the cuttings.
8. Put the tray in a sunny place and cover it by placing the aquarium over it, upside down.
9. Note any changes in the plants during the next few weeks.
10. Once a week, gently pull the African violet leaves out of the vermiculite and examine them. Note any changes, and then replace the leaves carefully in the vermiculite.

OBSERVATIONS

On a chart like this one, record any changes you observe.

	COLEUS	AFRICAN VIOLET
week 1		
week 2		
week 3		
etc.		

QUESTIONS

1. How do the two plants compare, in the amount of time it takes them to reproduce by this method?
2. Describe how each type of plant grew from the cuttings.
3. What was the reason for putting the aquarium over the African violet cuttings?
4. Explain why this form of reproduction is asexual.

It is possible to make most green plants reproduce by using cuttings. You could try growing some other types of plants in this way, on your own.

Another type of asexual reproduction, used by all one-celled organisms, is the fission process. Each cell divides itself into

A green plant growing roots from cuttings

two parts, each of which grows and becomes identical to the original parent cell. In fission, one parent cell is replaced by two new cells, called daughter cells. The parent cell ceases to exist.

Fission produces two daughter cells.

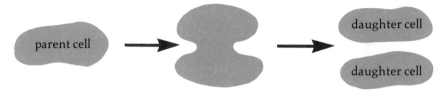

parent cell

daughter cell

daughter cell

This process is sometimes called division, because one cell divides to produce two daughter cells.

INVESTIGATION: To observe fission in one-celled protozoans

MATERIALS

microscope
prepared slide of amoeba or paramecium undergoing fission

PROCEDURE

1. Use the microscope to find a specimen of the organism. Refer to the sketches for help in finding it.
2. Move the slide so that you will be able to examine other specimens of the organism. Try to find several different specimens.
3. Examine each organism you find and note any differences between them. In each specimen note especially the dark region, which is the nucleus.

OBSERVATIONS

1. Sketch several different specimens of the organism you examined.
2. The organisms on your slide were at various stages of fission. Some were just beginning and others were almost finished. Label each of your sketches with an appropriate title from this list:

fission started   fission nearly completed
fission partly completed   fission completed

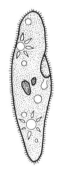

An amoeba (top) and a paramecium (bottom)

3. Write a brief description of what happens to the nucleus during fission.
4. Write a short comparison between the new cells and the parent cell.

QUESTIONS
1. What happens to a parent cell when it has undergone fission?
2. Explain why fission is an asexual method of reproduction.

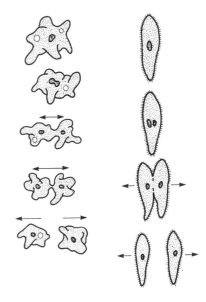

Still another kind of asexual reproduction is budding. In this process, a bud is produced on the parent organism, and this bud grows into a new organism. Once grown, the new organism breaks away and becomes a separate individual. Budding occurs in yeasts, which are one-celled organisms, and also in some simple animals, such as the hydra, which lives in freshwater ponds and marshes. After the budding process has been completed, the parent organism continues with its other normal life activities.

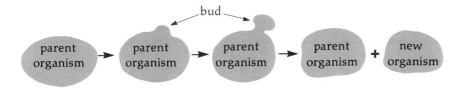

Yeast reproduces by budding.

INVESTIGATION: To observe budding in yeast and hydras

MATERIALS

microscope
prepared slides of yeast and hydras

PROCEDURE
1. Examine the yeast slide and note the structure of the yeast cells.
2. Look for organisms that have bumps on their outer edges.
3. Look for an example of a bud that has just separated from the parent organism.
4. Repeat steps 1, 2, and 3 for the slide of hydras.

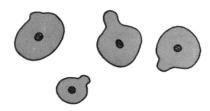

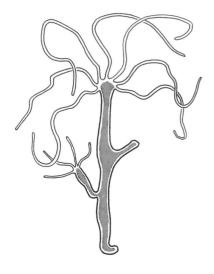

OBSERVATIONS

1. Write a description of each of the organisms you examined.
2. Draw a series of sketches to show the budding process in yeast.
3. Sketch a hydra that has a bud.
4. Describe how the buds compare in size with the parent organisms.

QUESTIONS

1. Are yeast and hydras able to grow buds at the same rate? Give reasons for your answers.
2. Explain why budding is a form of asexual reproduction.

Reproduction by the formation of spores is a form of asexual reproduction that is used by fungi, such as mushrooms and moulds, and by some plants and protozoans. The parent organism produces spores, which, like seeds, can develop into new individual organisms under suitable conditions. Each mushroom, for example, produces thousands of microscopic spores that are released by the parent and dispersed by wind and water. Again, only one parent is necessary to make the spores.

Mushrooms reproduce by forming spores.

INVESTIGATION: To observe spores of various kinds of fungi

MATERIALS

microscope
glass slides and cover-slips
clean sheet of paper
several types of fungi

PROCEDURE

1. Obtain specimens of a few types of fungi – mushrooms, tree fungi, and moulds.
2. Using a toothpick or small stick, probe under the cap of a mushroom while holding it over the sheet of paper.
3. Transfer some of the dust-like material to a slide and cover it with a cover-slip.
4. Examine the spores with the microscope, using the highest power.
5. Scrape some of the dust-like spores from the underside of a tree fungus.
6. Transfer the spores to a glass slide and cover them with a cover-slip.
7. Examine the spores with the highest power on the microscope.
8. Place a little mould on a slide, cover it with a cover-slip, and examine it.

OBSERVATIONS

1. Describe the appearance of each of the types of spores you examined.
2. Make a sketch of each.

QUESTIONS

1. Suggest why fungi produce so many spores.
2. Explain why the formation of spores is a type of asexual reproduction.

Sexual reproduction

Sexual reproduction usually involves two parent organisms. In some simple plants, such as the alga *spirogyra*, and in protozoans there is no difference between the two parent organisms. The more complex plants and animals have individuals of two sexes – male and female. In such organisms, each of the parent organisms donates a part of the necessary material for the formation of a new individual.

In one-celled protozoans and in simple plants, the reproductive process is called conjugation. In this process, two cells exchange material with each other. Each of the cells then undergoes fission.

Spirogyra is a species of alga that forms a green scum on the surface of ponds. It is made up of long strands of cells joined together. In the next investigation, you will examine *spirogyra* during the process of conjugation.

INVESTIGATION: To observe conjugation in spirogyra

MATERIALS

microscope   prepared slide of *spirogyra*

PROCEDURE

1. Locate a specimen of *spirogyra* with the microscope.
2. Examine other specimens on the slide until you find two strands of *spirogyra* lined up beside each other.
3. Examine these two strands closely and note whether there are any points of contact between them.

OBSERVATIONS

1. Sketch the specimens you examined in step 3.
2. Describe in your notes what you observed that suggests that two cells join to form a single cell.

QUESTIONS

1. What is the function of the bridge that forms between adjacent cells of *spirogyra*?
2. Explain why the conjugation you observed in this investigation is a form of sexual reproduction.

When *spirogyra* strands line up together, they sometimes form bridges, as you observed. The contents of one cell are transferred to the adjacent cell, where the materials of the two cells become mixed together. The cell containing a mixture of materials develops into a new strand of *spirogyra*.

The life cycle of an animal

Most animals use the sexual method of reproduction. Individuals of each of the two sexes, male and female, contribute material for the production of a new individual. The male parent produces sperm cells. These must combine with the egg cells produced by the female parent. The uniting of sperm and egg is called fertilization, and the resulting cell is called a zygote. The zygote undergoes cell division to form an embryo. From the embryo, the new animal develops.

When it has fully matured, the new animal is capable of producing egg or sperm cells, so that it can contribute to a repetition of the same process. In this way, each generation produces a new generation, and the species continues to exist.

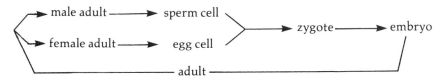

The life cycle of flowering plants

Flowering plants use the same method of reproduction as animals, with one important difference: most plants are able to produce both sperm and egg cells. The eggs may be fertilized by sperm from the same plant or from another plant of the same species. The flower of the plant includes all the parts necessary for the production of both sperm and egg cells.

The male part of the flower is called the stamen. It consists of a thin part – the filament – and an enlarged end – the anther. The anther is coated with many grains of pollen, each of which contains a sperm cell. The female part of the plant is the pistil. It consists of three parts – the sticky stigma, the style, and the ovary. The ovary contains ovules, each of which contains an egg cell.

You can see both male and female parts of this flower.

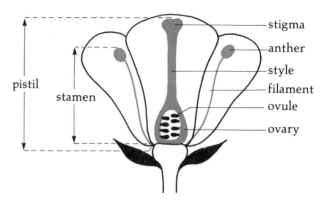

The first step of the reproductive process in flowering plants occurs when pollen is transferred from the anther to the stigma. This is called pollination. In the next two investigations you will observe this process.

INVESTIGATION: To examine a flower

MATERIALS

1 or 2 flowers, such as a tulip, lily,
  amaryllis, morning glory
magnifying glass
microscope
slides
scalpel or razor blade
small envelopes

PROCEDURE

1. Examine one of the flowers closely.
2. Locate and examine the petals.
3. Locate and examine the stamens.
4. Locate the pistil and touch the stigma with your finger.
5. Repeat steps 1 to 4 for a flower of another type.
6. Complete steps 1 to 4 in the observations before proceeding further.
7. Using the scalpel or razor blade, carefully cut one flower in half. Start at the stem and cut through the pistil so that you have two similar halves.
8. Examine the contents of the ovary, using the magnifying glass.

9. Carefully remove a stamen and brush the yellow pollen onto a microscope slide.
10. Examine the pollen, using the low powers on the microscope.
11. Remove the remaining stamens and place them in an envelope. Label the envelope with your name and type of flower.
12. Repeat steps 7 to 11 for the other flower.
13. Place the two envelopes in a safe place. You will need them in the next investigation.

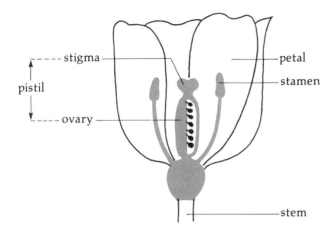

OBSERVATIONS
1. Describe the petals of each flower.
2. Sketch one of the stamens.
3. Describe the texture of the stigma.
4. Sketch one of the flower halves and label all the parts.
5. Describe the contents of the ovary.
6. Sketch the pollen grains you examined.

QUESTIONS
1. What are the functions of the petals of a flower?
2. Suggest why the stigma is sticky.
3. Explain how pollen might be transferred from the stamens to the pistil.

INVESTIGATION: To observe the function of pollen

MATERIALS

stamens from the last investigation
(or fresh ones from another flower)
1 g table sugar
medicine-dropper
microscope slides and cover-slips
Petri dish
microscope

PROCEDURE

1. Dissolve the table sugar in 10 mL of water.
2. Select a stamen and dust some of its pollen grains onto a microscope slide.
3. Examine the pollen with the microscope under low power.
4. Remove the slide and add three drops of the sugar solution on top of the pollen.
5. Cover the pollen with a cover-slip.
6. Examine the pollen again.
7. Place the slide carefully into the bottom half of the Petri dish and add a few drops of water to the dish.
8. Place the lid on the dish.
9. Examine the pollen again after a few hours, and then once more the next day.

OBSERVATIONS

1. Describe any changes that occurred in the pollen when you added the sugar solutions.
2. Describe the changes that had occurred by the next day.

QUESTIONS

1. The structure you saw growing from the pollen grains is a pollen tube. How many pollen tubes grow from each grain of pollen?
2. During pollination, the pollen grains land on the stigma of the pistil. Where must the pollen tube grow in order for the sperm to reach the egg?

After the pollination process, each pollen grain grows a pollen tube down to the ovary, which contains several ovules. The sperm cell in the pollen grain then travels down the tube and enters an ovule, where it unites with an egg to form a zygote. Once the egg has been fertilized, the zygote starts to develop into an embryo. The ovule that contains the embryo becomes the seed. The embryo will remain resting in the seed until the proper conditions of temperature and moisture cause it to germinate, or begin to grow.

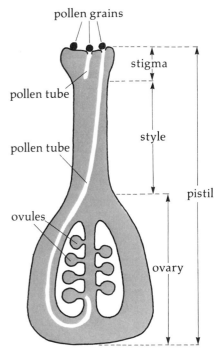

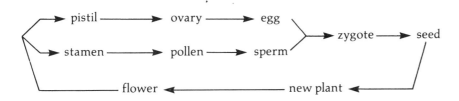

The life cycle of a fern

Ferns first appeared on Earth about 300 million years ago, which was more than 200 million years before the first flowering plants. They are commonly found in forests and near swamps and bogs. They thrive wherever the soil is always moist. The large, complex leaf with its many branches is the most obvious feature of the fern.

The life cycle of the fern is unusual because it consists of two separate generations, and one of these generations reproduces sexually and the other reproduces asexually. The large, leafy plant is the asexual stage. Many thousands of spores are pro-

The life cycle of a fern (left) and one of the two stages in the cycle (above)

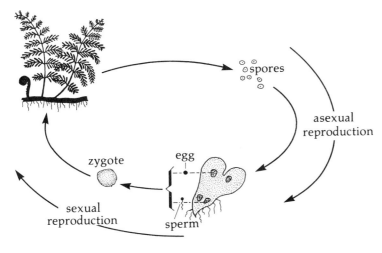

duced by each fern from spore cases on the undersides of the leaves. Under moist conditions the spores develop into the second-generation plant, which is the sexual stage. This heart-shaped plant, which is about 1 cm across, produces both sperm and egg cells. The sperm swim through the dew or water on the underside of the plant and fertilize the eggs. Each fertilized egg, or zygote, develops into another fern plant. The life cycle of the fern, then, consists of two different generations that alternate.

INVESTIGATION: To germinate spores from a fern

MATERIALS

fern plant
humus
2 pots
2 clear plastic bags
magnifying glass

PROCEDURE

1. Examine the large green leaves of the fern, using the magnifying glass. Take a close look at the under surfaces of the leaves.
2. Remove a few spore cases from the plant.
3. Examine the spores with the magnifying glass.
4. Fill each pot with humus, but do not press the humus down.
5. Moisten the humus thoroughly and allow the excess water to drain through the pots.
6. Sprinkle spores on the surface of the humus in each pot.
7. Place each pot in a plastic bag.
8. Put one pot in a dark cupboard that has a steady temperature of about 16°C.
9. Put the other pot in a bright place (not directly in the sun), also with a steady temperature of about 16°C.
10. Examine the spores once a week for any changes.

OBSERVATIONS

1. Describe a leaf of the fern in your notes.

2. Sketch the arrangement of the spore cases on the leaf you examined.
3. Record the changes you observed in the spores from week to week.

1. Which pot produced the most new plants? Suggest a reason for this.
2. Is this method of reproduction sexual or asexual? Explain your answer.

The life cycle of the earthworm

Earthworms are found everywhere on Earth except in very dry or cold areas. They burrow through the soil and feed on decaying plant and animal matter. Their activities in the soil make them very important to farmers. Their wastes, called castings, contain nutrients that help to make the soil more fertile. Their burrowing constantly brings fresh soil to the surface. In fertile soil, the earthworm population can add up to 1 cm of fresh soil to the surface in two years. The burrows allow air and water to penetrate more deeply into the earth, which helps the plants.

The body of an earthworm is long and slender and may be divided into over 100 segments, or sections. It is covered with a thick gooey substance called mucus that helps it to breathe, keeps it from drying out, and helps it to move through the soil. The most noticeable feature of the earthworm is the clitellum, which is a wide band about one-third of the way from the front of the earthworm. Depending on the species, earthworms may be reddish-brown, brown, green, or purple. The length varies from 6 to 15 cm in North American species to almost 3.5 m in a species found in Australia.

Although the earthworm reproduces sexually, there are no male or female worms. Each earthworm produces both sperm and eggs. Animals that are able to produce both sperm and eggs in each individual are called hermaphrodites. Other hermaphrodites include snails, clams, and oysters.

The reproductive process of earthworms is in two stages. During the first stage, two earthworms exchange sperm. In the second stage, the eggs are fertilized by the sperm. The external

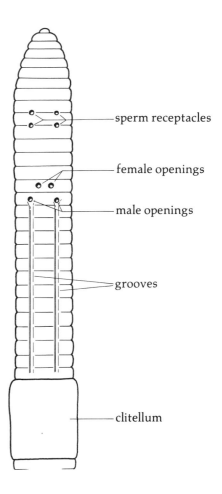

sperm receptacles

female openings

male openings

grooves

clitellum

parts of the earthworm that are involved in the reproductive process are shown in a diagram.

The exchange of sperm is usually done on the surface of the ground, at night or under the cover of vegetation. Two worms arrange themselves so that their bottom surfaces are in contact. A large amount of mucus is produced on these surfaces. The mucus forms what is called a slime tube between the two worms. The sperm from each worm swim through the mucus, along the grooves that are on the undersides of the worms, to reach the sperm receptacles of the other worm. Once the exchange of sperm has taken place, the worms return to their separate burrows.

Earthworms exchanging sperm

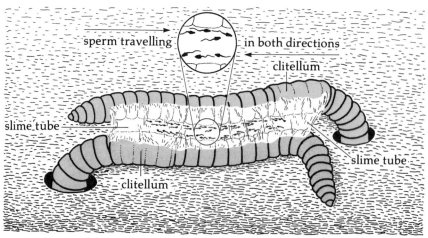

The second stage of the reproductive process takes place underground. The clitellum forms a mucus capsule, which separates from the skin of the clitellum. The capsule encircles the earthworm, as shown in a diagram. When the earthworm pulls its body back, the capsule is pulled off its front end. As the capsule passes the female openings, the eggs are released into it, and as it passes the sperm receptacles the sperm are also released. Fertilization of the eggs occurs at this time. The open ends of the capsule close as it comes off the body, and it dries, forming a cocoon.

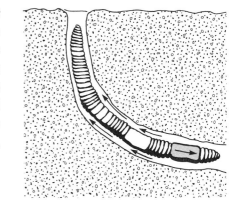

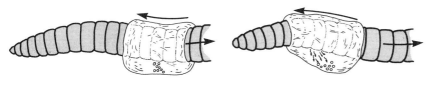

eggs released   sperm released

If the temperature and moisture conditions are suitable, about 15 young worms will emerge from each cocoon after 21 d. Within three months the worms will have fully matured and will be ready to reproduce.

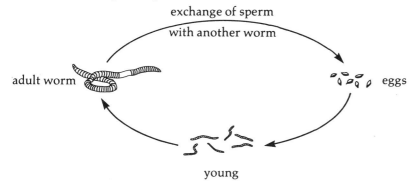

exchange of sperm
with another worm

adult worm   eggs

young

INVESTIGATION: To observe the life cycle of the earthworm

MATERIALS

wooden box (about 50 cm
  x 30 cm and 15 cm deep)
3 styrofoam cups
small stones or gravel
dry grass
corn meal

earthworms (about 6)
soil (from the site where you
  found the earthworms)
burlap or cotton cloth
small drill
magnifying glass

1. Drill about 50 small holes in the bottom of the box.
2. Cover the bottom of the box with a layer of small stones.
3. Cover the stones with a double layer of damp burlap.
4. Place a 2 cm layer of dry grass on the burlap.
5. Mix the soil with a few handfuls of decaying leaves.
6. Fill the box to about 2 cm from the top with the mixed soil.
7. Examine one of the earthworms closely with the magnifying glass. Note the colour, reproductive openings, and clitellum.
8. Place the earthworms on the surface of the soil and cover the box with damp burlap.
9. Store the box in a warm place out of direct sunlight. Stand it with a small piece of wood under each corner so that air can get at the bottom of the box.
10. Wet the burlap cover every day. It must be kept damp.
11. Once a week, sprinkle a little corn meal and some decaying leaves on the surface.
12. After about 21 d, turn the soil out of the box onto a sheet of newspaper. Sift through the soil and remove any cocoons you find. The cocoons are lemon-shaped and are pale yellow in colour when first deposited; later they turn a dark brown or purple.
13. Examine the earthworms before you return them with the soil to the box.(You may repeat steps 11 and 12 any number of times.)
14. Examine the cocoons closely.
15. Place about 2 cm of soil in each of the cups and place one cocoon in each cup. Fill the cups with soil and cover each with a piece of damp burlap. Keep the burlap moist.
16. Remove and examine the cocoons each day, then replace them as in step 15.
17. Any extra cocoons or young worms should be returned to the soil in a garden, or you can start new boxes for breeding worms.

OBSERVATIONS

1. Describe the earthworms you examined in step 7. Sketch one of them, and label the clitellum, the head, and the tail.
2. Record any movements of the earthworms that you observed when you lifted the burlap cover.

3. Describe what you found in step 12.
4. Compare the appearance of the worms in step 13 with your description for step 7.
5. Sketch and describe the earthworm cocoons you found in step 12.
6. Describe the appearance of the young worms that hatched from the cocoon (step 16).

1. What is the purpose of the dry grass and the decaying leaves?
2. Why were you told to drill holes in the bottom of the box?
3. Research the life cycle of another hermaphrodite.

The life cycles of insects

There are more species of insects than there are of any other class of animals. Insects are found everywhere on Earth except in mid-ocean. Most of them reproduce sexually and each species has separate male and female individuals. The life cycles vary between species, but all insects undergo changes as they grow from the young to the adult forms. The changes can easily be identified, since a change of form occurs at each stage.

Insects whose life cycles include four separate stages are said to undergo a complete change, or metamorphosis. The four stages are the egg, the larva, the pupa, and the adult. Butterflies, moths, bees, flies, and mosquitoes are examples of insects that go through a complete metamorphosis.

The life cycle of the mosquito

The life cycle of a mosquito begins when a male and a female mosquito mate. The male deposits his sperm inside the female, where fertilization of the eggs occurs. As with most flying insects, the mating takes place in flight. The female then deposits up to 400 eggs on a still-water surface. After a day or two, the eggs hatch into larvae. The larvae are very active and usually float upside down just below the surface of the water. After about a week each larva changes into a pupa.

In most insects, the pupa stage is not an active one, but the mosquito pupa is active. It floats and wiggles about just

The life cycle of a mosquito

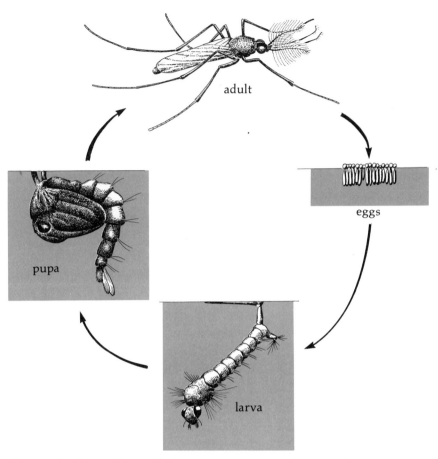

beneath the surface of the water. In 2-4 d, the adult mosquito that has been developing inside the pupa emerges and flies off. The male mosquito has bushy antennae and feeds on nectar from flowers. The female, whose antennae are often slender, feeds on the blood of mammals. Within 2 d of becoming adults, the females are able to mate and lay eggs. This cycle is repeated many times each year.

INVESTIGATION: **To observe the life cycle of the mosquito**

MATERIALS

aquarium with the fish removed and with a cover	transparent wrapping material
two 250 mL beakers	2 elastic bands
vegetable oil	magnifying glass
	mosquito eggs

1. Examine the eggs and estimate the number in a raft.
2. Note the shape, size, and colouring of the eggs.
3. Place the eggs in the aquarium and cover it.
4. Observe the eggs often for the next day or two, until half or more have hatched.
5. Note the location of the larvae in the water.
6. Half-fill each of the beakers with water from the aquarium and number them 1 and 2.
7. Remove about half of the larvae from the tank and put approximately equal numbers in each beaker.
8. Return the fish to the aquarium and cover it.
9. Add just enough oil to form a film over the surface of the water in beaker 1.
10. Cover each of the beakers with transparent wrapping and fasten the wrapping with the elastic bands.
11. Examine the aquarium and the beakers daily. Note any changes that occur in the larvae, and note the actions of the fish in the aquarium.
12. Within a week, any larvae that are still living will change in shape. Note carefully the changes that occur.
13. Observe the pupae frequently for the next 2-4 d, and try to observe the emergence of an adult from a pupa.

OBSERVATIONS

1. Describe the shape and colour of the eggs, in step 1.
2. Sketch the egg, larva, and pupa stages of the mosquito.
3. Describe the changes that occurred in the larvae in beaker 1 after you added oil.
4. Describe the actions of the fish in the aquarium.
5. Describe the changes in the larvae in beaker 2.
6. Describe the emergence of the adult from the pupa.

QUESTIONS

1. Suggest why the first three stages in the life cycle of the mosquito take place near the surface of the water.
2. How long did the life cycle take, from egg to adult?
3. Why did the larvae in beaker 1 not survive?
4. From your observations in step 4, suggest why a single mosquito lays so many eggs.

There are many insects that do not undergo complete metamorphosis. Their life cycle consists of only three stages – egg, nymph, and adult. The young that hatch from the egg usually resemble the final adult form and are called nymphs. Examples of insects that undergo an incomplete metamorphosis are the grasshopper, the cicada, the dragonfly, and the praying mantis.

The life cycle of the grasshopper

The different species of grasshoppers vary greatly in appearance, but they all have a life cycle that is an incomplete metamorphosis. The male grasshopper fertilizes the eggs of the female within her body. Later, the female lays about 50 eggs in the ground. At the end of the female's abdomen is an organ called the ovipositor. It is hard and sharp, and with it the female digs a hole in the earth in which she lays her eggs. She then covers the hole with earth.

If the eggs are laid early in the summer, they will hatch

The life cycle of a grasshopper

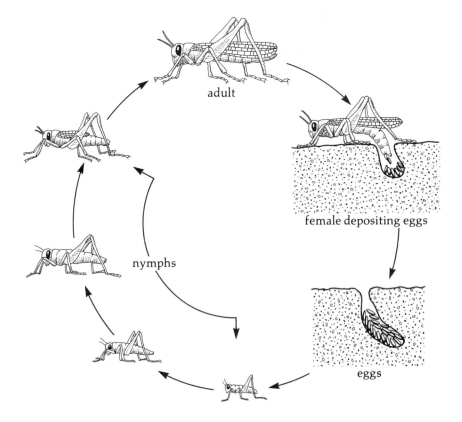

adult

female depositing eggs

nymphs

eggs

within a few weeks. If they are laid in late summer, they will remain dormant until the next spring. The nymphs that hatch from the eggs resemble the adults but are much smaller and lack wings. As they grow, the nymphs shed the outer covering of their bodies, which does not increase in size. This process is called moulting. It occurs several times before the adult form emerges. The adults are usually able to mate soon after emerging and the life cycle then repeats itself.

INVESTIGATION: To examine the stages in the life cycle of the grasshopper

---

MATERIALS
magnifying glass
prepared specimens of adult female grasshoppers, nymphs, and
    eggs

PROCEDURE
1. Examine an adult female grasshopper. Find the head, thorax, abdomen, wings, mouth, and legs.
2. Examine the end of the abdomen to find the ovipositor.
3. Use the magnifying glass to examine some of the eggs. Note their size, shape, and colour.
4. Examine the nymphs and compare them with the adults.
5. Compare the shapes, sizes, and structures of a number of developing nymphs.

OBSERVATIONS
1. Describe the size and colouring of the female grasshopper.
2. Describe each of the parts you located in step 1.
3. Sketch the ovipositor.
4. Describe the size, shape, and colour of the eggs.
5. List the differences you observed between the nymphs and the adults.
6. List the changes you found in the nymphs, in step 5.

QUESTIONS
1. Suggest why the grasshopper lays its eggs in the ground.
2. How do grasshoppers survive the winter?

A dragonfly nymph before shedding its skin (top left) and the skin beginning to open (top right). In the next four photographs, the head emerges (notice connecting tubes); the dragonfly flings its inner body back; it flips forward to pull out its tail; and it is out of its old skin. Its wings dry and expand (bottom left), and then it is in the adult stage (bottom right).

In the last two investigations you examined examples of the two types of insect life cycles. The mosquito has a life cycle with a complete metamorphosis. It develops through four distinct stages, and the adult form is usually very different from the larva. The grasshopper goes through an incomplete metamorphosis with only three distinct stages. The nymph may resemble the adult, as in the grasshopper, or it may be totally different, as in the dragonfly.

In each species of insect, the life cycle consists of a series of changes by which an egg develops into an adult that is able to lay eggs that develop into new adults. The life cycle ensures that the species will have a chance to continue to exist.

The life cycle of the frog

Frogs belong to a class of animals called amphibians. Amphibians are the only vertebrate animals that go through a metamorphosis. The young are usually water-dwelling creatures that breathe with gills. The adult forms normally breathe with lungs and are often very different in appearance from the young. Some examples of amphibians are toads, salamanders, and frogs. We will examine the life cycle of the frog.

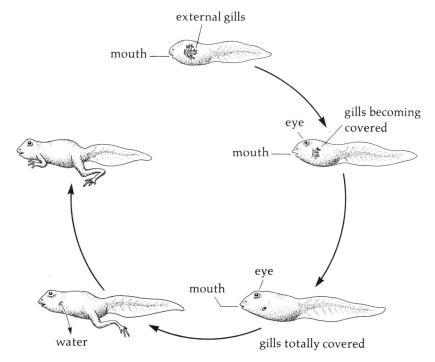

The development of a frog's respiratory system

During early spring the male and female frogs mate in the water. As the female releases her eggs in the water the male releases his sperm on top of them. The sperm swim through the water and fertilize the eggs. As with all animals, only one sperm is needed to fertilize each egg. The outer coat of the fertilized eggs swells in the water to form a jelly-like, rather sticky material. The eggs stick together in a mass and often become attached to water plants. The tiny black dot in each egg becomes an embryo that develops in about 4 d into a tadpole.

When the tadpole emerges from an egg, it has a head and tail and feathery external gills. The tadpole feeds by nibbling plants. In about 8 d the eyes develop, the mouth starts to grow, and the external gills begin to disappear. The tadpole now begins to feed on the flesh of dead animals, such as fish and other tadpoles.

In one month, the tadpole has increased in size and its gills have become covered. During the second month, the hind legs begin to develop and the mouth continues to grow. At this point the tail begins to get smaller, and, as the front legs

The life cycle of a frog

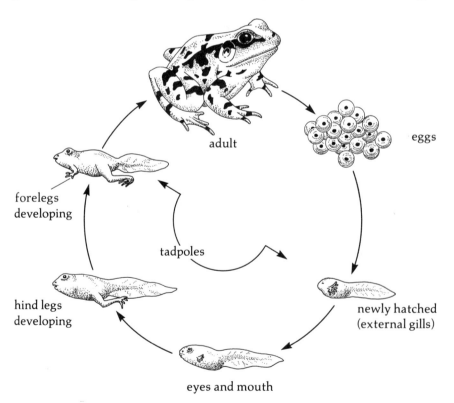

adult

eggs

forelegs
developing

tadpoles

newly hatched
(external gills)

hind legs
developing

eyes and mouth

develop, the tadpole comes to the surface more and more often in order to breathe. The tail continues to shrink as the frog grows in size. After about three months, the frog is able to come out of the water onto land. The tail eventually disappears completely, and the frog, now breathing only with lungs, continues to mature. By the following year it will produce sperm or eggs and the life cycle is repeated.

In the next investigation, you will examine the stages in the life cycle of the frog.

INVESTIGATION: To observe the life cycle of the frog

MATERIALS

aquarium with pond water and water plants (include a large rock that projects above the surface)
frogs' eggs

dissecting microscope
magnifying glass
Petri dishes
pail

PROCEDURE

1. In the spring, use the pail to collect a mass of frogs' eggs from a pond.
2. Use the magnifying glass to examine some of the eggs. Note their colour and shape. Note also the jelly coat that surrounds each egg. Place the eggs in the aquarium.
3. Place one or two eggs in a Petri dish with some water and examine them under the microscope. Return the eggs to the aquarium.
4. Repeat step 3 each day, and note any changes.
5. When the tadpoles emerge, examine them daily for several weeks. Note any changes that occur. The tadpoles may be fed dried fish food.

OBSERVATIONS

1. Describe the colour, shape, and size of the frogs' eggs.
2. Describe any changes you observed in step 3.
3. Sketch a newly hatched tadpole and label the head, the tail, and the exterior gills.
4. Name the two parts that appear on the tadpole's head as its external gills disappear.

5. Describe the changes that occur in the appearance of a tadpole as it develops into an adult frog.

QUESTIONS

1. The life cycle of the frog is sometimes referred to as a metamorphosis. Explain why this is a correct use of the word.
2. Suggest why a frog lays so many eggs.
3. Try to find out how the life cycle of a bullfrog differs from that of an ordinary frog.

Practical applications

In the investigation of the life cycle of the mosquito, you were required to pour oil on the surface of water containing mosquito larvae. You found that this effectively killed the larvae by cutting off their air supply. People have used the same method to control mosquitoes that carry malaria and encephalitis, diseases that are often fatal to humans.

Another method of controlling insects begins with the sterilizing of males grown in a laboratory. In the sterilization process, the insects are exposed to radiation that kills the sperm cells. The male insects are then released, and they mate with the females in the wild. Since the females usually only mate once before laying eggs, they will lay eggs that have not been fertilized and so will not hatch.

A much more important application of our knowledge of life cycles and reproductive processes is in the developing of new types of plants and animals. It is known that, in sexual reproduction, the sperm cells contain some of the characteristics of the male parent and the egg cells contain some of the characteristics of the female parent. When an egg is fertilized, the resulting offspring will show some of the characteristics of both parents. All members of a given species of organisms are very similar to one another but no two individuals are identical (except for identical twins). By selecting individual organisms with desirable characteristics, and allowing them to reproduce, man has been able to develop many useful varieties of plants and animals.

In plants, the process is called controlled pollination. It has been used to develop types of wheat that are more resistant to disease, grow faster, and produce more plentiful grain than naturally occurring types. Most of today's crop plants have been improved by the use of controlled pollination. Many new varieties of roses and other flowers and fruits have been developed in the same way.

In animals, the process is called selective breeding. Today's beef and dairy cattle have been developed through selective breeding, and they produce more meat and milk than cattle in the past. Dogs are bred selectively for certain characteristics.

These are just a few of the ways in which scientific knowledge of life cycles has been applied to the benefit of humans.

REVIEW QUESTIONS

1. What is meant by "life span"?
2. Why must organisms reproduce?.
3. Explain the difference between asexual and sexual reproduction.
4. Name four types of asexual reproduction.
5. Describe fission in one-celled animals.
6. What is a life cycle?
7. What occurs during the process of conjugation?
8. Name the two cells that are required for sexual reproduction.
9. What is a zygote?
10. Define "fertilization".
11. Name the male and female reproductive organs of a flower.
12. What is pollination?
13. Explain why the life cycle of a fern is sometimes described as an "alternation of generations".
14. Explain why earthworms are important to farmers.
15. What is a hermaphrodite?
16. Name two kinds of animals that are hermaphrodites.
17. What are the two steps in the reproductive process of the earthworm?
18. What is metamorphosis?

19. Name, in order, the four stages of complete metamorphosis.
20. What are the three stages of incomplete metamorphosis?
21. Explain the meaning of moulting as it applies to the grasshopper.
22. Describe the changes that occur during the development of a frog from egg to adult.
23. What is "selective breeding"?

IMPORTANT TERMS

vegetative reproduction—a form of asexual reproduction that occurs with plants when new plants develop from cuttings of a parent organism

fission—a type of reproduction in which a parent organism splits to form two daughter cells

budding—a type of asexual reproduction in which a new organism develops from a bump, or bud, on the side of the parent organism

spore—a microscopic stage in the life cycle of a fungus or fern

conjugation—a simple form of sexual reproduction in which two organisms exchange cellular material

fertilization—the process by which a sperm cell from a male parent joins with an egg cell from a female parent to produce a zygote

metamorphosis—a process in the life cycle of such animals as insects and frogs by which the developing animal changes its shape a number of times

ADAPTATION
AND BEHAVIOUR

About a million species of animals and nearly one-third that number of species of plants exist on Earth. These organisms live in almost every type of environment, from the extreme cold of the polar regions to the great heat and humidity of jungles near the equator. They live in fresh water and salt water, and in the arid desert regions.

Some organisms, for example, plants, are limited in their ability to move about. Others are able to walk, crawl, slither, hop, swim, or fly from place to place.

The Earth's organisms obtain their nourishment in many different ways. Plants make their own food from carbon dioxide, water, and sunlight. Animals use various methods of getting and eating plants or other animals. Some birds, for example, use their beaks to break open the seeds of plants. Others use their beaks to kill and tear the flesh of other animals on which they prey. The humming-bird uses its long, tube-like beak to suck nectar from flowers.

Animals have various ways of taking in food. The deer chews what it eats. The cougar tears its food apart with its teeth. Frogs and snakes swallow their food whole, while leeches and mosquitoes suck nourishment from the organisms they feed on.

Birds use their beaks to gather food.

Organisms also vary in the methods they use for reproduction. All flowering plants produce seeds; some produce just a few each year and others produce thousands. Fishes and frogs lay thousands of eggs each season; dolphins and whales produce only one young at a time.

Each species of organism has a method of movement, obtaining nourishment, and reproduction that suits the environment it lives in. Fishes and frogs must lay large numbers of eggs because many of the eggs and young will be eaten by larger fishes or frogs, and enough must survive to replace the original population. Dolphins and whales are able to protect their young, and each baby whale or dolphin has a good chance of growing to maturity.

The way each organism fits into its environment is called adaptation. A fish is well adapted for life in the water. Its streamlined body and the powerful muscles that run the length of the body help it to move through the water. A bird is adapted to flight. Its hollow bones give its skeleton strength without any excess weight, and its wings enable it to fly.

Environmental conditions all over the world are constantly changing. These changes are very gradual, as a rule. The changing of a pond into a marsh and then into a grassy field, for example, may take hundreds of years. Sometimes they are sudden – as when a tract of fertile land is flooded permanently by an overflow of ocean or lake water. Sudden changes simply kill many of the living things in the area that is affected. But when the changes take place gradually, as they nearly always do, plants and animals have time to move or to adapt to their altered environments.

The Mesozoic Era of Earth's prehistory began about 200 million years ago and ended about 60 million years ago. During those 140 million years, the climate over much of the land was warm and moist. Plant life was abundant and the reptiles dominated the animal kingdom. They were the most successful creatures at the time. They lived on land and in the sea, and some were able to fly. In size they ranged from lizard-like creatures the size of a chicken to the giant brontosaurus which sometimes grew to a mass of more than 20 t and a length of 20 m.

About 60 million years ago, conditions on Earth must have

changed. All the dinosaurs and many of the other reptiles became extinct within a few thousand years. Many other species of organisms also disappeared at about the same time, as far as we can tell from the fossils that have been found. Scientists have suggested that a change of climate may have caused the swamps to dry up and the temperature to drop. This would have affected the vegetation, and hence the dinosaurs, which depended on plants for food. The many species of dinosaurs that had existed for well over 100 million years presumably could not adapt quickly enough to the changes in environment and died off.

An organism's survival depends chiefly on whether it is well enough adapted to its environment. But it also depends on the organism's behaviour. The behaviour of an organism is the

An artist's view of life when dinosaurs dominated the Earth

way it responds to what is happening around it. An event that causes an organism to react is called a stimulus. The organism's reaction is called a response.

For example, if you were to touch a hot stove, the heat you would feel would be the stimulus and the immediate pulling away of your hand would be your response. Clearly, the way you respond to a stimulus such as the hot stove will help to determine how long you will survive. The same is true of all organisms: the way they respond to stimuli in their environment helps to determine their chances for survival.

In this chapter, we will examine some of the ways in which organisms are adapted to suit their environments, and also how they increase their chances of survival by the way they behave.

Plant responses – tropisms

A tropism is the response of a plant to a stimulus. Since plants are not able to move about physically, their response usually takes the form of a change in the way they grow, and thus is usually slow. The stimuli that plants react to include light, water, heat, and gravity. The tropism may be either towards the stimulus, in which case it is called a positive tropism, or away from the stimulus, in which case it is called a negative tropism.

In the next investigation, you will examine the tropism of the roots of a bean plant to gravity.

INVESTIGATION: To observe the growth of bean seeds

MATERIALS

4 Petri dishes
cotton batting.
masking tape
bean seeds

marking pen (waterproof)
cardboard or thin wood
   (about 10 cm x 15 cm)

PROCEDURE

1. Fill the bottom half of each Petri dish with cotton batting.
2. Add water until the batting is thoroughly soaked. Drain off any excess water.

MATLOCK COLLEGE LIBRARY

3. Place two seeds in each Petri dish on the surface of the cotton, as shown.
4. Cover each dish and tape it closed. If necessary, add more wet cotton batting, so that the seeds will be held in place.
5. Number the dishes 1, 2, 3, and 4 on the underside.
6. Arrange the dishes as shown.

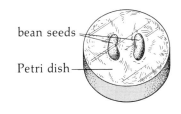

bean seeds

Petri dish

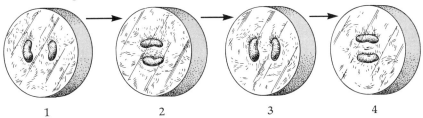

1   2   3   4

7. Tape the dishes together and mark the topmost edge of each dish.
8. Tape the stack of dishes to the cardboard, as shown.

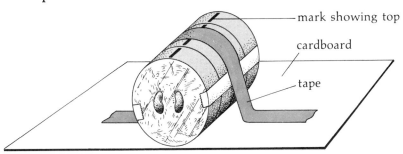

mark showing top

cardboard

tape

9. Place in a dark, warm (16°C) location.
10. Observe the beans each day through the covers of the dishes.
11. After the daily observation replace the dishes as in steps 6, 7, and 8.
12. When the roots are 1 cm or 2 cm long, rotate dishes 1 and 2 by 90°.

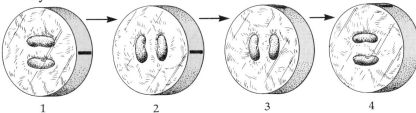

1   2   3   4

13. Tape the dishes together again, as shown in the diagram. Tape the stack to the cardboard so that dishes 3 and 4 are in the same position as originally.

ADAPTATION AND BEHAVIOUR   159

14. Observe each day for three or four more days and note any changes that occur.

OBSERVATIONS

1. Record your observations each day on a chart like the one illustrated.

	DISH 1	DISH 2	DISH 3	DISH 4
Day 1	◯	◯	◯	◯
Day 2	◯	◯	◯	◯
Day 3	◯	◯	◯	◯
Day 4	◯	◯	◯	◯

QUESTIONS

1. From which part of the bean did the root start?
2. In which direction was each root growing before you completed step 12?
3. What change occurred in the roots of the bean seeds in dishes 1 and 2 after you rotated those dishes?
4. What changes occurred in the beans in dishes 3 and 4 after you did step 12?
5. Suggest a reason for the change in the direction of the growth of the roots after step 12.
6. Does the growth of roots indicate a positive or a negative tropism to gravity?
7. Suggest a reason for including dishes 3 and 4 in this investigation.

8. When you plant seeds in a garden, does it matter which way up you plant them? Explain your answer.

From your observations in the last investigation, you were able to make an educated guess, or hypothesis, about the growth of the roots of a bean plant. Your hypothesis may have been like one of these: "The roots of bean seeds show a positive tropism to gravity", or "The roots of bean seeds grow towards gravity". In any case, it was a guess made after some observation.

Scientists work in exactly the same way. After observing an event or a series of events, a scientist will make a hypothesis to explain it. The hypothesis must then be tested to see whether it is true. Your hypothesis from the last investigation indicated that the roots of bean seeds always grow downwards. In order to answer question 8, you had to make a similar hypothesis about other types of seeds.

To prove or verify your hypothesis, you would have to repeat the investigation with many different types of seeds.

For the next investigation, you will be asked to make a hypothesis before you start. Before you decide on your hypothesis, think carefully about how plants grow.

INVESTIGATION: To determine the effect of gravity
on the stem of a bean plant

MATERIALS
2 bean plants in clay flower pots
empty clay pot

PROCEDURE
1. Before starting, remember to make a hypothesis for this investigation.
2. Place the two pots on a window ledge or counter in such a way that both will receive the same amount of light.
3. Support one of the bean pots on the empty pot, as illustrated. Leave the other pot upright.
4. Observe the bean plants for several days. Remove the tilted pot only for watering.

5. Remove the empty pot after a noticeable change has occurred and stand the two bean pots side by side.
6. Continue to observe the two plants for a few days.

1. In your notebook, record your hypothesis predicting how the bean stem will respond to the pull of gravity.
2. Draw a chart like this one in your notes and write your observations in it.

DAY	NORMAL BEAN POT	TILTED BEAN POT
1		
2		
3		
4		

1. Was your hypothesis correct? Was the tropism a positive or a negative one? Explain your answer.
2. Could any other factor or stimulus have caused the response you saw? Explain your answer.

There are a few plants that show fairly rapid positive or negative tropisms when they are touched. The Venus's fly-trap is a plant with a very sensitive leaf that can close quickly when it is touched the way an insect would touch it when walking across it. After the leaf closes, the plant uses the insect as food.

The Venus's fly-trap eats insects through its leaves.

The mimosa is a plant that shows a negative tropism to touch. When anything contacts the leaf or stem of this plant, its leaves fold up and its stem becomes limp. (See illustration on page 25.)

Climbing plants such as vines or ivies exhibit positive tropisms when touched. They grow towards any object they touch and go around it in order to attach themselves for support.

How do these patterns of behaviour increase the plants' chances of survival? The positive tropism shown by the roots of seeds to gravity ensures that the roots will grow into the ground to anchor the new plant and be able to draw moisture and nutrients from the soil. The negative tropism to gravity shown by the stems of plants ensures that the leaves face the light as much as possible and therefore that the plant is able to make its food. Plants show positive tropisms to moisture, warmth, and light – all of which they need for growth.

Animal responses

Animals, like plants, are able to respond to stimuli in their environments. Unlike plants, however, they are capable of locomotion, and so their responses are more immediate and much easier to observe.

Animal responses vary from simple movements to complex behaviour. If the response is simply a movement towards or away from a stimulus, it is called a taxis. When an earthworm is touched, it immediately draws away. This is an example of a negative taxis. Negative and positive are used with taxes in the same way as with tropisms – negative means away from the stimulus and positive means towards it. Insects exhibit a positive taxis to light when they fly towards an outdoor light or when they congregate about a lighted window at night.

In the next investigation you will examine a taxis of earthworms to light. Before you begin, you will again be asked to form a hypothesis about their response.

INVESTIGATION: **To examine the response of earthworms to light**

MATERIALS

4 earthworms
large aquarium or box (about 60 cm x 30 cm)
dark-coloured construction paper
light source (incandescent lamp)
4 small blocks or stones (about 1 cm in height)
piece of cardboard large enough to cover
   about one-half of the bottom of the
   aquarium (about 30 cm x 30 cm)
tape

PROCEDURE

1. Make a hypothesis for the response of earthworms to light.
2. Wash and dry the aquarium.
3. Cut one piece of construction paper to cover the bottom of the aquarium on the inside.
4. Cover the outside walls of the aquarium with construction paper.
5. Use the four blocks to support the piece of cardboard in one-half of the aquarium so that it forms a protected area.
6. Place the earthworms in the aquarium at the opposite end from the protected area.
7. Arrange the light so that it shines directly down on the earthworms.

8. Observe the movements of the earthworms for about 10 min, or until you can no longer see them.
9. Remove the earthworms and return them to their original container.

OBSERVATIONS

1. Record your original hypothesis.
2. Write a description of the movements of the earthworms.

QUESTIONS

1. Was the response of the earthworms a positive or a negative taxis to light? Explain your answer.
2. Could any other stimulus have caused the response you observed? Explain your answer.
3. Suggest how the investigation might be modified to test your answer to question 2.
4. Sowbugs are commonly found under most rocks and pieces of wood lying on the ground. Capture about 10 specimens in a jar, and repeat this investigation with them.

The last investigation demonstrated a simple response to a stimulus. The responses of animals are often much more complex than movements towards or away from a stimulus. The sowbugs, for example, curled up and remained motionless in response to being touched. How does this response help the sowbug?

Another example of a complex response may be observed in many kinds of organisms, including humans. A speck of dust in the eye will cause you to blink and produce tears. Both responses happen automatically and they will usually have the effect of dislodging the particle and removing it from your eye.

How do animals know how to respond to a certain stimulus? Why does each individual of a given species respond in a similar way? Why do members of different species of organisms respond differently to similar stimuli? These and other questions are being investigated by psychologists seeking a better understanding of human behaviour.

Psychologists are scientists who specialize in the study of behaviour. They classify the behaviour patterns of animals into two categories – those that are instinctive and those that are learned. Instinctive behaviours come automatically to an animal in response to a stimulus. They will occur in an animal even if it has been raised with no contact with other individuals of its species. A baby chick, for example, will peck at material on the ground even if it is hatched in isolation. The responses of the earthworms and sowbugs you investigated are also examples of instinctive behaviours.

Learned behaviours are behaviours that occur, or change, according to the experiences of the animal. Your response to the stimulus of a red light at an intersection is a learned behaviour. All young children in the city have to be taught that they must stop and wait when they are facing a red light at an intersection. You learned this behaviour to ensure your survival in city traffic.

How do animals acquire their patterns of behaviour? That is the next question you will be examining.

Inherited behaviour

All living things have inherited their physical characteristics from their parents. This is why there is often a close resemblance among the members of a family. However, since an individual inherits some of the father's traits and some of the mother's, a mixture of the characteristics of the two parents occurs in the offspring. Also, some characteristics will disappear for a generation or two and then reappear. So you may have a closer resemblance to one of your grandparents than to your parents.

In the next investigation you will examine some of your inherited characteristics.

INVESTIGATION: To examine some of the physical
characteristics of your family

MATERIALS

mirror
camera and film
    (the instant developing type is most useful)

pictures of your grandparents
(and great-grandparents, if available)
large display board

1. Take two pictures of the head of each member of your family, including yourself. One pose should be full face and the other a profile.
2. Examine yourself for each of these characteristics:
   (a) colour of eyes – choose from brown, blue, or other
   (b) natural colour of hair – choose from black, brown, blond, or red
   (c) shape of ears – choose between lobed and attached
3. Repeat step 2 for each member of your family. Complete the observations before doing step 4.
4. Compare your results with those of the other members of your class.

lobed   attached

1. Mount your photographs on the display board. Label each photograph and identify the family members you most resemble.
2. Record your information in your notebook, in a table like this one.

| | CHARACTERISTICS | | |
PERSON EXAMINED	EYE COLOUR	HAIR COLOUR	SHAPE OF EAR
—Yourself			
—Brothers list all of them by name			
—Sisters			
—Mother			
—Father			
—Paternal grandmother (your father's mother)			
—Paternal grandfather			
—Maternal grandmother (your mother's mother)			
—Maternal grandfather (etc.)			

1. (a) On the basis of your table, which member(s) of your family do you resemble most?
   (b) How does your answer to question 1(a) compare with your answer in step 1 of the observations?
2. Were your results similar to those of other members of your class? Suggest a reason for your answer.
3. The study of the transmission of traits from parents to offspring belongs to the science of genetics. Do further research on this topic by looking up genetics in a few reference books to find out why traits sometimes "skip" a generation.

Behaviours, like physical characteristics, can be inherited. Instinctive behaviour may be as simple as the taxis shown by earthworms and sowbugs to light or as complex as the spawning behaviours of the Pacific salmon. After a few years in the salt water of the Pacific Ocean, the salmon return to the same fresh-water stream where they were born, to lay their eggs.

Each year, large numbers of ducks and geese migrate in North America. These waterfowl spend the winter in the warmer, southern parts of the continent and return each spring to the same area of the northern part of the continent that they

Migratory waterfowl adapt to climate changes.

left in the fall. They mate and rear their young in the north and then head south again for the winter. Often the adults set off for the south ahead of the young birds, but the young are able to follow the same general route and arrive at the same destination as the adults.

There are many other birds that exhibit seasonal migratory behaviour. The arctic tern holds the record for long-distance migration. It spends each summer in the Arctic and each winter in the Antarctic. Homing pigeons show a perhaps even more remarkable direction-finding behaviour. They can be transported hundreds of kilometres in covered cages, and when they are released they find their way straight home.

All animals exhibit instinctive behaviour in some form or other. A new-born spider, for example, will spin a web identical to the webs spun by all the other individuals of its species without ever having seen one made. In a beehive, the worker bees have many tasks to perform – building the honeycomb, cleaning the hive, feeding the young larvae, making beeswax, and collecting nectar. Each task is done without instruction. The workers know by instinct what must be done, and they do it.

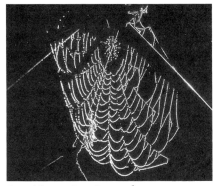

A spider spins its web instinctively.

In each of these examples, the instinctive behaviour of an animal helps it, in some way, to survive. Spiders make webs to capture food so that they will be able to mate and produce more spiders. Birds migrate to escape the cold of winter and return for the abundance of food in the spring and summer. The salmon return to the shallow water of streams to spawn, so that their young will have a better chance of surviving. All of these behaviours are passed on from generation to generation, helping each species to maintain itself.

Humans also show instinctive behaviours. Blinking and shedding tears when something gets in your eye and limping when your foot is sore are two examples. Human behaviour is often very complex, and it can be changed or modified by what we experience. Some forms of behaviour, such as reading and writing, are learned.

Your ability to read this page and understand it is a form of learned behaviour. It is not instinctive. You are only able to read because you were taught how to. Another example of a learned behaviour is your response to a traffic signal.

Learned behaviour

Learning how to respond to a certain stimulus occurs frequently in animals. It is common in the more complex animals such as the vertebrates, and particularly in mammals and birds.

Imprinting

A simple type of learned behaviour that occurs mainly in birds is one called imprinting. A young bird "learns" to follow the first large object it sees that moves and makes regular noises. Normally, the young bird will imprint on its mother. It is a common sight, in spring, to see a mother goose or duck followed by a brood of young. The young ducks or geese follow closely behind their mother for the first few months of their

Young ducks following their mother

lives, mainly for protection. But the mother can be replaced by almost any object that is large, moves about, and makes regular noises. The young birds will follow the object as if it were their mother. Naturalists who have found wild goose eggs, and have hatched the eggs artificially, have found themselves in the role of a mother goose.

Conditioning

Conditioning is a form of learning, in which a stimulus that causes a certain response in nature is replaced by a different stimulus.

Dogs can be conditioned to respond in a certain way.

Ivan Pavlov (1849-1936) was a Russian psychologist who performed some interesting investigations with dogs. He observed that a dog would often produce excess saliva (a response) when it was shown food (a stimulus). He set up an apparatus that recorded the amount of saliva produced by a dog. It also had a light that could be flashed on. When the dog was hungry, the light was turned on for 5 s before food was presented to it. From time to time the light was turned on but no food was given. Pavlov found that the dog produced just as much saliva in response to the light as it did when food was presented.

The dog had learned to respond to the light in the same way as it normally responded to food. It had been conditioned to respond in this way. Pavlov found that the new stimulus soon lost its effect when he stopped using the light.

In the next investigation, you will try a similar type of conditioning on a fish.

INVESTIGATION: To demonstrate conditioning

MATERIALS

2 goldfish from a pet store
small aquarium

light source
fish food

PROCEDURE

1. Before you get the goldfish, fill the aquarium with water and let it stand for 48 h.
2. Put the bag containing the goldfish in the aquarium and leave it there for 2 h before you open it and let the fish swim out.
3. Place the light source close to one side of the aquarium.
4. Turn on the light. (Observe any changes in the fishes' behaviour.) After 5 s drop a small amount of fish food onto the surface of the water.
5. Observe the fish for 5 min and then turn the light off.
6. Repeat steps 4 and 5 twice a day for a week, once in the morning and once in the afternoon.
7. At the end of the week observe the actions of the fish as the light is turned on. Do not add any food this time. After 5 min turn off the light.
8. At the next feeding time, feed the fish as in steps 4 and 5.
9. Every second day repeat step 7 and observe the actions of the fish.
10. Continue for one or two more weeks.

OBSERVATIONS

1. Describe the behaviour of the fish when the food was added in step 4.
2. Describe the behaviour of the fish in step 7. Record a description each time you do this procedure.

QUESTIONS

1. What was the original stimulus that caused a response in the fish?
2. What stimulus was paired with this in the investigation?
3. Describe how you might condition the same fish to a different stimulus, such as a tap on the glass.

B.F. Skinner, an American psychologist, has shown that the conditioning type of learning can be improved by the use of what is called reinforcement. A reward for a behaviour acts as a positive reinforcement, so that the behaviour is more likely to be repeated. Punishment for a behaviour acts as a negative reinforcement so that the behaviour is less likely to be repeated. Most of Skinner's research was done with pigeons and rats, but the methods he developed have been used successfully to train many kinds of animals.

In one of Skinner's experiments, a rat was placed in a specially prepared box. Inside the box was a lever that could be pressed by the rat, and various lights. There was a source of water and an opening where food would be deposited automatically each time a light flashed and the lever was pressed. Once inside the box, the rat would be rewarded with food only when it pressed the lever. After a few days, the rat learned, or rather was conditioned, to press the lever when it wanted food.

Then another step was added. The lever was made to operate and deposit food only when a light inside the box was on. At

Killer whales are trained by positive reinforcement.

first the rat would press the lever just as often when the light was on as when it was off, but after a day or so, it would press the lever much more frequently when the light was on. It had been conditioned by positive reinforcement to a certain behaviour.

Skinner performed similar experiments using negative reinforcements, such as electric shocks, to discourage certain behaviour. These experiments were successful, but not as successful as the ones in which he used positive reinforcement.

When you are teaching a dog to perform a trick or obey a command, for example, the positive reinforcement of a pat on the head, or a treat such as a biscuit, is much more effective than the negative reinforcement of yelling, scolding, or hitting.

The porpoises and killer whales that perform at marine parks are trained with positive reinforcement. If you watch carefully, you will see the trainer reward the animals with food after each trick.

In the next investigation, you will use positive reinforcement to condition an insect to a certain response. The insect you will use is the mealworm, the larval stage of a grain beetle.

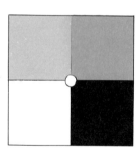

INVESTIGATION: To condition mealworms by positive reinforcement

MATERIALS

mealworms (from a pet store)   coloured paper

PROCEDURE

1. Make a four-coloured square as illustrated (Any four colours may be used).
2. Choose 10 active mealworms and place them in jars numbered 1-10.
3. Place one of the mealworms on the centre spot of the paper. Observe it for 2 min and record the direction in which it moves.
4. Repeat step 3 with each of the other nine mealworms. Note the colour that was *least* attractive to the mealworms. Put a small amount of bran in the centre of that colour. Repeat step 3 with each of the mealworms.

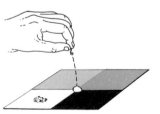

5. Remove the bran and repeat step 3 once more with each of the mealworms.

Record all your observations in your notebook in a table like this one.

| MEALWORM NUMBER | COLOUR TRAVELLED TO | | |
	TRIAL 1	TRIAL 2 (FOOD ON COLOUR)	TRIAL 3
1			
2			
3			
4			
5			
6			
7			
8			
9			
10			

1. What type of reinforcement is used in this investigation?
2. Give possible reasons for any differences between your results in step 3 and your results in step 4.
3. Compare your results in steps 4 and 5 and state what the results suggest.
4. The differences between the results in step 3 and the results in step 5 demonstrate conditioning. Explain why.
5. Why were you told to use 10 mealworms instead of just one or two?

Learning by conditioning is common in human society. Laws, rules, customs, regulations, and routines are constantly modifying our behaviour. It is unfortunate that a negative reinforcement is so often used to produce acceptable behaviour. A speeding driver is punished with a ticket and a bank robber with the loss of his freedom. Many of the rules in your school are probably enforced by the threat of a punishment. Such negative reinforcement works. It decreases such unacceptable behaviour as lateness. Can student behaviour also be improved by the use of positive reinforcement? To see how this might work, try rewriting the rules of your school so that they depend on positive reinforcement to encourage desirable behaviour instead of on negative reinforcement to discourage undesirable behaviour.

Advertising is a form of conditioning that is used widely in our society. The usual purpose of an advertisement is to make as many people as possible want to buy a certain product. The desire to buy is often stimulated by connecting, or pairing, the product with a response, such as being happy or feeling good. That is how Pavlov conditioned dogs to produce saliva in response to a flashing light. Most advertisements try to pair happiness or well-being with the use of a product. "You'll feel rich driving this new car." "Eat this breakfast cereal and you'll be as strong as an Olympic champion." The same message is repeated over and over again, and once you begin to pair the product with the message you are apt to rush out and buy some of it.

Protective mechanisms

To survive changes in the environment and to keep from becoming food for another creature, many animals have developed protective mechanisms, or ways of saving themselves. Some hide for protection. Others have developed colouring that lets them blend into their environment, so that it is hard for their enemies to see them.

INVESTIGATION: **To examine the coloration of a yellow perch**

MATERIALS

yellow perch or other fresh-water game fish
   (A preserved or stuffed fish may be used as long as it
   has its natural coloration.)

PROCEDURE

1. Examine the fish and note its general characteristics – eyes, mouth, fins, gill cover, and scales.
2. Hold the fish so that you can view it from above.
3. Hold the fish and view it from below.

1. Describe the colour and shape of the fish as it appeared from above and from below.
2. Sketch the fish to show the coloration.

QUESTIONS

1. When you are in a boat looking straight down into the water, why are fish difficult to see?
2. If you were at the bottom of the lake looking up, fish would also be difficult to see. Why is this so?
3. What animals might attack a fish from below?

A young deer is brown and has white spots that help to hide it in the forest. As it grows and becomes better able to run away from danger, the protective spots disappear. The arctic hare is white during the winter and a grey-brown during summer. In each season it blends in well with the background. Many insects are green so that they can hide in leaves or grass. Some are even shaped like leaves or sticks.

Not all animals hide from their enemies. Some are brightly coloured and easily seen. The monarch butterfly, for example,

Deer are camouflaged for protection.

A monarch butterfly

A viceroy butterfly

A wasp

A fly

is bright orange and black. Yet it is left alone by birds who depend on butterflies for food because it tastes bad to them. The bright colouring of bees and wasps serves as a warning: "Stay away, or I'll sting!" Many other dangerous or poisonous insects are also brightly coloured.

Mimicry

Still other insects take advantage of the fact that the dangerous insects are brightly coloured, and mimic or imitate them. The viceroy butterfly closely resembles the monarch and is often left alone by birds because of its similarity to the monarch, yet it would taste quite all right to a bird. Many kinds of flies mimic bees or wasps for protection.

Mimicry also occurs in other types of animals. The coral snake is a small and colourful snake that is found in southeastern parts of the United States. Although it is pleasant to look at, it is also very poisonous. The king snake closely resembles the coral snake and is thus protected from its enemies.

Monarch and viceroy butterflies (above and below, respectively) look alike.

Grouping

Some animals prefer to live in groups. In many cases, these are animals with few defences against the predators that hunt them. Deer, caribou, and musk-oxen normally travel in herds for safety. A single deer is easy game for a wolf, but three or four deer in a group can defend themselves against an attacking wolf and even inflict injury on it. Many birds and fish show similar grouping behaviour.

Some predators band together to hunt for prey. A pack of wolves will work to separate one or two deer from a herd, then share in the kill.

Protective behaviour

Grouping may be thought of as a kind of protective behaviour.

Bison band together for protection.

Individuals may form groups as a safety measure. Hiding, which is helped by coloration, is another kind of protective behaviour. Protective behaviours occur in the presence of danger, as when a predator comes near. Each species has its own way of reacting to danger. Some organisms remain motionless in the presence of danger while others take flight.

Animals must also protect themselves from the weather. Some birds and insects migrate to the south to escape the winter's cold. But plants, and many animals, are unable to get away. To survive the winter, they enter a resting stage that is called dormancy. For many plants, the resting stage is the seed. Seeds are able to survive the cold of a northern winter and still produce a new plant in the spring.

Many insects pass their dormancy as eggs or pupae, which are stages in their life cycles. Organisms that produce spores may rest in that stage of their life cycles. Some vertebrate animals have a resting stage to pass the winter, called hibernation. Hibernation is a kind of deep sleep that occurs with bears, squirrels, groundhogs, turtles, frogs, and many other organisms. It is a special type of dormancy that only starts when the temperature begins to drop, and ends when milder weather returns.

Most organisms have some kind of protective mechanism. These mechanisms may affect their appearance (coloration and

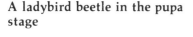

A ladybird beetle in the pupa stage

mimicry), or their behaviour (grouping and protective), or their habits (dormancy and hibernation). Whatever form a mechanism takes, its purpose is to help the organism to survive.

Body language is communication between animals that uses movement rather than sound. If you approach a friendly dog, it will wag its tail. If it is extremely happy to see you, its whole body will shake. A different dog may bare its fangs and cause the hair on its neck to stand up, showing that it is angry or afraid.

Have you ever seen a dog that is away from its home and is being chased by a larger dog? If you have, you may have seen the smaller dog exhibiting one or more of the following signals of body language:

- It may have rolled over on its back with its feet up in the air.
- It may have run homewards with its tail lowered and its ears down.
- It may have turned and faced its chaser, bristled the hair on its neck, and bared its fangs.
- It may have turned sideways and slowly backed off.

You can probably suggest the meaning of each of these signals by the little dog. Body language is used by many different kinds of animals. Scientists have found that it is widely used by insects, particularly insects that live in large colonies. Much research has been done on ants, termites, and bees.

A German scientist, Karl von Frisch, has spent his whole life studying the body language of honey bees. He received the Nobel Prize in 1974 for his work. His interest was born as he was observing some bees in a flower garden. First, he noticed a worker bee collecting nectar. It departed, and shortly afterwards a large number of bees arrived on the scene. He resolved to find out how the bees were able to locate the flowers.

Von Frisch spent years designing and carrying out experiments, and he repeated each experiment several times. He began by marking the bees in a hive with spots of various colours so that he would be able to identify the individual members of the hive, which had more than 20 000 inhabitants.

This enabled him to keep track of every bee. He found that bees that returned from the fields were able to communicate with the bees in the hive. They did this by body language. The bees had a number of different dances that they performed, to pass on information to other bees. The information that was conveyed in that way concerned the direction and distance to a food source, as well as the amount of time needed to fly to the source. During the dance, the performing bee allowed the other bees to taste some nectar. This told them the type of flower they would find.

Humans also use body language. In school, a child who is sure of the answer to a question will wave an arm frantically in the air. A child who is less sure of the answer will hold up a hand but will probably not wave it. A child who does not know the answer will simply avoid the teacher's eye. These are all examples of body language.

As we grow, we develop many types of body language. A smile when you greet someone conveys a certain message. The way you walk can express your mood. If your head is down, you are sad or dejected. Hold your head high and your shoulders back and you give people a different message.

QUESTIONS FOR INVESTIGATION

1. Make a list of examples of body language that you have observed, and in each case try to interpret the message.
2. List the types of body language that you use regularly.
3. Body language sometimes gives a misleading message. List some examples of this.

REVIEW QUESTIONS

1. Explain "adaptation".
2. Define "behaviour", "stimulus", and "response".
3. Explain the difference between a tropism and a taxis.
4. Name four possible stimuli for plants.
5. Explain the difference between a positive response and a negative response in an organism.
6. List three stimuli for animals.
7. What is a hypothesis?
8. Name two of your own characteristics that you probably inherited.

9. Name the two categories of animal behaviour.
10. (a) What is the meaning of "instinctive"?
    (b) Give an example of an instinctive reaction.
11. What is "migration"?
12. Explain why migration is an instinctive behaviour.
13. Name two types of learned behaviour.
14. Explain why imprinting is important to some young birds.
15. Explain the difference between a positive reinforcement for a behaviour and a negative reinforcement.
16. From your observations of animals, make lists of animals that display each of these types of protective behaviour: grouping, hiding, remaining still, and running away.
17. Explain why grouping can be a protective mechanism.
18. Define "dormancy" and "hibernation".
19. (a) What is body language?
    (b) What is a signal?
20. What kind of body language do honey bees use?

IMPORTANT TERMS

adaptation—the way an organism fits into its environment

behaviour—the response of an organism to what is happening in the environment around it

stimulus—an event or change in an organism's environment that causes it to react

response—an organism's reaction to a stimulus

tropism—the response of a plant to a stimulus such as light or water

hypothesis—an educated guess at the answer to a scientific question that is based on all existing information

taxis—the response of an animal when it moves towards or away from a stimulus

instinctive behaviour—the automatic response of an animal to a stimulus

learned behaviour—a response by an animal that is not instinctive but a result of the animal's experience

migration—the seasonal movement of animals in response to changes in temperature or food supplies

body language—communication between animals that uses movement instead of sound

signal—a movement by an organism that suggests a definite message

ROCKS AND MINERALS

The solid part of the Earth's crust consists of rock. You often see exposed rock as you drive through a road cut, explore a river bank, or walk beside a hill. Large chunks of rock are sometimes broken off by earthquakes and by explosions.

If you look closely at a piece of rock, you will probably find that it is built up from more than one kind of material. The different materials you see are called minerals. Some rocks consist entirely of one kind of mineral. Two rocks are considered to be the same type if they consist of the same minerals, or mineral.

Each mineral is made up of one or more of the 104 chemical elements that are known to exist. Graphite, for example, is a mineral that consists entirely of the element carbon. Quartz is a mineral made of the elements silicon and oxygen. Water, our most plentiful and useful mineral, is made of hydrogen and oxygen.

There are more than 2000 different minerals, but only about 12 of them are common all over the Earth.

Granite headlands in Lake Superior

An active volcano in Hawaii

ACTIVITY

From a collection of assorted rocks, choose one that appears to be made entirely of one mineral. Write a description of it, but do not mention colour. Put the rock back in the collection and give your description to a friend with a challenge to find the correct rock.

Types of rocks

Geologists classify rocks into three types, which they call igneous, sedimentary, and metamorphic.

Igneous rocks

Rocks of this type were formed when hot molten material cooled, changing from a liquid into a solid. "Igneous" means "formed by fire".

Some scientists believe that the Earth began as a mass of hot gases which eventually cooled and shrank into a great ball of hot liquid. As the liquid cooled, a crust formed on the outside – like the layer that forms on the top of pudding. From time to time the crust broke open and hot liquid flowed out on top, but eventually a thick solid crust formed over the liquid interior. Even today, molten rock from below (called magma) sometimes bursts through the crust and is squeezed out onto the surface. That is what happens when a volcano erupts. The lava is molten rock from beneath the Earth's crust.

The size of the crystals in a sample of igneous rock indicates how long the molten rock took to solidify. Large crystals indicate that the cooling happened slowly. Very fine, small crystals indicate that the cooling was rapid. Rapid cooling occurs when lava from a volcano pours into the sea.

Some of the common igneous rocks are granite, gabbro, basalt, pumice, and obsidian.

Granite is the most common igneous rock. It is generally pink or grey. It has a speckled appearance because it consists of three minerals with contrasting colorations. These are quartz, whose crystals are often milky, feldspar, which is usually

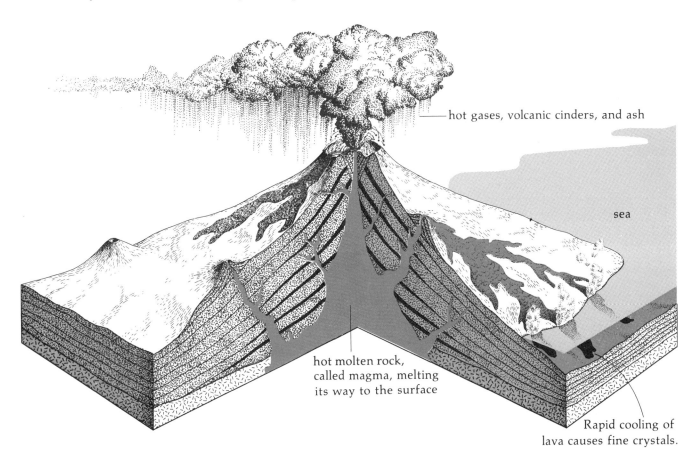

hot gases, volcanic cinders, and ash

sea

hot molten rock, called magma, melting its way to the surface

Rapid cooling of lava causes fine crystals.

Granite   Gabbro   Pumice

Obsidian   Basalt

white, and mica, which is usually brown and in thin, shiny layers. Granite is used in stone fireplaces and monuments. The crystals are medium-sized to large, indicating that the rock was formed from molten material below the Earth's crust and cooled slowly enough to allow large crystals to form.

Gabbro is a dark rock that may be grey, black, or brown. The crystals are medium-sized to large, showing that it also was formed below the Earth's crust.

Basalt is similar to gabbro, except that it is fine-grained. It is volcanic rock commonly formed from flowing lava. It has a dark colour and is heavier than granite.

Pumice is a volcanic rock that is filled with small holes formed by hot gases. This rock has so little density that it will float on water. It is sometimes used as a substitute for sandpaper.

Obsidian is also volcanic. It looks like black glass, and, in fact, it has the same composition as commercial glass. It cooled too quickly for crystals to form.

INVESTIGATION: To make a "working" model of a volcano

MATERIALS

ammonium bichromate (20 g)
magnesium ribbon (8 cm)
plasticine
clay flower pot
aluminum foil

PROCEDURE

1. Invert the flower pot and mould the plasticine around it, as illustrated.
2. Make a small cup with some aluminum foil, and press it into the top of the mound. This represents the volcano's throat.
3. Pour the ammonium bichromate into the aluminum-foil cup. (For an even more spectacular eruption, mix in 4 g of magnesium powder.)
4. Push one end of the magnesium ribbon into the centre of the cup, to serve as a fuse. Leave about 3 cm of the ribbon sticking out.
5. Ask the teacher to light the magnesium ribbon with a match. It may take a few matches to get it going. (*Caution*: Stand at least 2 m back from your volcano when it is being lit.)

OBSERVATIONS

Draw a picture to show how your volcano appeared as it was erupting.

QUESTIONS

1. In what ways does your volcano resemble a real one?
2. Where does a real volcano get its energy?
3. Name some volcanic rocks, and explain how you could recognize them.

WARNING
This investigation is for TEACHER DEMONSTRATION ONLY!

TO THE TEACHER:
Demonstrate *only* in well-ventilated area. Read *Teacher's Manual*, p. 94, before proceeding.

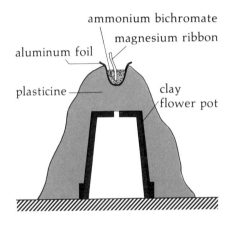

ammonium bichromate
magnesium ribbon
aluminum foil
plasticine
clay flower pot

MATERIALS

powdered sulphur
alcohol burner
2 beakers
magnifying glass
filter paper (or paper towel)
metal spoon

PROCEDURE

1. Heat some sulphur in a spoon slowly, until it melts.
2. Pour the melted sulphur into a paper cone resting in a beaker, as illustrated. Let the sulphur cool slowly.
3. Melt some more sulphur and pour it into a beaker of cold water.
4. Break open the solidified sulphur from steps 2 and 3 and compare the crystals in the two samples, using the magnifying glass.

OBSERVATIONS

In your notebook, write down your observations from step 4.

water

sulphur

INVESTIGATION: To examine a collection of igneous rocks

MATERIALS

collection of igneous rock samples
magnifying glass

PROCEDURE

1. Pick any four samples from the collection.
2. Examine each sample with the magnifying glass to see whether crystals are visible. Note the size of any crystals you see.
3. Draw and colour a diagram of each of the four samples.
4. Study a piece of granite with the magnifying glass, and try to identify quartz, feldspar, and mica crystals.

In your notebook, record your observations in a table like this one.

NAME OF ROCK	DIAGRAM	CRYSTALS

QUESTIONS

1. Describe how igneous rocks are formed.
2. Why are the crystals larger in some igneous rocks than they are in others?
3. What is magma?

Sedimentary rocks

Sedimentary rocks are formed from particles, or sediments, settling layer upon layer on the ocean floor over great periods of time, until they are so tightly compressed under their own weight that they become fused into rock.

There are three ways in which sedimentary rocks can form. The first is by the buildup of gravel, sand, or mud, carried down by streams and rivers, and deposited on lake and ocean bottoms. When many of the particles are gravel, the rock that forms is called conglomerate. If the particles are grains of sand, the rock is called sandstone. If the particles are flakes of clay or mud, the rock is called shale.

Another way in which sedimentary rocks can be formed is by the depositing, out of seawater, of chemicals such as salt and calcium carbonate. This happens when a body of salt water evaporates, or dries up. Rock salt, gypsum, and limestone are formed in this way.

Sedimentary rocks can also be formed from the shells and skeletons of animals and from plant remains. The shapes of organisms are sometimes preserved in the rocks as fossils. Limestone can be formed from the shells of shellfish. Coal,

Conglomerate

Sandstone

Shale

Limestone with fossils

Coal

Limestone

Folded sedimentary layers

another sedimentary rock, is formed from compacted plant remains.

Sedimentary rocks are usually arranged in layers. In a road cut or river bank, you can often see clearly defined layers. On closer inspection, you will probably find that the particles differ from layer to layer. One layer of rock may represent thousands of years of Earth-building.

In many places, compressive forces in the Earth have caused once-flat layers of rock to fold or bend. The Rocky Mountains are composed mainly of sedimentary rocks that were at one time flat and covered with water.

Sedimentary rocks are the kind you are most likely to see while travelling; they account for three-quarters of the rocks showing at the Earth's surface. However, sedimentary rocks make up only about 5% of the Earth's crust.

ACTIVITY

You can simulate the natural process of sedimentation with a tall glass jar and some natural soil. Each day add a handful or two of soil to the water and let it settle. Note how it forms layers. Imagine what might cause the thickness of the layers being deposited on the floor of a lake to vary from year to year. What could you add to your jar to make conglomerate?

INVESTIGATION: To make a model of a sedimentary rock bed

MATERIALS

sand
fine gravel
patching plaster
poster paints
milk carton
pie plate
nail

PROCEDURE

1. With the nail, punch about 20 holes in the sides of the milk carton.
2. Every day for six or eight days add a 2 cm or 3 cm layer of sand or gravel to the milk carton and enough paint to lightly saturate the layer. Use a different colour of paint each day.
3. Peel off the carton and expose the "sedimentary rock profile".

OBSERVATIONS

Make a coloured diagram of your rock bed.

QUESTIONS

1. What is the function of the paint?
2. In what season of the year is a layer of coarse particles likely to be deposited?
3. How can sand and other particles be transported, other than by flowing water?

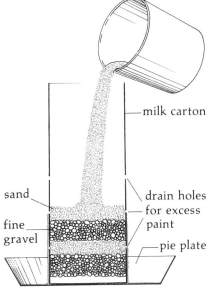

Making a bed of sedimentary rocks

INVESTIGATION: To examine a collection of sedimentary rocks

MATERIALS
collection of assorted sedimentary rocks
magnifying glass

PROCEDURE
1. Examine each rock carefully, with and without the magnifying glass.
2. Look for grains of sand, pebbles, fossils, and crystals in each sample.

OBSERVATIONS
1. Record in your notebook which of the rocks showed evidence of layering, and which contained fossils.
2. Make a coloured sketch of any three of the sedimentary rocks you examined.

QUESTIONS
1. Why do sedimentary rocks often occur in layers?
2. Describe the three ways in which sedimentary rocks are formed.
3. Were any of the rocks you examined formed as a result of the ocean drying up? Explain your answer.

Metamorphic rocks

These are formed when igneous and sedimentary rocks are subjected to intense heat and pressure. The changes may be slight, only causing the grains to be squeezed closer together. Or they may be so great that the original rock cannot be recognized. "Metamorphic" means "changed in form".

Metamorphic rocks are usually formed at depths greater than 12 km beneath the surface. The pressure there is intense due to the weight of rock above. If you have ever buried your feet in sand at the beach, you can probably remember feeling extra pressure on them. Can you imagine what the pressure is like under 12 km or 16 km of rock? No wonder the grains and fragments in sedimentary rock are squeezed together! Sometimes the pressure even forces the minerals to rearrange themselves into bands or layers. This process is called foliation and rocks that have been subjected to it are said to be foliated. Foliated rocks tend to split along the layers. Unfoliated metamorphic rocks do not have definite layers. Foliation is a sign of metamorphism, but not all metamorphic rocks are foliated.

There are two ways for metamorphic rocks to be formed closer to the surface than 12 km. When molten rock pushes its way towards the surface from the Earth's interior, it heats up the rocks along its path to temperatures ranging from 800°C near the molten rock down to 150°C a few metres away. 150°C is the lowest temperature at which metamorphism takes place. Metamorphic rocks can also be formed near the surface when the rocks are subjected to enormous compressive, or mountain-building, forces.

Study the illustration below. Where have rocks changed mainly because of heat? Where have they changed mainly because of pressure? Where have they changed because of heat and pressure? What do we call the metamorphic rock formed from sandstone? from shale? from granite? from limestone?

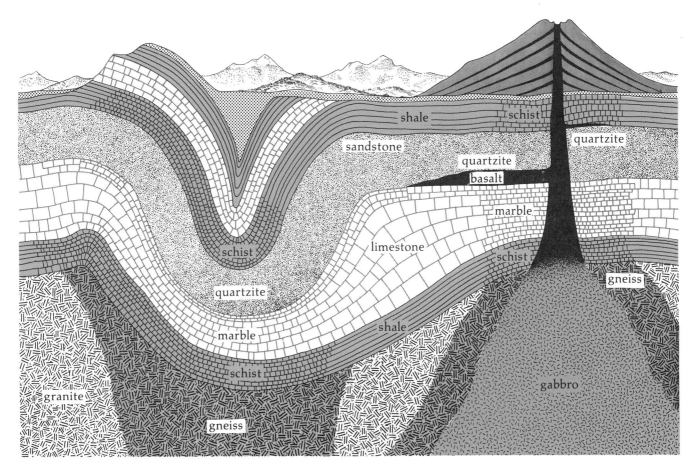

Slate

Marble

Quartzite

Geologists classify metamorphic rocks into two groups – foliated and non-foliated. Three common foliated (or layered) metamorphic rocks are slate, schist, and gneiss (pronounced "nice").

Slate is a fine-grained rock that is formed from shale. The foliation of slate is flat, allowing the rock to split easily into thin sheets. For this reason, slate has been used for blackboards, as flagstone, and as shingles. Slate is harder and shinier than shale. It rings when you tap it.

Schist is a rock with fine layers that can be formed from shale or basalt. The layering is clearly visible but often wavy. Crystals are small but can be seen with the naked eye.

Gneiss looks as though it had been formed from granite. It is coarse-grained rock and is easily recognized by its alternating light and dark layers.

Two common non-foliated metamorphic rocks are marble and quartzite. *Marble* is formed from limestone. Although it is often difficult to tell the two apart, marble is harder than limestone and has larger crystals. Marble may be pure white or coloured by the presence of iron. Any fossils present in limestone are squeezed and flattened.

Quartzite is formed from sandstone. It is denser than sandstone and has a glassy or sugary appearance. When sandstone breaks, it breaks around the sand grains, whereas quartzite breaks through the individual grains.

MATLOCK COLLEGE LIBRARY

INVESTIGATION: To make a substance that looks like
metamorphic rock

MATERIALS

plasticine
pennies (or washers)

PROCEDURE

1. Force as many pennies as you can into a ball of plasticine.
   Push them in from all sides. The pennies represent the
   crystals in a piece of igneous rock.
2. Leave your plasticine-and-penny "rock" in the hot sun or
   beside a radiator for 5 or 10 min.
3. Exert pressure on your hot "rock" by standing on it,
   causing it to be flattened.
4. After it has cooled, break your flattened new "rock" open,
   and note what has happened to the pennies.

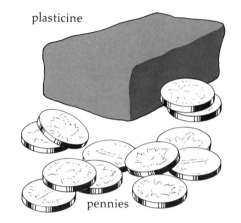

plasticine

pennies

OBSERVATIONS

1. Draw diagrams to show how the pennies were arranged in
   the "rock" before and after you applied heat and pressure.
2. Note how heat affected your "rock".

QUESTIONS

1. Describe how metamorphic rocks are formed.
2. What causes foliation in some metamorphic rocks?

INVESTIGATION: To examine some metamorphic rocks

MATERIALS

collections of assorted metamorphic rocks, sedimentary rocks,
    and igneous rocks
magnifying glass

PROCEDURE

1. Examine the collection of metamorphic rocks and decide
   which of them are foliated.

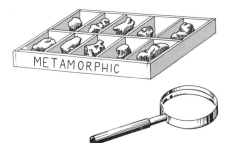

2. Decide which of the rocks have components that can be seen as individual crystals.
3. Find occurrences of slate, schist, gneiss, marble, and quartzite in the collection of metamorphic rocks. Then find the parent rock for each of these in the igneous or sedimentary collections. Compare each of the metamorphic rocks with its parent.

OBSERVATIONS

Enter your observations in a table like this one.

FOLIATED	NON-FOLIATED	INDIVIDUAL GRAINS VISIBLE	INDIVIDUAL GRAINS TOO SMALL TO SEE	META-MORPHIC ROCK	PARENT ROCK

QUESTION

Find out what geologists mean by "rock cycle" and write a brief note on it.

Rock classification chart

Here is a chart that summarizes the characteristics of igneous, sedimentary, and metamorphic rocks. If you find a rock and want to classify it, start at the top of the chart and work your way down, eliminating different possibilities until you are left with a particular type of rock. Use the chart to classify these three rocks.

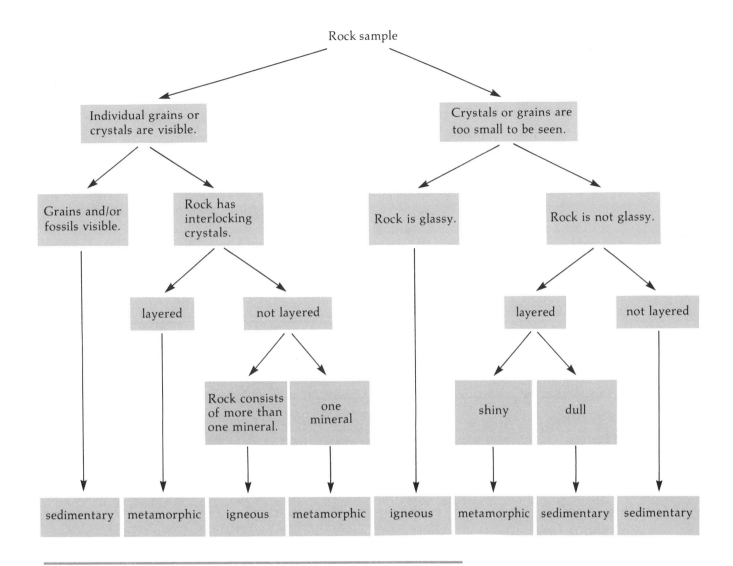

INVESTIGATION: **To collect and classify a variety of rocks**

MATERIALS

small paper bags
notebook
map (optional)
geologic hammer

knapsack
goggles
masking tape

PROCEDURE

1. Plan a trip to a local quarry, rock cut, building excavation, beach, field, or park where rocks are exposed.

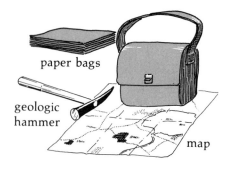

paper bags

geologic hammer

map

2. Find specimens of 5 or 10 different kinds of rocks. Samples need be no larger than your fist. Trim down larger ones with the hammer. Be sure to wear the goggles whenever using the hammer.
3. Put each specimen in a separate paper bag and write on the bag exactly where the specimen was found.
4. Make a sketch in your notebook of each of the rocks you collected.
5. Back at school, or at home, scrub your samples with soapy water, dry them thoroughly, and number them, using masking tape.
6. Using the classification chart, classify each rock as igneous, sedimentary, or metamorphic.

OBSERVATIONS

1. Make a catalogue of your rocks using a form such as this.

ROCK NO.	DATE FOUND	LOCATION	IGNEOUS, SEDIMENTARY, OR METAMORPHIC	NAME OF ROCK

2. Identify as many of your rocks as you can from the descriptions given earlier or by matching them with rocks in the collections you used in this investigation.

Weathering and erosion

Weathering is the breaking down of rocks into smaller fragments. Erosion is the carrying away of the fragments.

Weathering can be mechanical or chemical. Mechanical weathering breaks a rock down without altering the chemical composition. In other words, the pieces are just made smaller. In chemical weathering, however, new materials are formed.

Mechanical weathering can be caused by the expansion of water when it freezes, by the heating and cooling of rocks, by the growth of plant roots, by worms and other burrowing animals, and by wind action.

When water freezes, it expands by about 10% and exerts

tremendous force in doing so. The force is so strong that it will crack a car engine. It can also break open rocks where cracks have allowed water to seep in. At certain times of the year, the temperature is above the freezing point during the day and drops below the freezing point at night. Rocks break down rapidly under such conditions.

The heating and cooling of rocks causes them to expand and contract. Surprisingly, the effect is more noticeable where there are frequent rain showers because water combines with certain minerals in rocks causing them to swell. The result is that layers of rock peel off. The process is called exfoliation.

The roots of plants work their way into cracks in rocks, causing them to split and crumble. Worms, ants, and other insects, as well as larger animals such as ground hogs, open up the soil and expose rocks below the surface to the effects of weathering. The wind picks up grains of sand and turns them into a veritable stream of bullets, blasting away at everything they strike, including rocks.

The five agents of mechanical weathering

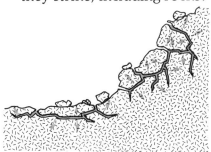

Freezing water

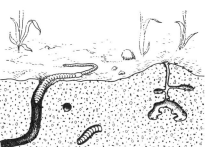

Worms

Plant roots

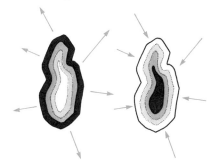

Heating and cooling

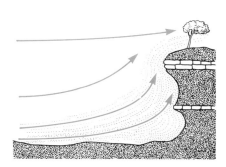

The action of wind and water

Chemical weathering usually accompanies mechanical weathering and is more pronounced in places where there is a lot of moisture. It can be caused by carbon dioxide in the air, by oxygen in the air, by water, and by acid conditions produced when plants and animals die.

Carbon dioxide is a gas forming a small natural part of air. In industrial areas, the atmosphere contains an unnaturally high percentage of carbon dioxide and the rain turns some of it into carbonic acid. This acid dissolves away limestone and certain minerals in other rocks.

Oxygen can cause rocks containing iron to rust, and the oxides of iron so formed are easily washed away by water. Water combines with many minerals, causing them to swell and break away from the rocks they belonged to. When plants and animals die, acids are formed that are capable of eating away at rocks.

INVESTIGATION: To observe the effect on various rocks of rapid heating and cooling

---

MATERIALS

electric frying pan and lid
samples of 6 different types of rocks (egg-sized)
pail
ice cubes
tongs
goggles

PROCEDURE

1. Heat the rocks to 100 °C or higher in the electric frying pan with the lid on. Stand well back, because some types of rock may explode on being heated. Wear the goggles.
2. Fill the pail with ice water, and with the tongs transfer the rocks from the frying pan into the pail. Listen for sounds of cracking.
3. Examine the rocks to see whether any of them have cracked or split open.
4. If you have time, repeat steps 1 to 3, using the same rocks.

hot rocks

ice water

OBSERVATIONS

Describe what you observed in steps 2 and 3.

QUESTIONS

1. Do heating and rapid cooling have the same effect on all rocks?
2. Describe two examples from nature of rocks being heated and cooled in rapid succession.

INVESTIGATION: To examine the weathering effect of moving water on a collection of loose rock fragments

---

MATERIALS

old brick (or rock that will crumble easily)
hammer
cloth
jar and lid
crayon

PROCEDURE

1. Cover the brick with the cloth and hit the corners with the hammer to break off chips.
2. Collect about 20 chips no larger than about 3 cm across.
3. Choose a chip that has sharp corners and edges and mark it heavily with crayon. Draw an outline of it in your notebook.
4. Half-fill the jar with water. Put the chips in the jar and seal it.
5. Shake the jar vigorously for 2 min and then take out the marked chip. Make another sketch of it and return it to the jar.
6. Repeat step 5 four more times, or more often if you have time, observing the same chip at 2 min intervals.

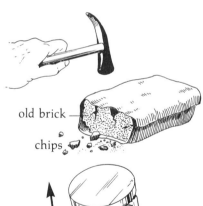

old brick — chips

shake

water and brick chips

OBSERVATIONS

1. From your sketches of the marked chip, write notes describing what happened to it during the investigation.
2. Write notes on any changes you saw in the clarity of the water and in the sediment at the bottom of the jar.

1. Describe three places where this kind of water action takes place in nature.
2. Could mud be formed in this way? Explain your answer.

INVESTIGATION: To demonstrate chemical weathering

MATERIALS

dilute hydrochloric acid (20% concentrated)
limestone or marble chips
test tube
goggles

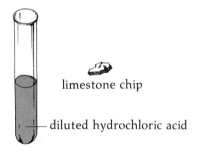

limestone chip

diluted hydrochloric acid

PROCEDURE

1. Pour about 5 cm of the acid into a test tube. Wear goggles and avoid getting acid on your skin.
2. Drop a chip of limestone into the acid in the tube.
3. When the action has stopped, add a little more acid.
4. Pour the remaining solution into the sink. Rinse off the limestone chip with water and examine it for any changes.

OBSERVATIONS

1. Write a description of what happened when the rock chip was added to the acid.
2. Note whether the chip changed, and if so in what way(s).

QUESTIONS

1. Where do rocks and acid meet in nature?
2. Why is rain more acidic today than 50 or 100 years ago?

Erosion. The carrying away of rock particles, called erosion, is caused by running water, glaciers, and wind.

Running water pours over rocks in streams and rivers, and along the shores of lakes and oceans. Stream erosion is greatest in the spring when the run-off from melting ice and snow causes rivers to swell their banks. Rivers carve out valleys by carrying away particles of rocks year after year. At first the

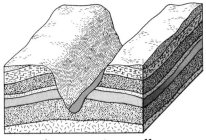

A young river valley

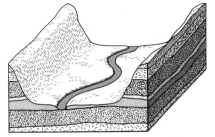

A mature, or old, river valley

valley is V-shaped. Then, as the years pass, the river widens the valley. Eventually, it wanders back and forth in a snake-like pattern.

Glaciers are huge streams of gradually flowing ice. The pressure of new ice forming at the top end, and the force of gravity, keep them moving slowly downhill. The rate of flow varies from 1 cm or 2 cm/d to more than 1 m/d. Glaciers push rock in front of them and carry it along on their undersides. Geologists believe that glaciers once covered most of what is now Canada and extended well into the United States. As the climate became milder, the glaciers receded northwards to

The Athabasca Glacier

Glacial boulders

Glacial striations

where they are today, high in the Rockies and in the arctic islands. There is much evidence to support this theory, including glacial boulders far from their place of origin and deep scratches in hard rock.

The wind carries away particles of earth, grains of sand, and even small rock fragments. This is a major problem wherever the soil is dry. Farmers worry when prolonged dry spells and high winds result in dust storms. Their fertile topsoil can be blown away completely. When the wind calms down, it may be deposited in hills, or dunes, several kilometres away.

A dust storm

MATLOCK COLLEGE LIBRARY

Energy Fuels

Nearly all the energy we use for heating homes, schools, and factories comes from the Earth. Similarly, we rely on the Earth to supply us with fuels to power cars, trucks, buses, trains, planes, and ships.

Coal, natural gas, and oil are three sources of energy we have depended on increasingly over the last 100 years. They are called fossil fuels since they were formed from the decayed remains of plants and animals. Recently, scientists discovered the energy of the atom. In the last 10 or 15 years nuclear reactors, which use uranium (an element found in certain radioactive rocks) for fuel, have been built in countries throughout the world.

Coal was one of man's earliest fuels. Its use dates back more than 4000 years. Coal begins to form when plants, including trees and bushes, die and are buried in a swamp. In peat, which is partly formed coal, it is possible to see outlines of branches and leaves. The longer the coal continues to form and the deeper it is buried, the harder it gets. Lignite is harder than

Bituminous coal

An open pit, or strip, coal mine

An underground coal mine

peat, and soft or bituminous coal is harder than lignite. But the hardest coal of all is anthracite. It is formed under such tremendous heat and pressure that it is classified as a metamorphic rock, rather than a sedimentary one.

Before about 1950, coal was used in almost every Canadian house. It was dumped through the basement window and later shovelled into the furnace. After 1950, coal furnaces were gradually replaced by oil furnaces, or converted to use oil. In years to come, coal may regain its old popularity, since it is in more abundant supply than oil or natural gas. It has been estimated that there is enough coal in the ground to last 300 or 400 years.

However, there are problems associated with coal. For one thing, it contains sulphur, which pollutes the air when it is burned. Also, the dirt that inevitably goes with it makes it a poor choice for heating houses, compared with oil, gas, or electricity. Soft coal can be mined in many places by the strip method, on the surface, but this leaves ugly scars on the landscape. Mining coal underground is unpleasant work and it is sometimes difficult to recruit men to do it.

Despite these problems, coal is a fuel that is bound to be used more and more as oil and natural gas become more expensive.

The *oil* we use today started to form millions of years ago, from the buildup over countless years on the ocean floor of animal and plant remains, and sediment. Layer upon layer was deposited and eventually a thick sedimentary rock was formed. A combination of heat and pressure converted the dead plants

If vertical holes were drilled at A, B, C, and D would they strike oil, gas, water, or a dry well in each case?

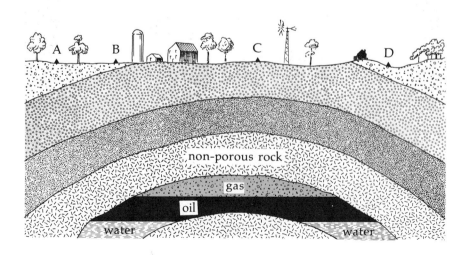

and animals in the rock into oil. The oil was trapped in layers of porous rock beneath layers of denser rock.

In Canada today, oil is used as an energy source almost as extensively as coal, wood, natural gas, and nuclear power combined. Canada has only 2% of the world's proven oil reserves but this does not include the Athabasca oil sands in northern Alberta. These sands contain one of the largest known oil deposits – an estimated 600 000 million barrels of heavy oil. The problem is to separate the oil from the sand at a reasonable cost. A consortium of petroleum producers invested $2500 million to start the job. It was anticipated that 125 000 barrels per day would be coming from the sands by the early 1980s. Despite this, serious shortages of oil were expected by 1985.

Natural gas is usually found along with oil and on top of it. Gas has 1.6 times the energy value of oil and burns without causing any great air pollution. Gas can be piped easily from the well to where it is to be used.

Nuclear energy is produced by splitting atoms of uranium-235 in a chain reaction. This process, called nuclear fission, releases enormous amounts of heat. One tonne of uranium provides as much energy as 20 000 t of coal. This energy is used to produce steam to turn electric power generators.

One barrel of oil equals 0.16 m^3. The cubic metre is the metric unit of measurement for expressing barrels of oil.

Pickering nuclear generating station, Pickering, Ontario

Canada has an abundant supply of uranium, but many people are concerned about the waste products of nuclear reactors, which remain dangerously radioactive for thousands of years and must somehow be stored or disposed of safely. At present, they are being stored in great water tanks at the reactor sites. For more permanent disposal, they may later be dumped into abandoned mines. Despite the so far unsolved problem of waste disposal, nuclear reactors are being built in many countries.

QUESTIONS

1. Why is energy conservation necessary, along with further exploration for coal, oil, and natural gas?
2. Name some of the alternative energy sources, apart from oil, gas, coal, and uranium, that are being studied by scientists.
3. Why are coal, oil, and natural gas called fossil fuels?
4. List as many ways as you can to conserve energy at home, at school, on the road, in recreational pursuits, and in industry.

Fossils

Fossils were discussed in connection with sedimentary rocks and the fossil fuels – coal, natural gas, and oil. They are believed to have been formed from plants and animals that died thousands, even millions, of years ago. They could be called imprints of the past, and some scientists use them in an attempt to piece together a picture of the climate, vegetation, and animal life during different periods of the Earth's history.

The earliest living things, nearly 3000 million years ago, were probably simple organisms living in warm oceans. They were like the algae, bacteria, and fungi of today. These were probably the chief forms of life for about 2400 million years, until about 600 million years ago when a biological revolution is believed to have occurred. Rocks of this age contain evidence of living things much larger and more varied than before. The revolution may have been a result of changes in the composition of the Earth's atmosphere. Oxygen had probably not been present in the atmosphere in sufficient quantities to support animal life. Then, as plant life developed, more oxygen was added to the air (since oxygen is given off by plants). By about 600 million years ago, the oxygen level was probably high enough to support more advanced forms of animal life. Over the next relatively short span of 20 million years, bacteria, fungi, and algae were joined by great numbers of larger and more complex types of animals and plants.

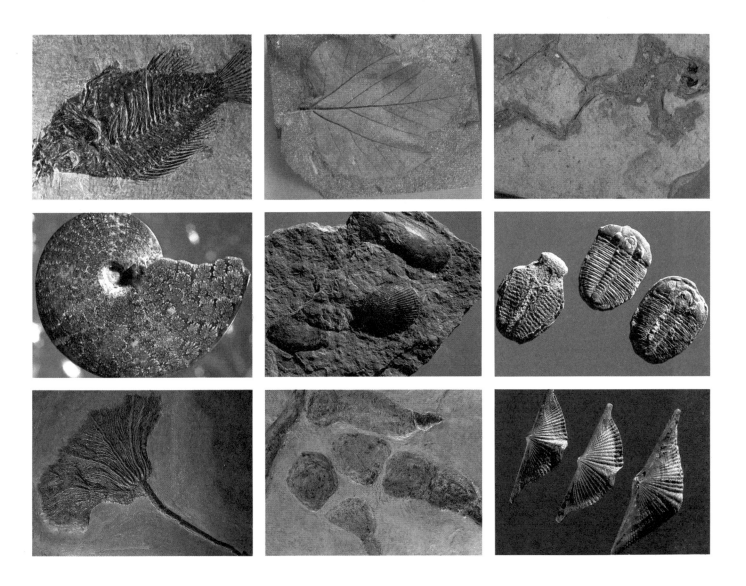

plaster of Paris

petroleum jelly

INVESTIGATION: To make models similar to fossils

MATERIALS

grease or petroleum jelly   plaster of Paris
assorted tree leaves   2 disposable plastic containers
shells

PROCEDURE

1. Mix some plaster of Paris with water in one of the containers.
2. Grease a leaf (or a shell).
3. Place it in the bottom of the second container and pour a layer of plaster on top.
4. When the plaster is hard, remove it from the mold. The leaf (or shell) should pull free from the plaster.

OBSERVATIONS

Draw a sketch of your "fossil".

QUESTIONS

1. What type of rock often contains fossils?
2. Why is it believed that a "biological revolution" took place about 600 million years ago?

Mineral identification

No mineral can be positively identified by a single test. It is necessary to make several tests of a mineral, and then match your results with data in a catalogue, before you can be certain what it is. Whether you are an amateur mineralogist or a professional one, when you need to identify a mineral you should try to answer the following questions about it.

1. *What is the mineral's lustre?* Lustre refers to the shininess of the surface. Every mineral may be said to have either a metallic or a non-metallic lustre, depending on whether its surface resembles that of a metal. Minerals with a non-metallic lustre may be further described as glassy, dull, pearly, silky, or sparkling.

Galena

Calcite

Galena has a metallic lustre while calcite has a non-metallic lustre.

2. *What is the mineral's colour*? Colour is sometimes an important characteristic. For example, malachite is always bright green, chalcopyrite is a golden yellow, and galena is silver-grey. However, some minerals' colours are of no help since impurities can change them. Quartz may be white or pink. Pink quartz contains an impurity – a small amount of iron oxide. Also, the surfaces of some minerals tarnish after long exposure to the atmosphere. A mineralogist will always break into a rock sample to see the true colour of a fresh surface.

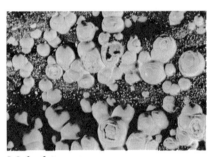

Malachite

Galena

Chalcopyrite

3. *Can the mineral be streaked*? To perform the streak test, rub the sample against a "streak plate" (or on the back of a porcelain tile). Some minerals will leave a mark on the plate. Such a mark is called a streak. The colour of the streak can help to identify the mineral. This test is especially useful for soft, metallic minerals. Hematite, for example, always leaves a brownish red streak although the colour of the mineral is silver-red, brown, or black.

4. *How hard or soft is the mineral*? The hardness of a mineral is judged by how difficult it is to scratch. The hardest mineral to scratch is diamond. The easiest to scratch is talc. Mineralogists use a hardness scale that ranges from one to 10:

Hematite

Scale of hardness

1. Talc (softest)
2. Gypsum
3. Calcite
4. Fluorite
5. Apatite

6. Feldspar
7. Quartz
8. Topaz
9. Corundum
10. Diamond (hardest)

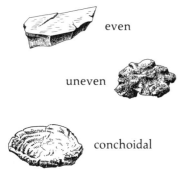

even

uneven

conchoidal

hackly

The four types of fracture

For a quick indication of a mineral sample's position on the scale of hardness, mineralogists have a few rules of thumb. If a mineral can be scratched with your fingernail, its rating is 2.5 or under. If it can be scratched with a copper penny, its rating is 3 or under. If it can be scratched with a knife, its rating may be as high as 5.5. If it takes a nail to scratch it, it may have a hardness of up to 6.5.

5. *Does the mineral show cleavage or fracture?* A mineral is said to possess cleavage when it breaks along smooth surfaces, indicating that its atoms are arranged in a regular pattern of layers. Mica has cleavage in one direction while salt (halite) cleaves in two directions. Calcite cleaves in three directions.

A mineral is said to fracture if it breaks irregularly. Even, uneven, conchoidal, and hackly are four words used to identify different kinds of fractures.

6. *Is a crystal form visible in the mineral?* In some minerals, it is possible to see parts of individual crystals. Crystals occur in six different forms, or shapes, as illustrated.

Some minerals have no crystal form, and they are called amorphous. They cooled too rapidly to form crystals. Glass is an amorphous mineral.

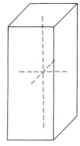
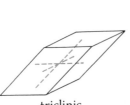

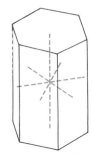

cubic   monoclinic   tetragonal   triclinic   orthorhombic   hexagonal

MATLOCK COLLEGE LIBRARY

Quartz crystals

Galena crystals

To which crystal system do quartz crystals belong?

To which crystal system do galena crystals belong?

7. *What is the relative density of the mineral?* The relative density of a mineral is the number of times the mineral is denser than water.

$$\text{relative density} = \frac{\text{mass of mineral}}{\text{mass of an equal volume of water}}$$

For example, corundum has a relative density of 4.0. This means that a piece of corundum has four times the mass of the same volume of water. Minerals with relative densities above 4.0 usually contain metals. You can get a rough idea of the relative density of a mineral by holding it in your hand and hefting it a few times.

8. *What special properties does the mineral have?* Other properties might include:

- It has a distinctive feel, smell, or taste.
- It is attracted to a magnet.
- It lights up when held under an ultraviolet lamp.
- It effervesces, or gives off vapour, in acid.

INVESTIGATION: To perform tests to identify certain minerals

MATERIALS

samples of three unidentified minerals
magnifying glass
porcelain streak plate

20% solution of hydrochloric acid
concrete nail
penny

PROCEDURE

1. If the samples are not numbered, attach numbers to them on bits of masking tape.

penny

concrete nail

unknown minerals

streak plate

dilute acid

2. For each mineral sample, perform the tests that have just been described. Keep a record of the results.
3. Consult the mineral chart, which follows, and try to identify the samples you tested.

OBSERVATIONS

Enter your results from step 2 in a table such as this one.

TEST	MINERAL 1	MINERAL 2	MINERAL 3
lustre			
colour			
streak			
hardness			
cleavage			
crystal form			
relative density			
magnetic			
effervescence			
other quality			

QUESTIONS

1. Having compared your test results with the mineral chart, write the names of the three minerals you tested.
2. In what way is a mineralogist like a detective?

Minerals with non-metallic lustre

MINERAL	COLOUR	STREAK	HARDNESS	RELATIVE DENSITY	CRYSTAL SHAPE	CLEAVAGE	OTHER QUALITIES
Gypsum	white or grey	white	2	2.3	monoclinic	1 direction	silky, dull, glassy
Calcite	white	white	3	2.7	hexagonal	3 directions	dull, effervesces
Fluorite	purple or light green or yellow	colourless	4	3	cubic	octahedral	glassy, fluorescent
Apatite	green or brown	white	5	3.2	hexagonal	conchoidal fracture	glassy, brittle
Feldspar	white or pink	colourless	6	2.5	monoclinic	2 directions	common in igneous rocks
Garnet	red or brown	white	7.5	3.5	cubic	none	glassy, common mineral

Minerals with non-metallic lustre (cont'd)

MINERAL	COLOUR	STREAK	HARDNESS	RELATIVE DENSITY	CRYSTAL SHAPE	CLEAVAGE	OTHER QUALITIES
Quartz	mostly colourless	colourless	7	2.65	hexagonal	conchoidal fracture	waxy or glassy
Topaz	white or yellow or blue	colourless	8	3.6	orthorhombic	1 direction	glassy
Tourmaline	black or green or brown	colourless	7	3.2	hexagonal	uneven fracture	glassy
Talc	white	white	1	2.8	monoclinic	1 direction	soapy, easy to cut
Sulphur	yellow	yellow to white	2.5	2.0	orthorhombic	conchoidal fracture	melts easily
Dolomite	white or grey-green	white	3.5	2.8	hexagonal	3 directions	glassy
Halite	colourless	colourless	2.5	2.1	cubic	cubic	glassy, salty taste
Hematite	reddish brown	reddish brown	6	5.3	hexagonal	none	dull, source of iron
Limonite	yellow or brown	yellow or brown	5.5	4.0	often powdery	none	dull, iron-rust appearance
Serpentine	white or red or green	colourless	2.5	2.4	monoclinic	none	silky, waxy
Asbestos	yellow	colourless	2	2.2	monoclinic	fibrous	silk threads
Bauxite	grey or red or white	grey	1.3	2.3	rounded mass	—	dull, source of aluminum
Hornblende	green or black	greyish white	5.5	3.4	monoclinic	2 directions	glassy
Kaolinite	reddish brown	white	2	2.6	triclinic	1 direction	dull, greasy
Augite	black or dark green	colourless	6	3.5	monoclinic	2 directions	dull
Olivine	olive green	colourless	6.5	3.5	orthorhombic	imperfect	glassy
Muscovite	white	colourless	2.5	2.8	monoclinic	1 direction	type of mica
Biotite	black to brown	colourless	2.5	3.0	monoclinic	1 direction	type of mica

Minerals with metallic lustre

MINERAL	COLOUR	STREAK	HARDNESS	RELATIVE DENSITY	CRYSTAL SHAPE	CLEAVAGE	OTHER QUALITIES
Graphite	black or grey	black	1.2	2.3	hexagonal	1 direction	greasy, smudges
Hematite	silver-grey	reddish brown	6	5.3	hexagonal	none	brittle, iron ore
Pyrite	yellow	greenish black	6.5	5.0	cubic	conchoidal fracture	"fool's gold"
Magnetite	black	black	6	5.2	cubic	conchoidal fracture	magnetic
Galena	grey	grey	2.5	7.5	cubic	cubic	source of lead
Copper	red or black	red	3	8.1	cubic	hackly fracture	malleable

Crystal formation

You have examined several crystals in rocks and discovered their beautiful shapes and varied colours. Now you will have an opportunity to grow your own crystals. Some people make a hobby of it, and consider it a challenge to grow the largest possible single crystals.

INVESTIGATION: To grow crystals

MATERIALS
100 g of copper sulphate (or 120 g of alum)
250 mL beaker
mason (or similar) jar
thread
needle
hot plate (or alcohol burner)
graduated cylinder

PROCEDURE
1. Measure 200 mL of water into the beaker and bring it to a boil.
2. Add 100 g of copper sulphate and stir until it has all dissolved.
3. Pour the solution into a clean mason jar. Make sure there are no undissolved particles.
4. Let the solution cool overnight. You should now have several small crystals on the bottom of the jar.
5. Pour all of the solution back into the beaker. Carefully remove one of the larger single crystals from the jar and set it aside. This is your "seed" crystal.
6. Transfer the other crystals to the beaker.
7. Heat the beaker until all the crystals have dissolved for a second time.
8. Carefully tie a piece of thread to your seed crystal, as illustrated.

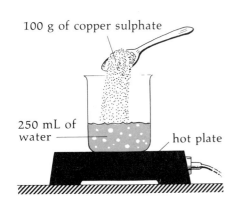

100 g of copper sulphate

250 mL of water

hot plate

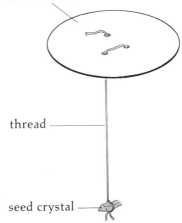

bristol board

thread

seed crystal

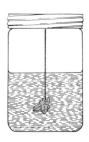

A seed crystal growing

9. Using a needle, run the other end of the thread through a circular piece of cardboard that fits inside the jar lid.
10. Wash the jar with water and then pour the solution back into it. Let the solution cool to room temperature.
11. You are now ready to add your seed crystal. Adjust the length of the string so that the crystal will hang freely in the centre of the solution. Screw on the lid and allow the jar to stand undisturbed for several days.

OBSERVATIONS

Draw diagrams of the seed crystal as it appeared at the start, and each day thereafter as it grows.

QUESTIONS

1. Can you tell which crystal form copper sulphate belongs to?
2. Why is copper sulphate sometimes called "bluestone"?
3. What difficulties did you have in following the crystal recipe?
4. Find out some uses of crystals.
5. Beach sand has been made over centuries by the weathering of rock. Quartz is a hard mineral that resists weathering, and for this reason quartz crystals (which are six-sided) are often found in sand. Examine some sand under a microscope, looking for quartz crystals.

Metallic Minerals

Canada has a variety of rich mineral deposits. The metals extracted from those deposits include gold, silver, nickel, iron, copper, and uranium. The chief properties and uses of these metals are given next.

Gold has been used at least since 10 000 B.C. in ornaments. It was treasured then, as it is now, because, in addition to being hard to find, it can be pounded into thin sheets, will not tarnish, and has an attractive yellow colour and a high metallic lustre. Gold has a relative density of 19.3, second only to platinum. This makes it one and one-half times as dense as lead. It melts at 1045 °C, which means it will not melt in a wood fire. Pure gold is softer than copper – too soft for any practical use. To harden it, it is alloyed, or mixed, with copper or silver. Pure gold is called 24-carat gold. Nine-carat gold contains nine parts of gold and 15 parts of another metal. Gold is extremely malleable, that is, it can be pounded into very thin sheets.

Gold is found in many countries. It usually occurs in pure form in small, irregular pieces, flakes, and scales. It is rarely found in crystal form. It often occurs in quartz veins and in stream beds.

Silver has been in use as long as gold. It, too, can be pounded thin, but it is not as malleable as gold. It is harder than gold but softer than copper. It leads all metals as a conductor of electricity. Its relative density is 10.5, and it melts at 960 °C. Silver tarnishes, turning black when exposed to air that contains sulphur.

Silver occurs in pure form and in argentite (silver sulphide). Pure silver is usually found in wiry masses or in scales, but it also occurs in crystal form. Argentite is a lead-grey mineral with a metallic lustre and is so soft that it can be cut with a knife.

Silver was used for making coins until its value increased beyond the face value of the coins. Then, other metals were substituted. Silver is used in jewelry and other ornaments. An alloy of silver and mercury, called amalgam, is used by dentists to fill teeth. Silver iodide is used in photography.

Nickel, a metal which resembles iron in appearance, was discovered in 1751. It is hard and white and can be highly polished. It has a relative density of 8.9 and melts at 1453 °C. Next to iron and cobalt, it is the most magnetic substance known.

Nickel is often plated on iron and steel for protection against rusting. Nickel and iron alloys are so tough that they are used in making armour plate. The mineral pentlandite (nickel iron sulphide) is the most common nickel ore. It is found in the Sudbury district of Ontario which is one of the world's principal sources of nickel.

Iron is the most useful of all metals. Iron ore occurs all over the world, yet it took man a long time to discover how to make a flame hot enough to separate the iron from the mineral. This was eventually achieved by mixing the ore right in with

Gold

Silver

Argentite

Pentlandite

Magnetite

Hematite

Limonite

Siderite

burning charcoal. Stories about the strength of iron and the ease with which it could be worked when hot spread rapidly. Iron became popular for tools and weapons.

Later, it was discovered that when carbon from the furnace got into the iron, it made the iron unusually hard. This new material was named steel. Steel, then, is iron with controlled amounts of carbon added.

Pure iron has a relative density of 7.9 and melts at 1535°C. It is silvery in colour and tends to rust in air. There are eight minerals that contain iron ore, the most important being magnetite, hematite, limonite, and siderite.

Copper. About 4300 B.C. it was discovered that heat could be used to extract a useful metal (later named copper) from certain rocks. It is believed that this discovery was made accidentally, perhaps by a potter whose kiln happened to reach a temperature of 1083°C – the temperature at which copper melts. The potter may have found copper metal in the bottom of his kiln that had been smelted out of the rocks from which the kiln was made. Early uses of copper were for weapons, tools, and ornaments.

Copper has a relative density of 8.96. It is an excellent conductor of heat, which makes it useful in cooking utensils. It is

Copper

Chalcopyrite

also an excellent conductor of electricity, and it is used extensively for electric wire.

In nature, copper is found in wiry, branching, irregular masses. It occurs in veins, volcanic flows, and sediments. Chalcopyrite (copper iron sulphide) is a common mineral containing copper. Other copper minerals include bornite, chalcocite, azurite, and malachite.

Uranium has recently become valuable as a fuel for nuclear reactors. In Ontario, uranium mines are found in the Elliot Lake and Bancroft areas. Common uranium minerals are uraninite, uranothorite, and brannerite.

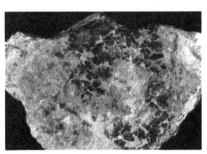

Uraninite

INVESTIGATION: To examine a number of metallic minerals

MATERIALS

samples of several metallic minerals
magnifying glass
magnet
streak plate
concrete nail
penny

PROCEDURE

1. Examine one of the mineral samples closely. Look for evidence that it contains a metal.
2. Take note of the lustre and colour, and whether crystals are visible.
3. Perform the streak test.
4. Test for hardness with your fingernail, a copper penny, and a concrete nail.

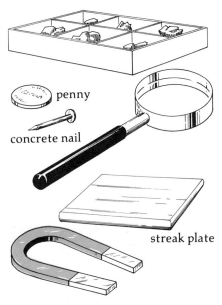

penny

concrete nail

streak plate

Metallic minerals

5. Scrape or file off a few grains, and test the grains with a magnet.
6. Heft the sample in your hand, and rate it high, medium, or low in relative density.
7. Repeat steps 2 to 6 for each of the other samples.

OBSERVATIONS

Record your results in a table like this one.

MINERAL	CRYSTALS	LUSTRE	COLOUR	STREAK TEST	HARDNESS	MAGNETIC	RELATIVE DENSITY
hematite							
galena							
chalcopyrite							

QUESTIONS

1. Why do you think gold was the first metal to be used by man?
2. Describe how copper might have been discovered accidentally.
3. Describe how iron was first produced.
4. How is iron turned into steel'?
5. Name one mineral that contains each of the following: copper, silver, nickel, iron, and uranium.

Non-metallic minerals

Graphite is a black mineral composed of carbon. It has a hardness of from 1.0 to 2.0, is greasy to feel, and has a relative density of 2.2. Its most common occurrence is in beds of highly metamorphosed rocks. Graphite is believed to have been formed from coal as a result of heat and pressure. It is used in paint, as a lubricant, and in making pencils.

Asbestos occurs most commonly in a form called chrysotile. Chrysotile is a silky, fibrous material with a hardness of 2.5 to 4 and a relative density of 2.5. Its colour ranges from grey-green to green. Fibres of chrysotile are semi-transparent and flexible. There are large, open-pit asbestos mines in the province of Quebec.

Asbestos is used to make fireproof fabric for drapes,

Graphite

Chrysotile

firemen's suits, and brake linings. It is mixed with pitch to make roofing cement, and is used as insulation in electric cables.

Asbestos workers must take special precautions to avoid breathing asbestos dust, which has been blamed for a respiratory ailment called asbestosis.

Mica is the name of a group of minerals the most common of which is muscovite. It has a hardness of 2 to 2.5 and a relative density of 3. Muscovite splits into thin, colourless sheets and was widely used in the past as window glass. Today, it is used primarily as an electrical insulator. It is found in granite and other igneous rocks.

Sulphur occurs as a yellow mineral that forms in tabular

Muscovite

Sulphur

crystals. It has a hardness of 1.5 to 2.5, a relative density of 2.06, and melts at 113 °C.

Sulphur also occurs in combination with copper and iron in the minerals iron pyrite and copper pyrite. It is recovered in the processing of both these ores as sulphuric acid. Sulphur and sulphuric acid have many industrial uses.

Talc, with a hardness of 1, is a soft, greasy mineral with a relative density of 2.7. Its colour ranges from white to pale green or yellow. It occurs in metamorphic rocks all over the world. In its solid form, it is called soapstone and can be carved to make ornaments. Tailors use it to mark fabric. Powdered talc is used extensively to make cosmetics and inexpensive soaps.

INVESTIGATION: To examine several non-metallic minerals

MATERIALS

samples of graphite, chrysotile,
    muscovite (or biotite), sulphur,
    and talc
concrete nail
magnifying glass
streak plate
penny

PROCEDURE

1. Examine one of the samples closely, looking for crystals and noting the lustre and colour.
2. Perform the streak test.
3. Test the hardness with your fingernail, a copper penny, and a concrete nail.
4. Scrape off a few grains, and determine whether any of them are magnetic.
5. Heft the sample in your hand, and rate its relative density.

OBSERVATIONS

Record your results in a table like this one.

MINERAL	CRYSTALS	LUSTRE	COLOUR	STREAK TEST	HARDNESS	MAGNETIC	RELATIVE DENSITY
graphite							
chrysotile							

QUESTIONS

1. Compare the relative densities of these non-metallic minerals with those of the metallic minerals you tested earlier.

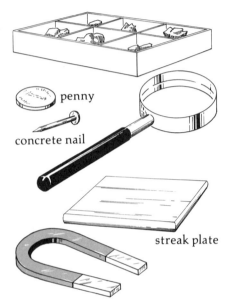

penny

concrete nail

streak plate

Non-metallic minerals

2. Can you tell a metallic mineral from a non-metallic mineral by its lustre?
3. Were any of the non-metallic minerals you tested magnetic?
4. Comment on the colours of the streaks of the minerals you tested, mentioning whether any of them surprised you.
5. Describe one use for each of the non-metallic minerals you examined.

Gem minerals

Many people collect mineral samples for their beauty. Unusual sparkle, peculiar arrays of colour, perfect crystal form and shape, interesting patterns, and phenomenal colour changes are some of the qualities they look for. Some stones are displayed just as they were found in nature. Others are cut, polished, and even engraved.

Diamonds consist of pure carbon, and are mined from the ground. The value of a diamond is based on its colour, its cut, its clarity, and its carat (or size). Rubies and sapphires are transparent varieties of the mineral corundum. Rubies are red while sapphires are bright blue or velvet blue. Large rubies are extremely rare and are worth more than diamonds of the same size.

Beryl, emerald, and aquamarine are from the same mineral. The crystals are hexagonal and the colour may vary from blue to light green to yellow. An emerald of rich green coloration ranks in value with a diamond.

Chrysoberyl is a rare mineral that occurs in shades of yellow, brown, light green, and dark green. One kind is dark green in daylight and red under artificial light. The chrysoberyl cat's eye changes from pale honey yellow to dark brown.

Collecting gem minerals and cutting gem stones can be exciting and profitable. To find out more, visit the mineral section of a museum, talk to a jeweller, or join a "lapidary" (gem) club.

A quartz crystal

1. What are the main differences between rocks and minerals?
2. Name the three rock types. Explain the geologists' theory of how igneous rocks were formed.
3. Name three types of igneous rock, describe each briefly, and tell what minerals it is composed of.
4. Some igneous rocks have very small crystals while others have much larger ones. Explain why this is so.
5. Describe three ways in which sedimentary rocks can be formed.
6. What clues should you look for when trying to decide whether a rock is of the sedimentary type?
7. Name three types of sedimentary rock.
8. Describe how metamorphic rocks were formed.
9. What caused some metamorphic rocks to be foliated?
10. Name three foliated metamorphic rocks and the rocks they probably came from.
11. Name two non-foliated metamorphic rocks and the rocks they probably came from.
12. What is the difference between "weathering" and "erosion"?
13. Describe two types of weathering, giving three causes of each.
14. Name three agents of erosion. How can you tell a young river valley from an old one?
15. Name the three most-used fuels, and explain why they are called fossil fuels.
16. Which of the three fossil fuels is the most abundant? Describe three obstacles to making greater use of this fuel.
17. Explain why the oil in the Athabasca oil sands has only recently come into production.
18. What concerns have environmentalists expressed over the building of more and more nuclear power generators?
19. Describe some immediate steps we can take, in view of the energy crisis.
20. What do fossils tell us about the earliest probable forms of life on Earth?
21. Why is a biological "revolution" believed to have taken place about 600 million years ago?

22. Describe briefly six tests mineralogists use to identify a mineral.
23. Name the softest and the hardest minerals in the scale of hardness.
24. Some minerals show cleavage and others show fracture. What is the difference between the two?
25. Every crystal belongs to one of the six crystal forms, or systems. Name and make a sketch to illustrate any three of these forms.
26. A mineral has a relative density of 5.0. If a sample of it has a mass of 50 g, what would be the mass of the same volume of water?
27. Describe the special properties a mineral may have that will help you to identify it.
28. What is a seed crystal used for?
29. Name four metals and describe how they are produced.
30. Name four non-metallic minerals and state one or two uses of each.
31. Explain what gem minerals are and name six.

IMPORTANT TERMS

rock—the solid part of the Earth's crust

mineral—a component part of a rock

igneous rock—rock that was formed when hot molten material cooled

sedimentary rock—rock that was formed under pressure from particles, or sediment, that had settled layer upon layer

metamorphic rock—rock that was formed when igneous or sedimentary rocks were subjected to heat and pressure

weathering—the breaking down of rocks into smaller fragments

erosion—the carrying away of rock fragments by water, glaciers, or wind

fossil—an imprint in rock of an ancient plant or animal

fossil fuels—coal, oil, and natural gas

streak—a mark left by a mineral when it is rubbed (streaked) on a piece of unglazed porcelain (a streak plate)

cleavage—the breaking of a mineral sample into layers

fracture—an irregular break in a mineral sample

relative density—the number of times a mineral is denser than water

metallic mineral—a mineral that contains metal

gem—a rare mineral of the kind used in making jewellery

lapidary—a person who cuts, polishes, or engraves gems

ASTRONOMY

Astronomy is the study of the universe. It is a study that challenges our wildest imagination.

Early astronomers sought answers to such questions as, "What are the sun, the moon, and the stars, which shine in the heavens?" "Why don't they fall to Earth?" "Why do they move?" Modern astronomers deal with such questions as the birth and death of stars, the possibility of life on other planets, the building of space stations, moon walks, quasars, pulsars, and black holes. The more scientists find out about the universe, it seems, the more mysteries they uncover. Astronomy is a story without an end.

We will take a look at how people long ago pictured themselves in relation to the universe. Then we will trace the history of man's knowledge of the universe. Finally, we will examine the sun and its planets, the moon, the stars, and other phenomena of space.

The history of astronomy

Imagine how the heavens must have appeared to people 4000 or more years ago. Much the way they do to a northern camper

The Great Nebula in Orion

today, sleeping in the open. The skies were particularly clear and still: no pollution, no city lights, no jets or noisy cars. And there were no books or television programs to help fill the hours of darkness. No wonder astronomy was the first science of ancient civilizations!

People believed that the Earth was flat. They were afraid to go on long voyages in case the ship might sail over the edge. They learned to use the stars to guide them in their travels, and often took advantage of the light of the moon and the stars to travel at night.

They realized the importance of the sun for growing plants to use as food and as a source of heat and light. Some early people adopted the sun as their god, and attached great importance to heavenly signs. When comets lit up the sky or the moon caused an eclipse, they thought their god was angry with them and prayed for forgiveness.

The day, naturally, was their unit of time. They also noticed that a new moon appears in the sky every 29 or 30 d. They called this period a moon, or month.

As time went on, they discovered that the night sky seemed to turn, very slowly. The stars shifted their positions slightly from one night to the next. Some stars disappeared from view, but after a long time (365 d) they reappeared. They called this span of time a year, and realized that it held almost 12 months. From this information, they built a calendar to remind them when to sow seeds and reap the harvest.

Historical records show that the Egyptians made careful, accurate observations of the stars and planets about 2000 years before the birth of Christ. They produced a 365 d calendar based upon the rising of Sirius, the brightest star in the sky. This calendar helped them to predict the annual flooding of the River Nile.

All this knowledge did not prevent the Egyptians from devising some far-fetched models of the universe, inspired by their religion. They believed, for example, that the universe was shaped like a rectangular box, with the long sides running in a north-south direction. Their sky was a flat ceiling supported by four pillars. A river was supposed to flow across the sky, carrying the Sun and the other gods (planets).

In India, it was taught that the Earth was flat, that it was

held up by 12 pillars, and that during the night the sun wove its way silently through these pillars without bumping into them. Then there was a Hindu theory that pictured the Earth being carried on the backs of four elephants standing on the shell of a tortoise.

The early Chinese were careful observers. They recorded eclipses as early as 4000 B.C. It is said they believed the eclipses to be caused by a hungry dragon that was trying to eat the sun.

There is a tendency for us to laugh at the ideas ancient civilizations had about the universe. We must remember that they had few observations to build their ideas on. Their remarkable works of art, literature, and architecture tell us that they were of the same level of intelligence as ourselves.

Great advances in understanding the universe were made by the ancient Greeks, in the period from 600 B.C. to 200 A.D. They were the first truly scientific astronomers. They developed the branch of mathematics called geometry, which proved to be most useful in astronomy.

One of the first of the great Greek philosophers was Thales, who advanced the novel idea that the Earth was round. Another was Pythagoras, who said that the Earth was moving through space. Then Plato (4th century B.C.) and Aristarchus (3rd century B.C.) maintained that the Earth rotated on an axis and moved through space in an orbit. Later, Seleucus said that ocean tides were related to the phases of the moon, and, in the 2nd century B.C., Hipparchus said that the sun, the moon, and the planets were all travelling around the Earth. This incorrect theory was developed further around 140 A.D. by Ptolemy, and it remained the accepted one for 14 centuries.

Copernicus. By the end of the 15th century, scientists had learned how to make very accurate astronomical measurements. They realized that many of their measurements did not make sense if everything rotated around the Earth.

The man who recognized the discrepancy was Nicolaus Copernicus (1473-1543), a Polish astronomer. In 1507, he wrote: "The centre of the Earth is not the centre of the universe . . . . All spheres revolve round the sun, as if it were in the middle of everything, so the centre of the world is near the sun." Copernicus also stated correctly the order of the known planets in distance from the sun. He made one major error in his theory: he assumed that the planets revolve around the sun in circular paths.

Copernicus's theory was contrary to the teachings of the Church at the time and was considered heresy. It is said that one of his followers was burned at the stake for promoting his ideas.

Galileo Galilei (1564-1642) was the first scientist to observe the sky through a telescope. He found overwhelming evidence to support Copernicus's theories and let this be widely known. The Church forced Galileo to say that he was wrong and placed him under house arrest. He was forbidden to talk about a sun-centred universe ever again.

Johannes Kepler (1571-1630), a German astronomer and mathematician, showed that the planets do not move in perfect circles as earlier astronomers believed, but travel in elliptical paths with the sun at one focus. He also showed that the planets speed up as they move nearer to the sun and slow down again as they move away from it.

Isaac Newton (1642-1727), a British mathematician and scientist, used Kepler's laws and Galileo's discoveries to arrive at what is called the Universal Law of Gravitation. This law is

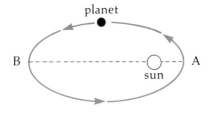

Kepler said that the planets travel in elliptical paths, not circles. They move fastest at A and slowest at B.

The Milky Way Galaxy

one of the great milestones in the advance of science. It says that all objects in the universe exert a pull on each other with a force he named gravity. This law also says that the greater the masses of two objects and the closer they are to each other, the stronger will be the pull drawing them together.

Newton used his law to explain why the planets stay in their elliptical orbits around the sun, as described by Kepler. He was even able to calculate the strength of the force with which the Earth pulls on the moon and to show that ocean tides are caused by the moon's gravitational pull on the Earth. The Universal Law of Gravitation marked a revolution in our knowledge of the universe. The law made it crystal clear why the planets move as they do about the sun, and why the moon circles the Earth.

Albert Einstein (1879-1955) added to and corrected Newton's law after it had been found that the law did not fully explain the movement of objects travelling in very strong gravitational fields or at speeds approaching the speed of light. Einstein's

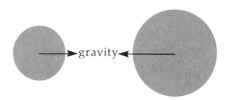

Gravity is the force pulling all objects in the universe together.

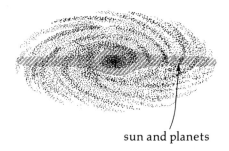

The sun is not in the centre of the Milky Way Galaxy.

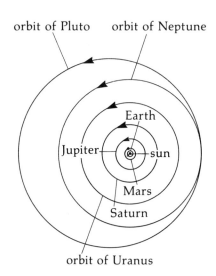

Approximate orbits of the planets. Mercury's and Venus' orbits are too small to show. Notice that the orbits appear to be circles but are actually ellipses.

theory, called the Theory of Relativity, is extremely complex. It is applied to many areas of science, including astronomy.

Harlow Shapley (1885-1972), an American, proved in 1918 that the sun is not at the centre of the universe but is one star in a galaxy of stars called the Milky Way. Shapley plotted the positions of hundreds of stars and showed that the Milky Way is shaped like a disc that bulges near the centre. The sun is far removed from the centre of the Milky Way, and it makes one orbit of the galaxy's centre every 200 million years.

Edwin Hubble (1889-1953) was observing the night skies during the early 1920s when he sighted and managed to photograph what appeared to be two distant gas clouds. He measured the distance to these clouds and concluded that they were galaxies like our own Milky Way. Up to that time, many astronomers had believed that the universe did not extend beyond the Milky Way. Hubble provided the basis for an expanding concept of a universe consisting of many galaxies.

The solar system

There are nine planets revolving in elliptical orbits about the sun. Starting with the one nearest to the sun, they are Mercury, Venus, Earth, Mars, Jupiter, Saturn, Uranus, Neptune, and Pluto. Except for Pluto, the orbits are nearly circular. It takes precise measurement to show that they are elliptical. When viewed from the north, all the planets revolve counterclockwise around the sun, and they are all in approximately the same plane, called the plane of the ecliptic. The plane of Pluto's orbit is tilted at an angle of 17° from the plane of the ecliptic.

Planet	Diameter (km)	Average distance to sun (km)	Time to orbit sun	Average speed (km/s)
Mercury	4 900	58 million	88 d	48
Venus	12 000	110 million	225 d	35
Earth	13 000	150 million	365 d	30
Mars	6 800	230 million	687 d	24
Jupiter	140 000	780 million	12 years	13
Saturn	120 000	1400 million	29 years	9.6
Uranus	51 000	2900 million	84 years	6.3
Neptune	49 000	4500 million	165 years	5.4
Pluto	3 000	5900 million	248 years	4.7

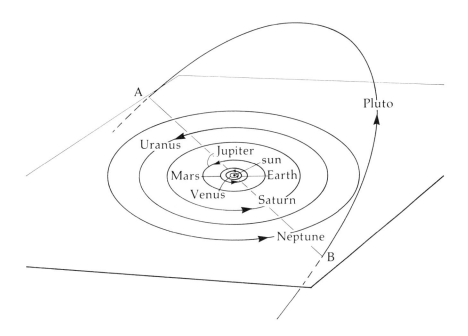

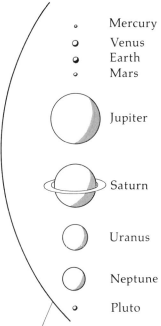

Mercury
Venus
Earth
Mars

Jupiter

Saturn

Uranus

Neptune

Pluto

edge of the sun's disc

This scale drawing shows how much larger the sun is than the planets. The mass of the sun is about 1000 times the combined mass of all the planets.

From the table, you can see that planets closer to the sun move faster. Mercury moves about 10 times as fast as Pluto. Note also that Pluto takes 248 years to orbit the sun and Mercury takes only 88 d.

A planet's speed changes slightly as it revolves in its elliptical orbit. It travels fastest when it is closest to the sun, at what astronomers call the perihelion, and slowest at the other end of the orbit, the aphelion. At the perihelion, Mars travels at 36 km/s but at the aphelion its speed is only 23 km/s.

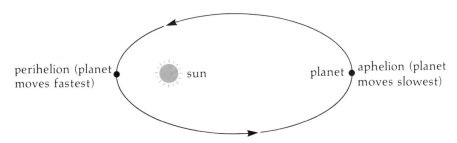

Planets move in elliptical orbits with the sun at one focus.

Each planet rotates on an imaginary axis as it orbits the sun. The time required for a planet to make one rotation about its axis is its day.

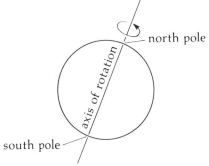

The planets spin or rotate on an imaginary axis as they orbit the sun. The time required for a planet to make one rotation about its axis is called the planet's day.

INVESTIGATION: To draw an elliptical orbit

MATERIALS

string
pencil
2 tacks
cardboard

PROCEDURE

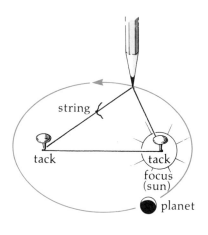

1. Make a loop in a piece of string or thread about 16 cm long.
2. Force two thumb tacks into a piece of paper. Heavy cardboard under the paper will help to hold the tacks in place.
3. Loop the string around the tacks, hold the pencil vertically, and place the point of the pencil on the paper, as illustrated.
4. Keep the string tight and slowly move the pencil point around the tacks. The curved shape traced out by the pencil is an ellipse.
5. Move one of the tacks to reduce the space between them, and repeat step 4.
6. Move the same tack again, to make the tacks farther apart than they were originally, and repeat step 4.
7. Make a fourth ellipse using a larger loop of string.
8. Draw a circle around the tack that you did not move, to represent the sun. Draw smaller circles, one on each elliptical orbit, to represent planets. Shade in the dark side of each planet. Use arrows to indicate that the planets rotate counter-clockwise around the sun.

QUESTIONS

1. On one of your elliptical orbits, indicate the aphelion and the perihelion.
2. Where would you put the two tacks if you wanted to draw a circle rather than an ellipse?
3. Which two planets in our solar system have the most noticeably elliptical orbits?

INVESTIGATION: To demonstrate that planets close
to the sun move faster than those
farther away from it

MATERIALS

washer
string (about 1.5 m)
small rubber ball or
rubber stopper

PROCEDURE

1. Tie a small rubber ball to one end of the string.
2. Slip the other end of the string through the washer, and hold the washer firmly in your right hand so that the string can slide easily through it.
3. Hold the string with your left hand and swing the ball over your head with your right hand, as illustrated.
4. When the ball is swinging in circles, gradually pull in some string with the left hand so that the ball ("planet") moves in a new orbit closer to the "sun".

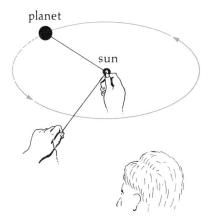

OBSERVATIONS

Record what happened to the speed of the ball when you reduced the size of its orbit.

QUESTIONS

1. The ball was held in a circular path by the tension of the string. Why are strings not needed to keep the planets in their orbits?
2. Compare the orbital speed of Pluto, the planet farthest from the sun, with the orbital speed of Mercury, the planet closest to the sun.
3. What would happen to the planets if gravity were suddenly switched off? Describe how you would use your ball and string to demonstrate this.

Planet Earth photographed from Apollo 10. The west coast of North America can be seen through the clouds.

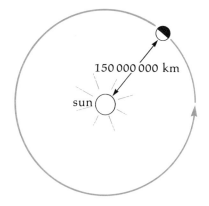

150 000 000 km

sun

The Earth's orbit is nearly circular with a radius of 150 million kilometres.

The Earth

Orbital characteristics. The Earth is the third planet out from the sun. It orbits the sun at an average distance of 150 000 000 km. It makes one complete orbit in about 365 d, or one year.

While it is whirling around the sun, the Earth is also rotating on an imaginary axis. It requires 24 h to make one complete rotation. We experience daylight when we are on the side of the Earth that is facing the sun. The Earth is rotating, so that sunlight is eventually blocked off and we experience darkness. It seems to us that the sun has disappeared over the western horizon.

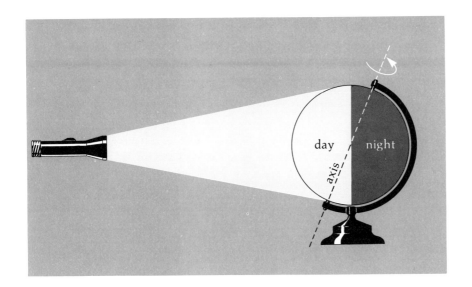

You can use a flashlight (or filmstrip projector) and globe to demonstrate the cause of day and night.

Why do we have seasons? The Earth's axis is tilted at an angle of 23.5°, as illustrated. It is always tilted in the same direction, no matter where the Earth is in its orbit. To see why the Earth maintains this tilt, obtain a gyroscope and make it spin. While it is spinning rapidly, try to tilt it. You will find that it resists. The Earth is like a huge gyroscope that behaves in the same way.

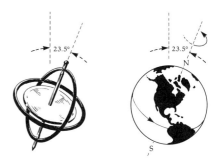

The Earth is like a huge gyroscope.

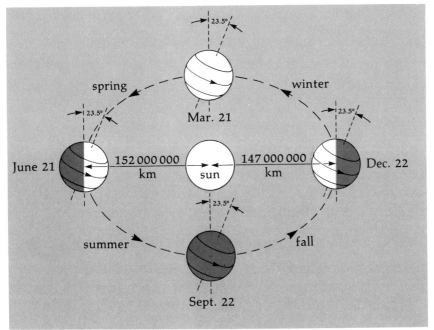

The seasonal changes we experience on Earth are explained by this diagram. The Earth is shown at four different positions as it orbits the sun.

The seasonal changes we experience are explained by the diagram showing the Earth at four different positions in its orbit. On December 22, the first day of winter, the northern hemisphere is tilted away from the sun. The effect of this tilting is to spread the solar rays that reach the Earth over a greater area of the Earth's surface, making them less intense. So our air temperatures in the northern hemisphere are lower at that time of year. At the same time of year, it is warmer in the southern hemisphere because that part of the Earth is tilted towards the sun, causing the sun's rays to be more concentrated there.

In this illustration the northern hemisphere is experiencing winter. Can you explain why? Why would temperatures be higher in the southern hemisphere?

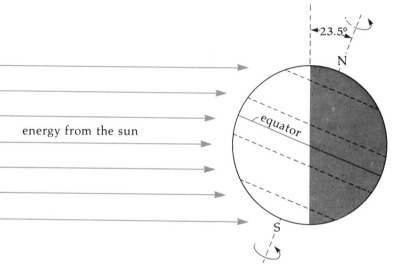

energy from the sun

During winter, the days in the northern hemisphere are shorter than the nights, while at the same time people in the southern hemisphere are experiencing long, warm days and short nights.

Physical characteristics. Nobody had doubted the idea that the Earth was flat until about 2400 years ago when Aristotle, a Greek philosopher, observed the curved shape of the Earth's shadow on the moon. He concluded that the Earth must be round. You can obtain this effect by holding a basketball in the beam of a filmstrip projector.

Unfortunately, people laughed at Aristotle's suggestion that the Earth was round. They clung to the idea that things would fall off the Earth if it was round. Yet everyone knew that the hull of a ship sailing out to sea disappears first, and then the sails.

When a ship is on the horizon only the sail is visible.

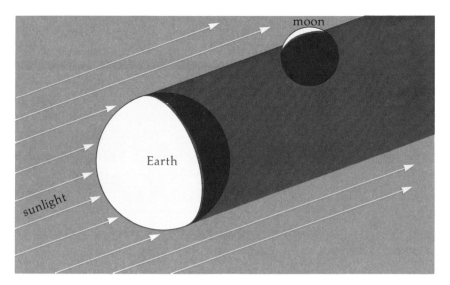

The sun casts a curved shadow of the Earth onto the moon.

There is visible proof that the Earth is round — for anyone who might doubt it — in the photographs of the Earth that have been taken from high-altitude balloons, aircraft, rockets, satellites, and space vehicles.

Careful measurements have shown that the Earth is not a perfect sphere but is slightly flattened at the poles. The polar radius is 6357 km and the equatorial radius is 6378 km. Newton explained that the slight bulge at the equator is the result of the spin of the Earth. Jupiter and Saturn spin even faster than the Earth and have larger equatorial bulges.

Surrounding the Earth is an atmosphere of air about 500 km thick. Air is composed mainly of nitrogen and oxygen, with small amounts of other gases. Dry air consists of:

78.1% nitrogen
20.9% oxygen
 0.8% argon
 0.1% carbon dioxide, neon, helium, krypton, xenon, hydrogen, nitrous oxide, and methane

Water vapour may also be present, up to 4%, depending on the degree of humidity.

Our bodies need oxygen, and the Earth is believed to be the only planet whose atmosphere contains enough oxygen to support life as we know it.

The Earth has a magnetic field, which behaves as though the Earth had a huge bar magnet at its centre. This field enables us

Earth summary

ORBITAL CHARACTERISTICS

Earth to sun distance, about 150 million kilometres
length of a year, about 365 d

rotation time, 24 h

seasons are due to tilt of Earth

Earth has one moon

PHYSICAL CHARACTERISTICS

radius at the equator, 6378 km

atmosphere has about 78% nitrogen, 21% oxygen, and 1% argon
temperature range, –88°C to 58°C
water covers about 71% of surface

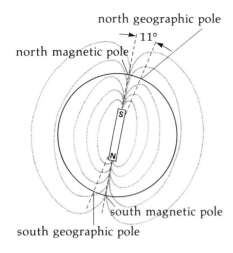

north geographic pole

11°

north magnetic pole

S

N

south magnetic pole

south geographic pole

to use magnetic compasses to find direction. The magnetic axis and the axis of rotation are separated by about 11° (see illustration). The magnetic field is also partly responsible for the northern lights.

The temperature of the Earth ranges from $-88\,°C$ to $58\,°C$. Temperature is another important factor in determining whether a planet can support life. The average surface temperature on Venus, for example, is about $527\,°C$, which obviously rules out life as we know it. Volcanoes and geysers are evidence that the Earth's interior is much hotter than the surface.

Water covers about 71% of the Earth's surface and is another necessity for life.

The Moon

Why does the moon appear to change its shape from one night to the next? What causes the strange patterns on its face? Where does it get its light? What causes an eclipse of the moon? Is there life there? These are questions that have intrigued man since the earliest times.

Characteristics. The moon is a satellite of the Earth and is held in its nearly circular orbit by the force of the Earth's gravity. It takes the moon 27.3 d (a short month) to circle the Earth once. Its average distance from the Earth is 380 000 km.

From Earth, we always see the same side of the moon. This is because the moon rotates slowly as it revolves around the Earth, turning exactly once in each revolution. Pictures of the far side of the moon were taken for the first time in 1959 when the Soviet Union sent a space vehicle around it.

The diameter of the moon is 3500 km. This is only about one-quarter of the diameter of the Earth. The face of the moon would fit easily inside North America, stretching from Vancouver to Quebec City.

On the moon, the downward pull of gravity is only one-sixth as great as that on Earth. This means that your weight on the moon would be only one-sixth of your weight on Earth. If you have seen a film of Neil Armstrong's moon-walk, you know the effect of this difference.

Because of its weak pull of gravity, the moon is unable to hold on to gases, so it has no atmosphere. Sound requires a

medium in which to travel. Since there is no air on the moon, it is an utterly silent place. There is no wind, no rain, no snow — not even clouds.

The temperature on the surface of the moon ranges from about −150°C at night to more than 100°C during the day. These wide extremes are explained by the lack of atmosphere there, and especially by the lack of water vapour. The presence of water in the Earth's atmosphere has a strong moderating effect on our temperatures.

INVESTIGATION: To make a scale model of the Earth
and the moon

MATERIALS

| plasticine | string or thread | balance |
| metre stick | paper-clips | |

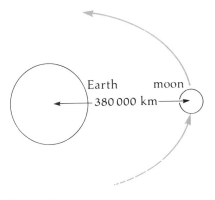

The Earth-moon system

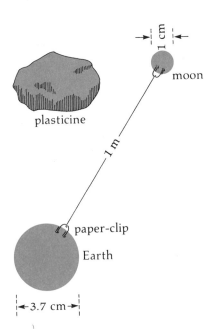

plasticine

moon

1 cm

1 m

paper-clip

Earth

3.7 cm

PROCEDURE

1. Make two balls of plasticine, one 1 cm and the other 3.7 cm in diameter. These balls represent the moon and the Earth, approximately to scale.
2. Determine the mass of each ball, using the balance.
3. Place the two balls on a table 1 m apart.
4. Push a paper-clip into each ball and join the balls by a string or thread.
5. Move your moon slowly around your Earth, keeping the string tight.

OBSERVATIONS

Record the masses of your moon and Earth.

QUESTIONS

1. How many times more massive is your Earth than your moon? (The Earth is actually 80 times more massive than the moon. The difference is due to heavier material in the Earth's core.)
2. The sun is about 500 times farther from Earth than it is from the moon. How far away would the sun be in your scale model?
3. How long does it take the moon to orbit the Earth?

Surface features. In 1609, Galileo Galilei became the first person to see the moon through a telescope. He noticed dark areas that appeared to be low and flat, almost like bodies of water. For this reason he called them "maria", or seas. We now know that there is no water on the moon, but "maria" is still used.

Many astronomers have studied the moon since the time of Galileo. In addition to the maria, they have observed great craters, mountains, and cliffs. One cliff, known as the Straight Wall in Mare Nubium, is about 100 km long and 400 m high. Some of the moon mountains are higher than Mount Everest.

The bright areas in the moon photograph are made up largely of craters. These craters are believed to have been caused by chunks of rock from space striking the moon's surface. In places there is a pattern of lines radiating out from a large crater. These lines are called rays, and they are believed to

Rills in a lunar "sea" photographed by Ranger IX at an altitude of 430 km above the moon's surface.

have been caused by material splashing out at the time of a major collision. You can see rays near the Kepler and Copernicus craters.

What created the seas was long debated by scientists, but the mystery is believed to have been solved as a result of the Apollo moon missions. Examination of the 380 kg of moon rocks and soil that were brought back to Earth has led to the conclusion that something big crashed into the moon, and that the moon's surface cracked open. When that happened, it is thought, hot lava poured out to form a sea of molton rock that later cooled and solidified.

Crossing the moon's surface are long valley-like depressions, called rills. Some rills extend for hundreds of kilometres, cutting across mountains and maria. The rills may be cracks in the moon's surface.

INVESTIGATION: To make craters like those found on the moon

MATERIALS

baseball or rock   small stones (or marbles)
box of sand

PROCEDURE

1. Fill a box with loose sand, representing the surface of the moon.
2. Stand on a chair and toss into the sand a rock representing a stray object from space. Do this with rocks of various sizes.
3. Mix several stones into the sand, and then drop in more rocks.

OBSERVATIONS

1. Make diagrams of the craters you made by dropping rocks of various sizes into the sand.
2. Make a diagram of the pattern that was created when you threw a rock into the mixture of sand and stones.

QUESTIONS

1. How, in the opinion of scientists, were the moon craters formed?
2. Scientists believe that many craters have formed on the Earth and that most of them have since disappeared.
   Why might a moon crater last longer than a crater on Earth?
3. What is believed to have caused the rays near certain moon craters?
4. How do scientists think maria were formed?
5. What are rills?
6. Would you like to live on the moon? Explain your answer.

INVESTIGATION: To observe the surface features of the moon with binoculars

MATERIALS

binoculars (or telescope)

PROCEDURE

1. On a cloudless night, observe the moon through a pair of binoculars.
2. Look for maria. These are the large dark areas.
3. Look for mountain ranges. These often show up well when the moon is crescent-shaped.
4. Look for craters. These are circular areas with raised edges. Look for rays running out from some of the craters.
5. Look for rills, which look like long valleys.

OBSERVATIONS

1. Describe and draw sketches of as many of the following as you were able to see. (a) maria (b) mountain ranges (c) craters (d) rays (e) rills
2. Refer to the photograph of the moon on page 247. Write down the names of features you were able to observe with binoculars.

QUESTIONS

1. Why did Galileo name the large dark areas on the moon's surface "maria"?
2. How can an observer on Earth use the shadows of mountains on the moon to compare their heights?

Phases of the moon. The moon does not give off light but reflects light from the sun. Only the half of the moon that is facing the sun is lighted. The other half is dark. As the moon travels around the Earth, we see varying amounts of its lighted surface. We say that the appearance of the moon, as viewed from the Earth, goes through a sequence of phases. It takes 29.5 d to see the complete sequence of phases.

When the moon is in position 1 (new moon), we cannot see it

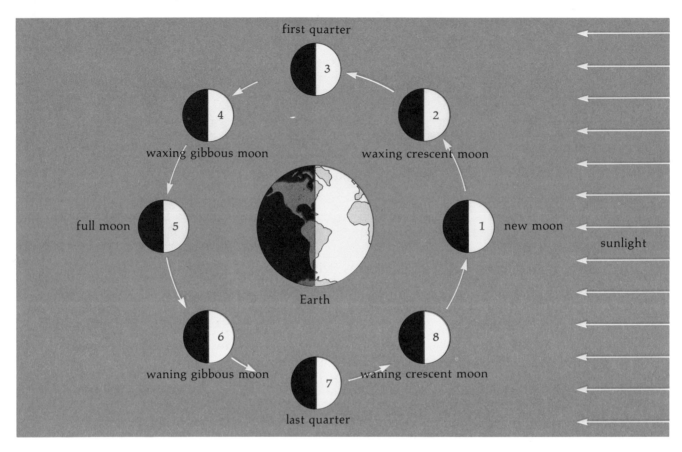

first quarter

3

4

waxing gibbous moon

waxing crescent moon

2

full moon

5

new moon

1

Earth

sunlight

6

8

waning gibbous moon

waning crescent moon

7

last quarter

because its dark side faces us. However, in one or two days, as it moves towards position 2, we begin to see a crescent shape. About a week after the new moon, the moon is in position 3, called the first quarter. Now we can see a half circle. In position 4, we see a gibbous, or bulging, moon. In position 5, the moon appears full. In position 6, the moon appears gibbous again. In position 7, we again see a half circle. This is called the last quarter. Finally, the moon is back at position 1, and will soon become a new moon once again.

The phases of the moon — numbers correspond to the positions of the moon shown in the illustration at the top of the page.

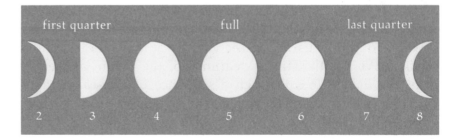

first quarter

full

last quarter

2   3   4   5   6   7   8

INVESTIGATION: To demonstrate the phases of the moon
(a class project)

MATERIALS

basketball
white tissue paper
filmstrip projector

PROCEDURE

1. Cover the ball with paper.
2. Choose one student to be the moon. The others are "earthlings".
3. Arrange the moon, the earthlings, and the projector as illustrated. Darken the room and turn the projector on.
4. The moon moves in a circle around the earthlings. It should move slowly to give the earthlings a chance to identify each of the moon's phases.

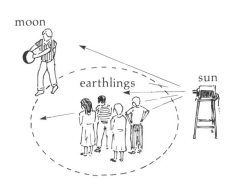

OBSERVATIONS

Make a sketch of the moon as it appeared in each of its phases.

QUESTIONS

1. Why do you think the term "new moon" is used?
2. What do "waxing" and "waning" mean?
3. How much of the moon's surface can you see during a full moon?

ACTIVITY

Keep a record of the appearance and position of the moon at the same time (say 18:30) each evening for a month. This will give you an opportunity to see all the phases.

Lunar eclipses. Sometimes the Earth gets between the sun and the moon and blocks off the sunlight, leaving the moon in total darkness. This phenomenon is called an eclipse of the moon, or a lunar eclipse. The moon is in the Earth's shadow. Total eclipses of the moon happen about twice a year.

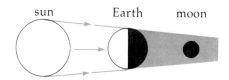

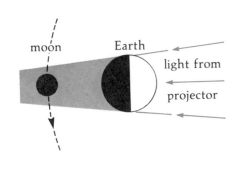

moon Earth
light from
projector

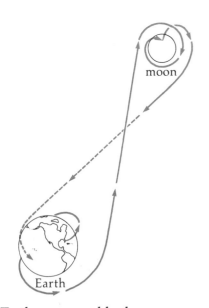

To the moon and back

INVESTIGATION: To simulate a lunar eclipse (a class project)

MATERIALS
globe
filmstrip projector
ball about one-quarter the
  diameter of the globe
  (representing the moon)

PROCEDURE
1. Position the projector, the globe, and the moon as illustrated. Place the projector as far away as possible.
2. One student walks the moon in a circle around the Earth. The others observe the brightness of the moon as it changes position.

OBSERVATIONS
Write notes on the relative brightness of the moon in its various positions.

QUESTIONS
1. Why is it difficult for us to see the moon during a lunar eclipse?
2. What is the phase of the moon at the time of a lunar eclipse?

Lunar explorations. On July 20, 1969, Neil Armstrong and Edwin Aldrin stepped onto the moon's surface. Armstrong descended to the lunar surface first. As he took the first step, he said, "One small step for man, one giant leap for mankind." While on the moon, the two men set up a television camera and a device to measure moonquakes. They also planted a United States flag and gathered samples of moon rocks and soil to bring back to Earth.

After that, five other Apollo landings were made on the moon. The last was in December 1972. It has been determined that some moon rocks taken from the maria are much like rocks that occur on Earth. They appear to be from lava flows, and are believed to be about 4000 million years old.

Astronaut Aldrin uses a scoop to make a trench (left), and Apollo 8 blasts off using a Saturn 5 space vehicle, December 21, 1968 (above).

Instruments left on the moon have recorded moonquakes every 28.4 d. Moonquakes are believed to be caused by the force of gravity because they occur when the Earth and the moon are closest together. Tests have also shown that the moon is magnetic, but its magnetism is very weak compared to that of the Earth.

The Apollo spacecraft that was used to get to the moon employed a three-stage Saturn V launch vehicle, as illustrated. The spacecraft was first launched into an orbit around the Earth. Then, when all appeared to be well, it blasted off for the moon. As one rocket was used up it separated and the next stage took over. After about 60 h, the spacecraft approached the moon. Rockets were fired to slow it down and bring it into an orbit around the moon.

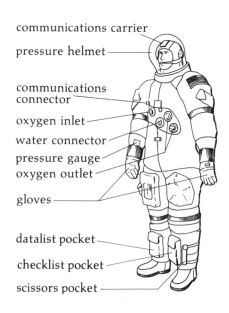

communications carrier
pressure helmet
communications connector
oxygen inlet
water connector
pressure gauge
oxygen outlet
gloves

datalist pocket
checklist pocket
scissors pocket

The spacecraft was in three sections — a command module, a service module, and a lunar module. Michael Collins circled the moon in the command module (with the service module attached) while Armstrong and Aldrin, in the lunar module, descended to the moon's surface. After 22 h on the moon, the lunar module blasted off from the moon's surface to link up again with the service and command modules. Armstrong and Aldrin rejoined Collins in the command module, and the lunar module was released. The rockets in the service module then blasted off for Earth. Just before re-entering the Earth's atmosphere at 40 000 km/h, the service module was released. The command module splashed down in the ocean near Hawaii.

The astronauts were kept in quarantine for several days, to make sure they had not picked up any dangerous bacteria in space. Later, it was concluded that there is no life of any kind on the moon.

The planets

"Planet" comes from an old Greek word that means "to wander". Ancient astronomers knew that the planets differed from stars because they wandered around the heavens, whereas stars kept fixed positions. Nobody has travelled to another planet yet, though a total of 12 earthlings have been to the moon. Instead of sending people to study the planets, scientists are sending unmanned spacecraft. Radar and television cameras are used to send information back to Earth.

Plans were made to send two spacecraft on a grand tour of the outer planets in the late 1980s. This time was chosen for the start of the tour because the planets would then be lined up fairly close to each other, making it possible to plan a "short" nine-year tour.

Mercury is the second smallest planet of our solar system. In 1974, the Mariner 10 spacecraft passed within 740 km of it and sent back pictures of the surface. The pictures revealed that Mercury is covered with craters and cracks, much like the face of the moon. It also has large flat plains that may have been formed by molten material flooding the surface through cracks. Mercury is 80% iron, which makes it the densest planet.

The surface of Mercury with its craters is similar to the surface of the moon.

Because Mercury is three times closer to the sun than the Earth, it is much hotter. Its temperature ranges from 425°C during the day to −150°C at night. This, with the fact that Mercury has no atmosphere, rules out any possibility of life.

Mercury is difficult to study by telescope because of its small size and nearness to the sun. It can only be seen near the horizon before sunrise and after sunset. It is sometimes called the morning star, or evening star, but it is really a planet. The Greeks called the evening planet Mercury, and the morning planet Apollo. Later they realized they were the same planet.

Characteristics of Mercury

average distance to sun	58 000 000 km
length of year	88 Earth days
rotation time	59 Earth days
diameter at equator	4850 km
atmosphere	none detected
temperature range	–150°C to 425°C
colour	lead-grey
surface features	resembles the moon

Venus is the second planet from the sun and passes closer to the Earth than any other planet. It is often called the Earth's twin because its size and mass are almost the same as those of the Earth, and it, too, has swirling white clouds around it. Venus is the brightest planet in the sky. No wonder it was named after the Roman goddess of love and beauty! It remains a mystery why Venus rotates clockwise, whereas the other planets rotate counter-clockwise.

Venus would be a most uncomfortable place to live. Instruments on the Mariner 10 spacecraft in 1974 determined that its clouds are poisonous. They are composed of carbon dioxide and a little sulphuric acid, which would quickly kill you if you tried to breath it. The sun's energy whips up these gases to speeds of more than 300 km/h. The temperature range is −45°C to 530°C, and the atmospheric pressure is 90 times that on Earth.

Like Mercury, Venus is an evening or morning "star", since it is only visible for about three hours after sunset or before sunrise. Venus goes through phases like the moon's. You can

A view of Venus taken by the television cameras of the Mariner 10 Spacecraft, February 6, 1974. The clouds are thought to be carbon dioxide and sulphuric acid.

observe its changing shape through binoculars, or with a low-power telescope.

Venus moves about a great deal, and you should consult a book called the *Observer's Handbook* to find out where to look for it. This book gives the positions of the planets as well as other current information about astronomy. (It may be obtained from the Royal Astronomical Society of Canada, 124 Merton Street, Toronto, Ontario, M4S 2Z2.)

The visible planets are always to be found in a narrow band in the sky that is called the zodiac. This happens because the planets all orbit the sun in approximately the same plane. Knowing where and when to look for the zodiac band will help you to locate the planets.

Characteristics of Venus

average distance to sun	108 000 000 km
length of year	225 Earth days
rotation time	243 Earth days
diameter at equator	12 000 km
atmosphere	mainly carbon dioxide
temperature range	−45 °C to 530 °C
colour	bright silver
surface features	only clouds visible

Mars is the fourth planet from the sun. Its diameter is only about one-half the Earth's. Astronomers have studied Mars in greater detail than any other planet. The Viking spacecraft flew around the "red planet", mapped it, landed, dug its soil, and checked for the possibility of life. So far, no signs of life have been found.

The surface of Mars has craters, some volcanoes, and some large canyons. The canyon Valles Marineris is the grand canyon of Mars. It is about 8 km deep and 5000 km long — more than 100 times the size of our Grand Canyon. Mars also has a volcanic mountain, called Olympus Mons, that is three times as high as Mount Everest. The poles of Mars are covered with ice-caps, the size of which fluctuates with the seasons. Mars has two small moons shaped somewhat like potatoes.

You can distinguish Mars from the stars by its red colour and its unblinking appearance. To see the surface detail, you will require a good 200-power telescope.

Characteristics of Mars

average distance to sun	227 000 000 km
length of year	687 Earth days
rotation time	24½ h
diameter at equator	6760 km
atmosphere	mostly carbon dioxide
temperature range	−100 °C to 30 °C
colour	orange-red
surface features	craters, mountains, canyons, volcanoes, polar ice-caps
moons	two

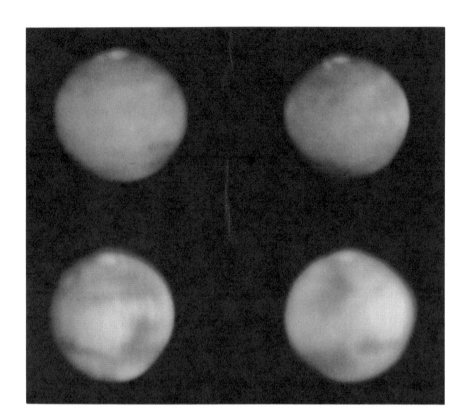

Four photographs of the planet Mars. The white spot at the top of each picture is the north polar cap. Other white markings are clouds or haze.

Artist's concept of Jupiter and its moons

OLLEGE LIBRARY

Jupiter, the fifth planet from the sun, is the largest planet and has 13 moons. It is made up mostly of gases and liquids, and has no solid surface. Because it is shrinking, its rate of spin is increasing. The rapid spinning causes its atmosphere to surround it with clouds hundreds of kilometres deep. The famous Great Red Spot of Jupiter is the centre of a massive hurricane that has been going on for a very long time.

Four of Jupiter's moons can be seen with binoculars.

Characteristics of Jupiter

average distance to sun	780 000 000 km
length of year	12 Earth years
rotation time	10 h
diameter at equator	140 000 km
atmosphere	helium, methane, ammonia, hydrogen
temperature range	−150 °C to 38 °C
colour	whitish yellow
surface features	clouds of gas
moons	13

Saturn and its rings, photographed from Earth through a telescope

Saturn, scheduled to be visited by Voyager spacecraft in 1980 and 1981, is the sixth planet from the sun and the second largest. A Pioneer spacecraft closely approached and photographed the planet in September 1979. Saturn has several rings that orbit its equator. They are believed to consist of ice and dust.

Saturn has 10 moons, the largest of which is Titan. Titan is the only moon known to have its own atmosphere, composed mainly of methane gas.

In spite of its great distance from Earth, Saturn can be seen without binoculars. It moves so slowly that it stays in the region of the same star constellation for more than a year at a time. In the early 1980s, it will be amid the constellations Libra and Scorpius. Once you know where it is, you will be able to find it night after night.

Characteristics of Saturn

average distance to sun	1 400 000 000 km
length of year	29 Earth years
rotation time	10 h
diameter at equator	120 000 km
atmosphere	helium, methane, hydrogen
temperature	perhaps −175 °C
colour	yellow
surface features	probably a ball of gases
moons	10

Uranus is the seventh planet from the sun. It was not discovered until 1781, when William Herschel, a British astronomer, spotted it with his telescope. Another gaseous planet, it appears to be surrounded by clouds.

The axis of rotation of Uranus differs from those of other planets. It lies almost in the orbital plane. The illustration shows how the poles of Uranus face the sun alternately.

You cannot see Uranus or the other two outer planets with the naked eye. That is why these planets took so long to be discovered.

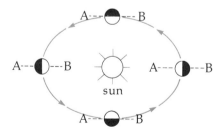

The axis of Uranus lies flat.

Characteristics of Uranus

average distance to sun	2 850 000 000 km
length of year	84 Earth years
rotation time	23 h
diameter at equator	55 000 km
atmosphere	hydrogen, methane, helium
temperature	?
moons	five or more rings

Neptune was discovered in 1846 after two mathematicians had predicted where it would be found. Astronomers had noticed a slight wobble in the path of Uranus and wondered whether some unknown planet might not be pulling it off course with its force of gravity. Their hunch was correct, and the mathematical calculations led them to the discovery of Neptune. It is believed that Neptune is surrounded by a thick layer of ice and frozen ammonia and methane. Through a telescope, Neptune appears pale green.

Characteristics of Neptune

average distance to sun	4 500 000 000 km
length of year	165 Earth years
rotation time	15 h 48 min
diameter at equator	48 600 km
atmosphere	?
temperature	?
moons	two
colour	pale green

Pluto is so far away that it appears only as a dot with the help of the largest telescope. Like Neptune, Pluto was predicted before it was discovered. Astronomers noticed slight shifts or wobbles in the orbits of Uranus and Neptune and thought that another planet must be near by. Pluto was finally discovered in 1930 after years of searching.

Some astronomers think Pluto was once a moon of Neptune and that it escaped. This could explain why Pluto's orbit is tilted in a strange way and why Pluto passes inside Neptune's orbit.

Characteristics of Pluto

average distance to sun	5 900 000 000 km
length of year	248 Earth years
rotation time	6 Earth days
diameter at equator	3000 km
atmosphere	none (?)
temperature	below $-200\,°C$ (?)
moons	one

ACTIVITY

Observing planets with the naked eye or with binoculars is fun. *Science and Children* magazine prints a monthly sky calendar. It tells you where and when to look for the planets and also has information about the moon and the stars. The *Observer's Handbook* is also helpful.

Jupiter, the largest planet, appears like a ball slightly flattened at the poles. It spins so fast that its atmosphere has a streaked appearance.

Saturn, the second largest planet, has beautiful rings that make it a real showpiece.

Venus looks like a small moon, through binoculars. It even has phases. Its cloud-covered surface makes it appear bright silver.

Mars is a red planet and does not blink. With a telescope you can see the markings on its surface.

The sun

The sun is classed as a star because it emits its own heat and light. It is so close to us (150 000 000 km) that it seems much bigger and brighter than any other star in the sky. But it is only slightly brighter than any of the other billions of stars in our galaxy, the Milky Way.

The sun is so big that over a million Earths would not fill the same space. It is a ball of very hot gases, mainly hydrogen and helium. It is the source of energy for the entire solar system. The sun's nine planets are held in their orbits by its pull of gravity on them.

The sun's surface may be thought of as three layers of gases. The inner layer, the photosphere, consists of gas. It has a

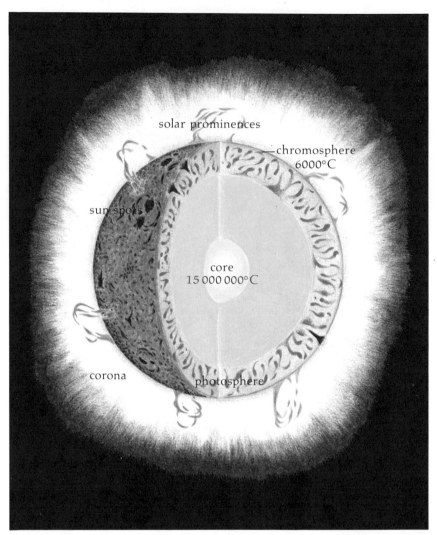

temperature of about 6000°C, and gives off light. The photosphere is surrounded by another layer of gas, the chromosphere. This layer is bright red and can be seen only during an eclipse. The outer layer, the corona, is like a halo around the sun. It extends out more than a million kilometres.

There are dark areas called "sunspots" on the sun's surface. They measure from 1500 km to several thousand kilometres in diameter and expand as they move across the sun. These areas are a cool 4000°C compared to the normal 6000°C on the sun's surface. Sunspots come and go, often lasting several months. The number of sunspots rises and falls in an 11-year cycle. Often huge "solar flares" burst out from the region of sunspots,

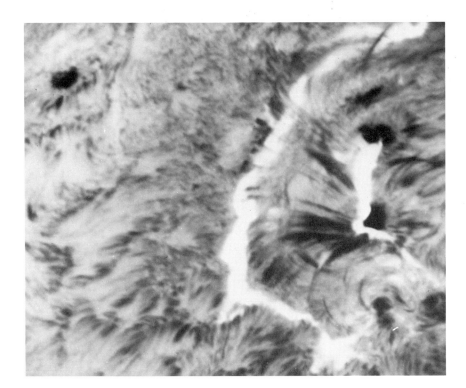

sending streams of electrically charged particles into space. Some of these particles reach Earth, causing radio and television interference. They are deflected by the Earth's magnetic field towards the north and south poles. This is what causes the northern lights and the southern lights. Smaller arches of hot gas sometimes stream between sunspots. These are called "prominences".

The sun rotates on its axis in an unusual way. Since it is made of gas and is not solid, some of its parts are turning more rapidly than others. Gases at the sun's equator rotate once every 25 d while gases near the poles take 35 d for one rotation.

The sun's interior is much hotter (15 000 000 °C) than the surface, and the pressure is very high there. Hydrogen is changed into helium in a process called nuclear fusion. This releases enormous amounts of energy, which makes its way to the surface and from there is radiated into space.

The effects of the sun on the Earth

The sun is our main source of energy. It enables plants to grow and keeps us warm. Without the sun, there would be no life on

An annular solar eclipse

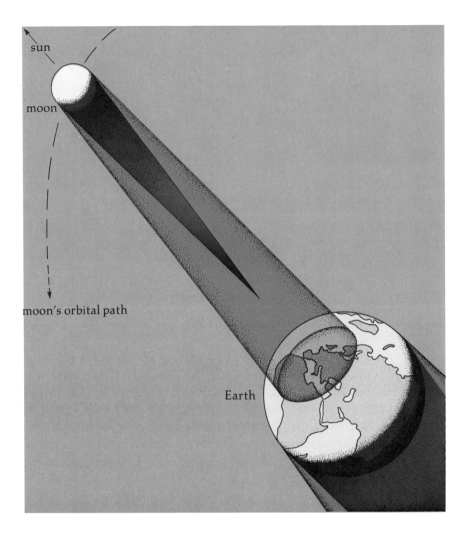

sun

moon

moon's orbital path

Earth

Earth. No wonder early civilizations worshipped the sun. The Earth receives only a tiny percentage of the sun's total energy output. This is because the Earth has a relatively small surface with which to collect the sun's rays and because clouds reflect much of the sun's radiation before it can reach the surface of the Earth.

Scientists have determined that the sun has a small but measurable effect on ocean tides. The gravitational pull of the sun and moon together, however, causes water on the Earth's surface to rise higher than the normal sea level. The sun also gives us day and night, the seasons, and changes in the weather.

A solar eclipse occurs when the moon comes between the sun

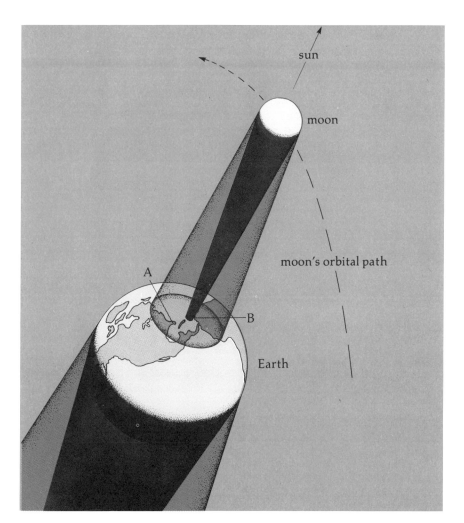

sun

moon

moon's orbital path

A

B

Earth

and the Earth. The moon then prevents the rays of the sun from reaching a portion of the Earth's surface. In other words, the moon's shadow appears on the face of the Earth. There are three types of solar eclipse: annular, partial, and total.

An annular eclipse occurs when the moon's disc blocks off the central part of the sun, leaving only an outer ring visible. From the Earth, the sun appears slightly larger than the moon, and a bright ring shows around it. "Annulus" means ring.

Partial eclipses and total eclipses occur when the moon, in its elliptical path, is close to the Earth. This causes an inner, dark, circular shadow (umbra) and an outer, not so dark shadow (penumbra), as illustrated. To a person standing in the penumbra (position A), part of the sun is still visible. This is called a

A total solar eclipse

partial eclipse. However, anyone standing in the umbra (position B) experiences a strange darkness; the moon totally blocks off the sun and only the outer corona is visible. Total eclipses may last for 5 or 6 min, during which time it may be possible to see bright stars. Flowers have been known to close and some animals even act as though night is approaching.

Total solar eclipses are rare. The last one for this century that was visible in North America took place on February 26, 1979.

Caution: It is dangerous to observe an eclipse (particularly a total eclipse) with the naked eye. When the sun reappears, the sudden brightness can cause permanent eye damage. Even sunglasses do not provide sufficient protection.

The life cycle of the sun

Over the years, scientists have suggested many theories about how the sun was formed. As new information became available from careful observations, older theories were rejected and modified versions of them were developed.

The star cluster Omega Centauri, which is more than 12 000 million years old

Carl F. von Weizsäcker, a German astronomer, developed an explanation in the 1940s which some scientists still accept. First, he suggested, huge clouds of gas and dust particles gathered together in space, pulled by the force of gravity. Over a period of millions of years, a ball of gas was formed, which continued to contract. It got hotter and hotter until it reached the temperature at which hydrogen atoms fuse together, as in a hydrogen bomb. The hydrogen was changed into helium, producing enormous amounts of energy in the form of heat and radiation. Weizsäcker and others believe that some parts of the original gas cloud formed smaller gas balls moving around the new star, and that these smaller balls eventually formed planets orbiting the central star.

The fusion reaction in a star is thought to continue for millions of years, gradually using up the star's hydrogen. When the star runs out of hydrogen, it begins to expand and assume a bright red colour. Stars at that stage are called "red giants". Aldebaran, hundreds of times as big as our sun, is an example of a red giant.

The red giant stage in the life cycle of a star is relatively short. Soon the red giant, its energy running low, contracts again, until it is a tiny "white dwarf". White dwarfs continue to radiate energy into space. They give off less and less light and eventually fade away.

The life cycle of a star

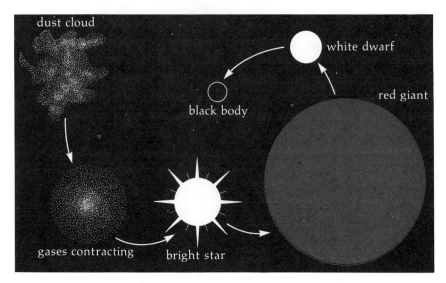

Scientists estimate that our sun is 5000 million years old and has used up about half of its hydrogen. The complete life cycle (from dust cloud to bright star to red giant to white dwarf to dark body) may take 50 000 million years in all.

INVESTIGATION: **To examine sunspots**

MATERIALS

cardboard box (about 50 cm long)	fine nail
aluminum foil	scissors
white paper	masking tape

PROCEDURE

Caution: Never look directly at the sun. Temporary and even permanent damage to your eyes could result.

1. Cut a square hole about 10 cm x 10 cm in one end of the box, and tape a piece of aluminum foil over it.
2. Using a nail, make a small hole in the centre of the foil to allow light from the sun to enter the box.
3. Cut away one-half of a side of the box, as illustrated.
4. Tape a sheet of white paper opposite the nail hole on the inside of the box, as a screen.
5. Hold up the end of the box so that the hole faces the sun.
6. Observe the image of the sun by looking into the box through the open side.

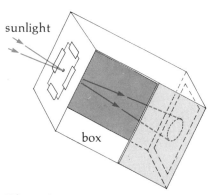

Observing sunspots

OBSERVATIONS

Draw a diagram of the sun's image and any sunspots you saw.

QUESTIONS

1. What causes sunspots on the sun's surface?
2. How long do sunspots last and how large are they?

INVESTIGATION: To demonstrate the cause of solar eclipses

MATERIALS

globe
baseball (or balloon)
masking tape
string
table lamp

PROCEDURE

1. Remove the lamp shade and position the lighted lamp several metres from the globe.
2. Suspend the ball by string and position it between the lamp and the globe.
3. Observe the shadow of the "moon" on the "Earth". Slowly move the moon towards the sun, until the shadow is uniformly grey. This is what happens during an annular eclipse.
4. Slowly move the moon even closer to the Earth. Form a shadow that is composed of an outer grey circle and an inner dark circle. This is the condition that exists during partial and total eclipses.

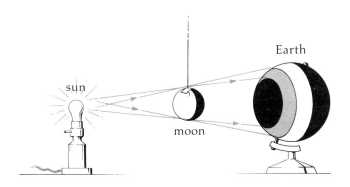

Make a sketch of the shadows you saw.

1. Why is it dangerous to observe an eclipse of the sun with bare eyes?
2. What causes an annular eclipse?
3. What causes a total eclipse?
4. What are the "umbra" and the "penumbra"? Use a diagram in your explanation.

The stars

When you look at the sky on a clear night, you can see about 2000 stars. With a telescope, you could see many thousands more. Stars, like our sun, are balls of luminous gas in space, but they are much farther away than the sun. In fact, stars are so far away that it takes starlight, travelling at the speed of light (300 000 km/s), several years to reach us. Astronomers sometimes call the distance light travels in a year a "light year". One light year is about 10 million million kilometres. For example, the distance to our next nearest star (after the sun) is 4.3 light years, or 40 million million kilometres.

All stars are believed to generate their energy by the same fusion process as the sun. But stars differ from one another in many ways — including temperature, colour, size, and brightness.

Star colour depends on temperature.

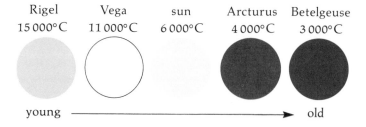

Rigel	Vega	sun	Arcturus	Betelgeuse
15 000°C	11 000°C	6 000°C	4 000°C	3 000°C

young ⟶ old

The colour of a star depends on its temperature. If you were to heat a steel nail in a hot flame, you would find that as it got hotter it changed in colour from a dull red to orange to yellow and, finally, to a bluish-white. Much the same is true of stars.

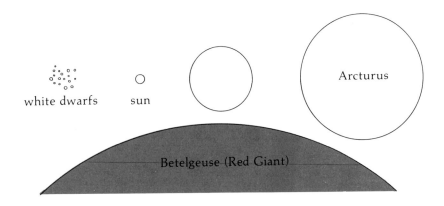
white dwarfs   sun   Arcturus

Betelgeuse (Red Giant)

The stars we see in the sky are of various colours, indicating that some are hotter than others. Our sun is classified as a yellow star. The colours of stars are easy to distinguish with a telescope.

Stars vary greatly in size. The smallest, the white dwarfs, are smaller than the Earth. At the other extreme are the red giants like Betelgeuse, which is about 300 times the size of the sun.

The brightness of a star depends upon its temperature, its size, and its distance from the Earth. We call the apparent brightness of a star its "magnitude". A scale of brightness for stars was first used about 2000 years ago by the Greek astronomer Hipparchus. He classified about 1000 stars on a six-point scale. The brightest stars he called "first magnitude", while stars he could barely see he called "sixth magnitude". Today, a similar scale is used to compare the brightness of all objects in the sky, including the moon and the planets. The red giant star Aldebaran is given a rating of 1. Brighter objects are given negative magnitudes.

OBJECT	MAGNITUDE
sun	−26.5 (brightest)
full moon	−12.5
Venus	−4
Jupiter, Mars	−2
Aldebaran	1.0
bare eye limit	6.5
binocular limit	10
powerful telescope limit	20 (faintest)

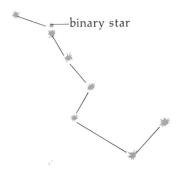

binary star

The Big Dipper

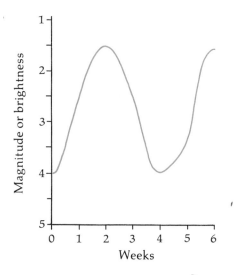

A variable star changes its brightness.

Unusual stars

Binary stars, also called double stars, consist of two stars rotating around one another. They are held together by the force of gravity. The most famous binary star is the second star in the handle of the Big Dipper. If you look carefully, you will see that it is really two stars close together. The bigger star is Mizar and the smaller is Alcor. Astronomers have determined that about half the stars in the universe are binaries.

Variable stars are stars whose brightness varies. This happens when a star explodes, or shrinks and then grows again. The brightness of Mira Ceti, a red giant, drops from magnitude 3 to magnitude 9.5 in 47 weeks and then increases to magnitude 3 over the next 47 weeks. The brightness is irregular for some stars, including the red giant Betelgeuse. Astronomers cannot predict how bright it will be at a given time. Delta Cephi, on the other hand, has a very regular pattern of brightness with a five-day cycle.

Novae and Supernovae. A nova was once considered to be a new star ("nova" means new). Then it was discovered that novae are not new at all. They are stars that erupt, displaying sudden and dramatic increases in brightness. As they erupt, they fling matter into space. About 100 novae have been observed among the stars of our galaxy.

Supernovae are stars that disintegrate in an explosion. A supernova in our galaxy occurs only about once every 100 years. The Chinese observed and recorded a supernova in the year 1054. A cloud of gas and dust known as the Crab Nebula may still be seen at the place where that supernova occurred.

Quasars, Neutron stars, and Black Holes are mysterious objects in space. Astronomers hesitate to call them stars and are trying to figure out their nature. Quasars are the most energetic bodies in the universe. One quasar throws off more energy in a year than the sun in its entire life.

Neutron stars are small but very massive objects in space. They are smaller than planets yet have masses greater than the sun's. Neutron stars spin several times per second. As they rotate, they flash pulses of light. For this reason they are often called "pulsars". There is a rotating neutron star or pulsar in the Crab Nebula. It turns and flashes light about 30 times/s.

Black Holes may be described as the reverse of stars.

Whereas stars give off light, black holes may absorb or pull in everything that comes near them – including light. Black holes cannot be seen, but astronomers have discovered at least one such object by observing the effect of its gravitational pull on a nearby star.

The constellations

These are groupings of stars that were conceived in ancient times to form patterns. In all, there are 88 of these patterns, named after gods, heroes, heroines, animals, and objects. For most of the groupings, you must stretch your imagination. A few of them, such as the Big Dipper, are obvious. Most of them are hard to discern. Still, the constellations make it easier to describe where a heavenly body is located.

As the Earth turns on its axis, it appears to an observer that the whole sky is turning. All the constellations appear to move in a circle, the centre of which is directly over the Earth's north pole. A star named Polaris lies near this turning point. For this reason, Polaris is sometimes called the North Star. It is the only star in the sky that appears not to move in a circle. It is the last star in the handle of the Little Dipper.

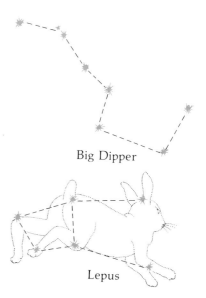

Big Dipper

Lepus

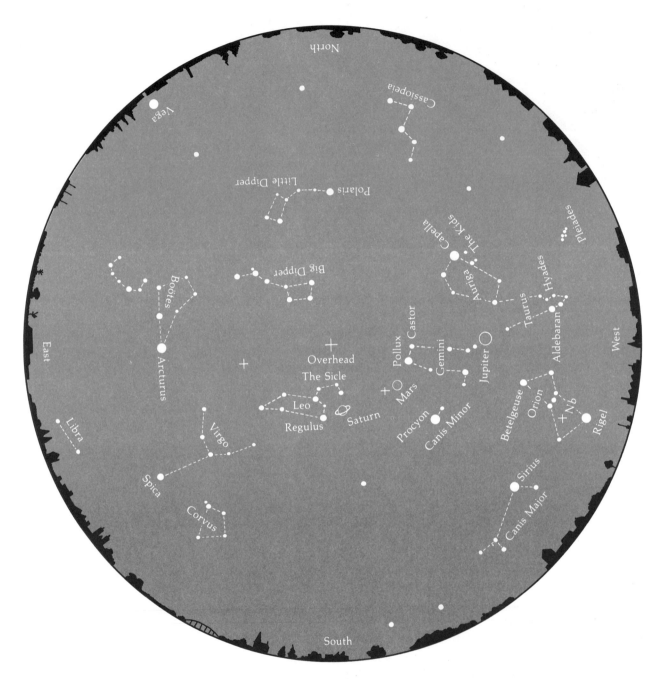

April evening skies — this chart is drawn for latitude 40° north, but should be useful to stargazers across mid North America during the month of April.

The night sky also appears to change with the seasons. This is because, as the Earth orbits the sun, our angle of view of the constellations is steadily changing. Many are even out of sight at certain times. If you travel to the southern hemisphere, you will of course see different constellations than you saw in the north. For these reasons, every star chart, or map of the night sky, is dated and specifies the latitude (number of degrees north or south of the equator) of the observer who made it.

Star trails — the camera was left pointing at the sky while the Earth turned during the night.

INVESTIGATION: To demonstrate the apparent rotation of the sky

MATERIALS

black umbrella
chalk

PROCEDURE

1. Use chalk dots to mark "stars" on the inside surface of the umbrella, as illustrated.
2. Begin by marking Polaris near the centre of the umbrella.
3. Mark the Big Dipper constellation. Note that a line joining the two stars at the end of the dipper points towards Polaris.
4. Mark the five stars in the constellation Cassiopeia. Note how they form the letter "M".
5. Mark the two bright stars, Vega and Capella. Note that they are almost in line with Polaris.
6. Mark the other six stars of the Little Dipper.
7. Mark two or three other stars that appear on the star chart on page 276.
8. Point the umbrella rod in a north-south direction at an angle of about 45°. This is approximately the angle of Polaris above the horizon.
9. Slowly rotate the umbrella counter-clockwise and note what happens to the stars.

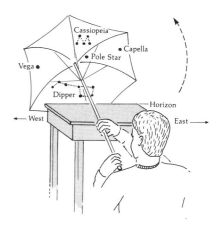

The sky seems to rotate from east to west.

OBSERVATIONS

Write a description of what happened to the stars, in step 9.

QUESTIONS

1. Does the sky really turn? Explain your answer.
2. Why is Polaris also called the Pole Star?
3. Why were you told to hold the umbrella rod at an angle of about 45° to the horizon?
4. How long does it take for the sky to appear to make a complete circle?
5. If you took a time exposure of Polaris, using a camera on a tripod and leaving the shutter open for 30 min, how would the developed picture of the night sky appear?

INVESTIGATION: To use an overhead projector as an aid in learning the constellations

---

MATERIALS

construction paper   star chart
compass   overhead projector and screen
pin

PROCEDURE

1. On a piece of construction paper about 20 cm in diameter, draw a circle. On it mark "N", "S", "E", and "W" to indicate the compass points.
2. Using the star chart and a pencil, carefully mark the positions and names of Polaris and several constellations. Use larger dots for the brighter stars.
3. Make pin-holes in the paper wherever you marked a star. For the brighter stars, make larger holes.
4. Place the paper on the projector and examine the patterns on the screen.
5. Try to remember the names of the constellations you see on the screen.
6. Make the sky rotate around Polaris by turning the paper while it is on the projector.

QUESTIONS

1. What is a constellation? Suggest why constellations were conceived.

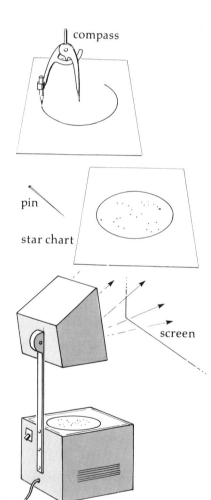

compass

pin

star chart

screen

overhead projector

2. Look up the meaning of "astrology". What is a "horoscope"? Do you believe that your future is "written" in the stars? Would you call this science?

INVESTIGATION: To identify constellations in the night sky

MATERIALS

star chart
flashlight

PROCEDURE

1. On a clear night, around 21:00, examine the sky, and get your compass bearings.
2. Find the Big Dipper, and count its stars.
3. Locate Polaris. (The two stars at the end of the Big Dipper point to it, and it is the last star in the handle of the Little Dipper.)
4. Use the star chart to find other constellations, such as Virgo, Boötes, Gemini, Orion, Cassiopeia, and Leo.
5. Put away the star chart, and find the constellations from memory.

OBSERVATIONS

Make a sketch of each of the constellations you saw.

QUESTIONS

1. If you came back an hour or two later, would you find the constellations in the same places? Explain your answer. What star would still be in the same place?
2. Why are the stars brighter on a moonless night?

flashlight

star chart

Other sky objects

Comets and Meteors. Comets are chunks of icy material about 1 km or 2 km in diameter. They orbit the sun in long elliptical paths that cut across the plane of the ecliptic. Some comets pass near the sun only once and then go off into space. This happens when the pull of gravity between the sun and the comet is not strong enough to keep it in orbit.

Comets' tails always point away from the sun.

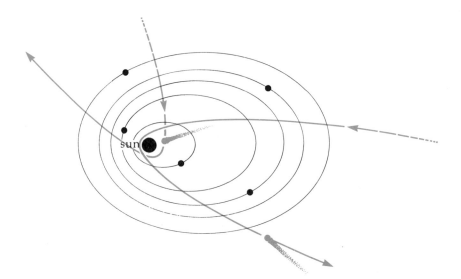

Visible comets appear only once in about three years.

The tail of a comet, believed to consist of vapour, always points away from the sun. This is caused by the pressure of the sun's light. Comets that are visible to the naked eye appear only every few years. Encke's comet returns every 3.5 years. The famous Halley's comet returns every 76 years and was last seen in 1910.

Meteors are chunks of rock flying through space. They range in size from sand grains to huge boulders of up to 50 or 60 t. Many are composed of iron and nickel. Billions of meteors are pulled into the Earth's atmosphere every year by gravity. After entering the atmosphere, they become so hot that they light up the sky. Some people call them falling stars, which is what they were believed to be long ago.

Meteor "showers" occur whenever the Earth crosses the path of a comet, and many meteors enter the Earth's atmosphere at once. This leads us to believe that some meteors are streams of debris from a comet.

Most meteors are small and burn up before reaching the Earth's surface. Others reach the Earth's surface, and some of these make huge craters, such as the Sudbury Basin in Ontario and Meteor Crater in Arizona. Meteors that reach the Earth are called meteorites.

ACTIVITIES

1. Look up comets in the library. Write a report on comets

that reappear. Find out about their tails, orbits, and composition.

2. Prepare a report on meteor showers. Go to your local museum and examine some meteorites. Find out what meteorites are made of.

Star clusters and nebulae. Star clusters are groups of stars. There are "open" clusters and "globular" clusters. In open clusters, the stars are loosely packed while in globular clusters they are closely packed. At least 350 open clusters, containing up to several hundred stars each, are known to exist. Only about 150 globular clusters are known, but each contains up to a million stars.

A nebula is a cloud of gas and dust particles. Sometimes one shows up as a bright patch of haze when light from nearby stars is reflected by its particles. In other instances, nebulae absorb starlight and dark patches result, such as the Horse Head Nebula.

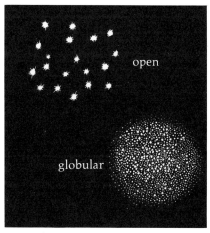

Star clusters

The Eta Carinal Nebula, a group of bright young stars still embedded in the cloud of gas and dust from which they formed.

The Milky Way Galaxy — a disc of stars

sun and planets

sun

10 000 light years

100 000 light years

Galaxies. These are great collections of stars, gas, and dust, held together by gravity in the shape of whirling discs. The centre of the disc is thicker and contains most of the mass. There are billions of galaxies in the universe. Ours is called the Milky Way. Our sun is located near the outer edge of the Milky Way and orbits the centre approximately every 200 million years. The Milky Way is so big it would take light 100 000 years to travel along its diameter.

If you look at the sky on a clear, moonless night, you may notice a faint whitish band extending across it. This is the Milky Way, believed to contain at least 100 000 million stars.

REVIEW QUESTIONS

1. Why have people been interested in astronomy from the earliest times?
2. List some of the ideas about the universe that were put forward by the early Greeks.
3. (a) Why was Ptolemy's theory about the planets incorrect?
   (b) What was Copernicus's theory?
   (c) What was the chief error in Copernicus's theory?
4. Why was Galileo Galilei arrested?

5. What contributions did Johannes Kepler make to Copernicus's model? Illustrate your answer.
6. (a) State Newton's Law of Gravitation.
   (b) What phenomena did this law help to explain?
7. What did Harlow Shapley discover?
8. What were Edwin Hubble's accomplishments?
9. Draw and label a diagram of the sun and the planets. Use arrows to show the direction in which each planet moves.
10. How does the plane of Pluto's orbit differ from the plane of the ecliptic?
11. Which planets travel the slowest?
12. (a) What is meant by a planet's day?
    (b) What is meant by a planet's year?
13. Explain, with the help of a diagram, what causes the Earth to have seasons.
14. What were some of the early arguments supporting the idea that the Earth was round?
15. The Earth is slightly flattened at the poles and bulges at the equator. What causes this?
16. What are the percentages of the two main gases in the Earth's atmosphere? Name some of the other gases in the Earth's atmosphere.
17. Make a diagram of the Earth's magnetic field. How many degrees are there between the magnetic axis and the rotational axis?
18. (a) Give a possible explanation of the origin of the moon's maria.
    (b) Give a possible explanation of the origin of the moon's craters.
19. Using a diagram, explain why we see phases of the moon.
20. What causes a lunar eclipse?
21. What scientific investigations were carried out on the moon by the Apollo astronauts?
22. Explain the role of each of the three sections of the Apollo spacecraft — command module, service module, and lunar module.
23. Why did ancient astronomers use the word' "planet" for certain objects they saw in the sky?
24. Why has our knowledge of some of the planets increased recently?

25. (a) How is Mercury's surface similar to that of the moon?
    (b) Why is Mercury difficult to see with a telescope?
26. (a) Why is Venus sometimes called the Earth's twin?
    (b) In what way is Venus different from the other planets?
    (c) Why is the zodiac band like a highway in the sky?
27. Describe three surface features of Mars.
28. How can you distinguish Mars from the stars in the sky?
29. What are Saturn's rings thought to be made of?
30. (a) In what way is Uranus's axis of rotation unusual?
    (b) Why did Uranus remain undiscovered for so long?
31. Why was Neptune known to exist before it was found?
32. What evidence is there that Pluto may have been a moon of Neptune?
33. (a) What two gases are believed to be the main components of the sun?
    (b) What are sunspots? What causes them?
    (c) Where does the sun get its energy?
34. (a) Name the three types of solar eclipse.
    (b) Make illustrations to show how they come about.
35. Trace the life cycle of a star from dust cloud to black body.
36. How is it possible for some stars we see at night to have burned out months or even years before?
37. (a) What determines the colour of a star?
    (b) What determines the brightness of a star?
38. What are (a) binary stars? (b) variable stars? (c) novae?
39. What are (a) quasars? (b) neutron stars? (c) black holes?
40. What are constellations?
41. What causes the night sky to "rotate" about Polaris?
42. Why does the sky change with the seasons?
43. (a) What are comets?
    (b) Why do comets' tails always point away from the sun?
44. (a) What are meteors?
    (b) Why are they called falling stars?
45. (a) What are star clusters? (b) nebulae? (c) galaxies?
46. What is the shape of our Milky Way galaxy? Where is the sun located within the Milky Way?

IMPORTANT TERMS

astronomy—the study of the universe

revolve—to move in an orbit

aphelion—the point in a planet's orbit that is farthest from the sun

perihelion—the point in a planet's orbit that is closest to the sun

ecliptic—the plane in which all the planets revolve

rotate—to turn about an axis

maria—the parts of the moon's surface that have the appearance of seas when viewed from the Earth

rill—a long valley-like depression

phases of the moon—the different appearances of the moon

lunar eclipse—what happens when the moon passes into the Earth's shadow

sunspot—a relatively cool dark patch on the sun's surface

solar flare—a jet of flaming hot gases rising from the sun's surface

photosphere—the inner layer of the sun's surface

chromosphere—the layer of the sun's surface that is outside the photosphere

corona—the outer layer of gas around the sun, which appears as a halo

solar eclipse—what happens when the moon gets between the sun and the Earth

umbra—the dark inner circular shadow of the moon on the Earth

penumbra—the outer, not so dark, circular shadow of the moon on the Earth

binary star—two stars revolving around one another

variable star—a star whose brightness varies

nova—a star that erupts, or explodes

neutron star—a small but very massive object in space that spins and gives off flashes of light

black hole—an area in space that absorbs light and anything else that comes near it

constellation—a grouping of stars conceived in ancient times to form a familiar pattern

comet—a chunk of icy material that orbits the sun in a long elliptical path

meteor—a chunk of rock flying through space

star cluster—a group of stars

nebula—a cloud of gas and dust particles

galaxy—a great collection of stars, gas, and dust, held together by gravity in a whirling disc

WATER

Water is as important to us as air. We could not live without it.

If fresh water comes out of a tap in your home, consider yourself fortunate, because in many parts of the world rain seldom falls. It is not uncommon in the dry parts of Africa and India for a housewife to walk 10 or 15 km every day to fetch water for her family. Yet we have so much of it, and use it so freely, that we hardly give it a thought.

Water is a commonplace thing to us, but most of us know little about it, or its perpetual cycle involving the rivers, the oceans, and the sun. Then there is the matter of what water is and what its chemical and physical properties are. You will be exploring these questions here, and learning about the importance of water to living things.

The water cycle

Powered by the energy of the sun, water moves in a continuous cycle from the ocean to the air, then to the land, and then back to the ocean. The sun causes evaporation to take place at the ocean's surface. The vapour rises, and as it rises it cools and condenses, forming clouds. The clouds are carried towards

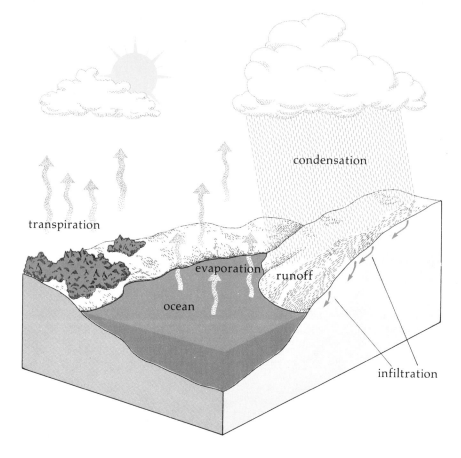

land by winds and then release their moisture as rain (or snow). After the rain reaches the ground, it collects in pools, which overflow into streams that flow down and across the land into lakes, which feed rivers flowing into the ocean. Some of the water soaks into the ground and travels back to the ocean at lower levels within the soil and rock. This process is called infiltration. The roots of trees and plants absorb some of this groundwater, which travels up through the stems and is given back to the air through the leaves. This process is called transpiration.

The chemistry of water

One way to find out about something is to take it apart and examine the pieces. In England, about 200 years ago, scientists did this to water with the help of electricity. They collected two gases and after testing them concluded that water is composed of hydrogen and oxygen.

Chemists call water a compound and they call hydrogen and oxygen elements. Compounds are made up of two or more elements.

$$\underset{\text{(compound)}}{\text{water}} \longrightarrow \underset{\text{(element)}}{\text{hydrogen}} + \underset{\text{(element)}}{\text{oxygen}}$$

This word equation shows how chemists describe the decomposition of water. The word equation for combining hydrogen and oxygen to make water is

$$\text{hydrogen} + \text{oxygen} \longrightarrow \text{water}$$

There are 91 elements that occur in nature and another 13 that have been made artificially, making a total of 104. There are thousands of different compounds.

A molecule is the smallest particle of an element or compound that displays all the properties of that element or compound. Molecules are so small that a drop of water, for example, contains about 10 000 000 000 000 000 000 000 000 of them, and each water molecule is identical in every respect to every other water molecule. However, a water molecule is unique – it is different from the molecules of all other substances.

Scientists have determined that water molecules are shaped as shown in the illustration. Note that the two hydrogen ends of the molecule have positive electrical charges while the oxygen end has a negative charge. This explains why water molecules attract each other: one of the positive (hydrogen) ends of one molecule is attracted to the negative (oxygen) end of its neighbour, and so on.

Because of this attraction, some water molecules link up with others to form clusters. This explains why droplets of water form when a little water is spilled on a piece of waxed paper or plastic. Without the force of attraction between water molecules, the water would just spread out.

ACTIVITY

Make some water "molecules", using plasticine of two colours. Make them as identical as possible. Form a cluster of "molecules", using wire to link hydrogen and oxygen ends together.

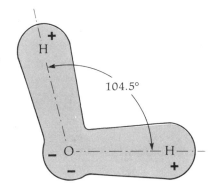

Water molecule enlarged about 200 million times

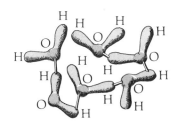

A cluster of water molecules made from plasticine

INVESTIGATION: **To decompose water into its components, oxygen and hydrogen**

MATERIALS

250 mL (or larger) beaker
insulated copper house wire (about 1 m)
dilute sulphuric acid
6 V battery (or four 1.5 V dry cells)
matches and wood splints
graduated cylinder
2 test tubes
paper towels
2 solid rubber stoppers

PROCEDURE

1. Cut the wire in half and remove about 4 cm of insulation from each end of both pieces.
2. Half-fill the beaker with water. Place the stoppers upside down on the bottom. Then fill the two test tubes completely with water and invert them into the beaker, as illustrated.
3. Bend one end of each wire and insert the bent end in each tube.
4. Connect the wires to the battery. Then slowly add about 15 mL of dilute sulphuric acid to the water.
   Caution: Do not get any acid on your skin or clothes. If this should happen, wash with plenty of water.
5. Disconnect the battery as soon as one of the test tubes is nearly full of gas. Compare the amounts of gas that have collected in the two tubes.
6. Without removing the test tubes, slip the wires out of the beaker.
7. Push the open ends of the test tubes down onto the stoppers, which are still in the beaker. Now lift them from the beaker.
8. Test the gas in the half-filled test tube. Have a *glowing* splint ready when your partner removes the stopper, and quickly insert the splint into the gas. If it is oxygen, the glowing splint will burst into flame.
9. Test the gas in the filled tube. This time hold the test tube upside down as you remove the stopper and have your partner insert a *flaming* splint up into the tube. If the gas is hydrogen you will hear a "pop".

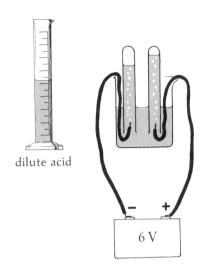

dilute acid

Changing water into hydrogen and oxygen

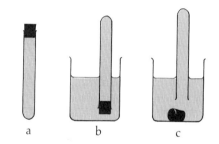

a   b   c

Poke out the stopper with a pencil.

OBSERVATIONS

Record what happened in steps 4, 8, and 9. Also note how the amounts of gas you collected in the two tubes compared.

QUESTIONS

1. What is meant by the "decomposition" of water?
2. What is water made of?
3. What is a test for oxygen? For hydrogen?
4. What was the source of energy in this investigation?

The universal solvent

Water has the ability to dissolve larger amounts of more different substances than any other liquid. For this reason, it is often called "the universal solvent". Water does not exist in pure form in nature. It always has other materials dissolved in it. The ability of water to transport other materials is of great importance to plants and animals, which obtain nutrients essential for their life activities from the water they take in. Natural water contains as many as 40 different mineral salts, dissolved from the rocks through which it flows on its way to the ocean.

For homes and industries, water is the cheapest and most convenient solvent for many uses. There is a seemingly endless supply of it in our rivers and lakes. Once it has been used, it must be disposed of, and too often it is simply flushed back into the rivers and lakes instead of first being treated to remove poisonous wastes. The result is severe pollution problems that threaten or destroy certain types of plants and animals in many areas. Careful testing of river and lake water is necessary, as part of a program to keep the concentrations of various chemicals in the water within safe limits.

Chemical testing of water

Water-testing kits are available that enable you to make quick and fairly accurate measurements of the levels of certain chemicals in water. These kits can test for oxygen, carbon dioxide, water hardness, phosphates, and "pH level".

Oxygen. The test for dissolved oxygen (D.O.) is the most important single test for determining the condition of water. If the D.O. level is high, the lake, river, or pond in question probably contains a healthy variety of fish and other aquatic life. If the D.O. level is low, fish may be non-existent and life may be reduced to certain types of worms and insects that require little oxygen.

Oxygen enters water in two ways: from the atmosphere by mixing with water at the surface, and from green water plants, which give off oxygen in the sunlight. If the water bubbles over rocks or dams, this helps it to absorb oxygen from the air. On the other hand, water that lies still in a pond has to rely mainly on the wind for help in taking oxygen from the air. Plants give

off oxygen to the water only when they can obtain sufficient sunlight. If the water becomes cloudy with sediment stirred up by boats, or by the addition of wastes, the D.O. level falls and plants begin to die.

The oxygen in a pond is used by its populations of animals, such as fish, and also by smaller organisms that inhabit the bed of the pond. These are called decomposer organisms because they break down dead animal and plant matter that sinks to the bottom.

The D.O. level is affected greatly by temperature. In general, the higher the temperature of the water, the less oxygen it will contain. Many industries and all thermal generating stations use water as a coolant, and discharge the hot, used water into a river or lake. Where this is done, the aquatic life can be severely affected. Certain types of fish that are plentiful upstream from a plant situated on a river may not survive below the plant, where the water is warmer.

Carbon dioxide is given off, and absorbed by the water,

when dead plant and animal matter is broken down by decomposers. This can happen at any depth, but it occurs mostly in the lower regions of lakes and ponds. Fish also give off carbon dioxide as they breathe. Water with a high carbon dioxide level can corrode certain metals and kill aquatic animals.

Water hardness is a measure of the concentration of calcium and magnesium salts in a sample of water. These are the salts that the water dissolved out of rocks through which it flowed. Rain water is called soft water because it contains only minute amounts of salt picked up from the atmosphere. Hard water is difficult to wash with, because it reacts with soap to produce an ugly scum. It also leaves a deposit in pots and kettles.

Phosphates enter the lakes and streams wherever phosphate detergents are used for washing and the dirty water is not treated to remove most of the phosphates. A high concentration of phosphates makes lake water too fertile. Huge amounts of green algae develop. A whole lake may become clogged with weeds, which die and absorb oxygen as they decay. One result of this is that there is not enough oxygen left for the fish. The lake becomes an unsightly tangle of weeds, dangerous for swimming and boating and useless for fishing.

What is called the "pH" of water is a rating on a scale that goes from 0 to 14, indicating whether the water is acidic, neutral, or alkaline. Pure water has a pH of 7.0 and is said to be neutral. When an acid such as vinegar or lemon juice is added to water, the pH falls below 7.0. Pure lemon juice has a pH of 2.3. There are also substances that raise the pH. For example, when milk of magnesia (with a pH of 10.5) is added to water, the pH goes above 7.0 and the water is then said to be alkaline.

Nature has its own ways of keeping the pH of water close to the desirable level of 7.0. When water is polluted, the pH may rise or fall, depending on the polluting chemicals. The pH of water is important because fish and other aquatic organisms are highly sensitive to it. Only a few fish can tolerate a pH that fluctuates by as much as four points on the scale, that is, from 5 to 9.

The Ontario government has revealed that the Muskoka Lakes are becoming acidic. This is a result of pollutants from industrial areas being transported through the atmosphere for

hundreds of kilometres by high winds. The pollutants form an acid, which drops into the lakes with the rain, gradually lowering the pH of the water. Unless a way is found to increase the pH again, most of the fish in the lakes may eventually be killed.

The pH of ponds or lakes usually drops as they get older. This is caused by an increasing amount of dead plant and animal material. As the carbon dioxide level rises the pH falls and the water becomes acidic. A typical boggy, decaying pond could have a concentration of 8 parts of oxygen per million parts of water, a carbon dioxide concentration of 10 parts per million, and a pH of 6.5.

INVESTIGATION: To use test kits to check the quality of the water in a stream or pond

MATERIALS

test kits for oxygen, carbon dioxide, hardness, phosphates, and pH
thermometer

PROCEDURE

1. Practise using the kits in the classroom, with water from an aquarium.
2. At a nearby pond (or stream), pick several points at which to take readings. If a pond you are using has an inlet and an outlet, test the water near each, as well as in the middle. Record all your observations in a table like the one below.
3. Draw a map showing where you took the readings.

OBSERVATIONS

TEST	LOCATIONS				
	A	B	C	D	E
Oxygen (D.O.)					
Carbon dioxide					
Hardness					
Phosphates					
pH					
Temperature					

QUESTIONS

1. Note where the oxygen level was highest and lowest, and compare the water temperatures at the two locations. Is this what you would expect? Explain your answer.
2. Was the water acidic, neutral, or alkaline? Note any significant fluctuations in your pH observations.
3. Examine your carbon dioxide readings for the various locations and write a paragraph commenting on the variations.
4. Work out the average hardness of the water in the pond and write a brief explanation of what causes water to be hard.

5. Examine your phosphate readings. Write a paragraph stating whether they were high or low and whether or not they varied substantially. In each case, suggest possible reasons.
6. From all your results, would you expect to be able to catch fish in your pond or stream? Explain your answer.

The physics of water

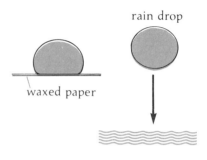

rain drop
waxed paper

Surface tension. Place a few drops of water on some waxed paper. Notice how they roll into little balls, or spheres. Photographs of raindrops show that they are both round and smooth. To understand why a very small quantity of water assumes a rounded shape, we must think of the forces that are acting on the individual water molecules. Remember that water molecules attract each other (see page 289). Each of the molecules near the surface is pulled inward by the molecules nearer the centre. The drop of water tries to reduce its surface area by forming a sphere. The result is what is called surface tension.

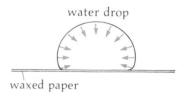

water drop
waxed paper

Surface tension gives water a "skin". One of the effects of this is to allow certain insects to walk on top of it without getting wet.

ACTIVITY

"Float" a steel pin on the surface of some water in a beaker. The easiest way to do this is to place the pin on a small piece of toilet paper or tissue paper. The paper will soon get soggy and sink, leaving the pin free. A little grease spread on the pin ahead of time will help. While the pin is "floating", add a drop of detergent to the water and note how quickly the pin sinks. Try the same experiment with duplicating fluid (methyl alcohol). The surface tension is not sufficient to support the pin on the surface. Scientists have measured the surface tension of hundreds of liquids. They have found that (with the exception of mercury) water has the highest surface tension.

Capillary action. If you place drops of water on smooth surfaces of various materials, you will find that water sticks to

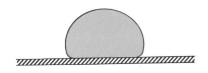

Water beads on plastic but sticks to glass.

some surfaces better than others. For example, water forms beads on plastic but spreads out on glass. It spreads out on glass because glass molecules and water molecules have a stronger attraction for each other than water molecules have for each other. We say that water adheres to glass.

This explains why the surface of water in a glass test tube curves up around the edges. It also explains why water tends to rise in a narrow glass tube. We call this effect capillary action. Capillary action is very important in nature. It enables water to find its way up through narrow channels in the soil from the water table below. Without capillary action, water from the earth below would never reach the roots of plants.

Water moves by capillary action in the soil to get to the plant.

Water rises up narrow glass tubes by capillary action.

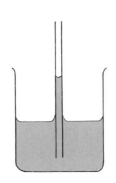

water table

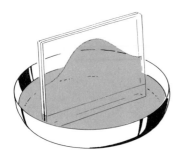

ACTIVITY

Stand two plates of glass parallel to each other and a few millimetres apart in a pan of water. Note how the water rises in the space between the plates. This is a demonstration of capillary action. Colouring in the water will help you see the liquid rising.

Heat capacity. Gram for gram, water can hold more heat than any other substance. In other words, water has great capacity for absorbing heat. Because of this capacity, the lakes and oceans help to moderate extremes of air temperature. During the day, lakes absorb the sun's radiation and warm up. At night, the water loses its heat to the cool air above it. In this way the difference between day and night air temperatures is reduced.

The temperatures of cars and other machines are lowered by circulating water. Similarly, our blood, which consists largely of water, helps to keep our body temperature steady.

The effect of temperature on volume. Most liquids contract as the temperature drops. They do this because their molecules come closer together as they cool. This is only partly true of water, as the next investigation shows.

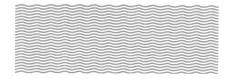

During the day water in lakes and oceans absorbs heat from the sun. At night water loses this heat to the air.

INVESTIGATION: To observe the effect of decreasing
temperature on the volume of water

MATERIALS
crushed ice
ice bucket or large beaker (1000 mL)
2-hole rubber stopper
glass tubing (30 cm)
250 mL flask
clock
salt
thermometer
ruler
food colouring

PROCEDURE

1. Mix the ice with a half cup of salt in the beaker.
2. Fill the flask with coloured water.
3. Fit the thermometer and glass tubing into the rubber stopper and push the stopper into the flask until the water rises at least 20 cm in the tubing. Place the flask in the ice bucket. *Caution*: This should be done by the teacher.
4. Measure and record the height of the water column in the tubing every minute, until the temperature is almost 0 °C.

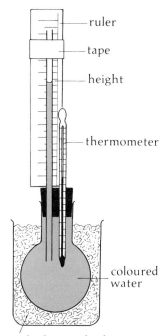

crushed ice and salt

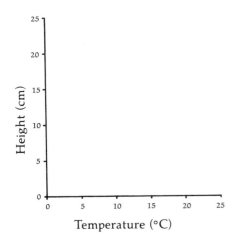

1. Record your results in a table like this one.

TIME (min)	WATER TEMPERATURE (°C)	HEIGHT (cm)
0		
1		
2		
3		
. . .		
. . .		

2. Plot a graph of height against temperature.

QUESTIONS

1. Describe what happened to the volume of the water as the temperature decreased. At what temperature did the water have the smallest volume? At what temperature do you think the mass of the water was most compacted?
2. Suppose that you have two glasses of water, one at 20 °C and the other at 4 °C, and you put a coloured ice cube in each. Which direction will the coloured water travel, in each glass, as it moves away from the melting ice cube? Explain your answer.

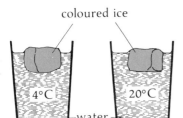

coloured ice

4°C   20°C

water

Why don't lakes freeze from the bottom up?

In the last investigation, you saw that water has its smallest volume (and greatest density) at 4 °C rather than at its freezing point, 0 °C. As the water cooled below 4 °C it was actually expanding, and becoming less dense.

This characteristic of water is important in nature. It means that in autumn when a lake cools, the water near the surface becomes denser, causing it to sink. When the surface water does that, it carries oxygen with it to the fish deep below. Eventually the entire pond is cooled to 4 °C and the circulation of water ceases. If the surface water is then cooled to below 4 °C, it will stay on top because it is less dense than the water below it. The cold air will continue to cool the water at the surface, and finally, at 0 °C, it will freeze. If water reached its maximum density at 0 °C, ponds and lakes would begin to freeze at the bottom. You can imagine what that would do to aquatic plants and animals.

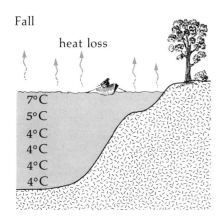

Fall

heat loss

7°C	
5°C	
4°C	
4°C	
4°C	
4°C	

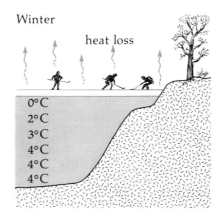

Winter

heat loss

0°C	
2°C	
3°C	
4°C	
4°C	
4°C	

The water at the bottom is at 4°C because it has the greatest density.

What happens when water freezes?

Most substances contract when they freeze – but not water. This most unusual substance expands when it changes state from a liquid to a solid. In other words, the molecules move farther apart. You can demonstrate this by filling a can to the very top with water and, with its lid removed, carefully placing it in a freezer. Later, you will find that ice has risen over the lip of the can. You may also have seen what happens to a bottle or can of pop that is accidentally left in a freezer.

The expansion of water when it freezes has two major beneficial effects in nature. First, it means that ice is less dense than water, and therefore floats. If ice sank, then lakes would freeze from the bottom up, and this would exterminate most aquatic life. Some deep lakes would probably never thaw completely. Second, it enables water to play a big role in the weathering of rocks. Water that has seeped into cracks in a rock during the day will freeze at night, splitting the rock open by the force of its expansion. Farmers know that large lumps of soil are broken down during the cold months by the action of frost. This happens because groundwater freezes and thaws repeatedly. The effect is to allow air to enter the soil and make it more fertile.

This expansion can also have undesirable effects. You know

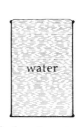

before freezing   after freezing

water   ice

what can happen to water pipes in a cottage if they are not properly drained in the fall, or to the radiator of a car in the winter if the owner forgets to put antifreeze in it.

What happens when water changes to vapour?

When water evaporates or boils, its molecules are pushed far apart. It takes a great deal of heat energy to do this. In fact, to change 1 kg of water into steam at the boiling point requires 2268 kJ (kilojoules) of heat energy – more than for 1 kg of any other substance. If the same steam cools, and condenses back to the liquid state, the same amount of heat is given off.

You can demonstrate that evaporation takes away heat by wetting your hand and holding it up in a breeze. Your hand feels cool because heat is being drawn away from your skin. Perspiration helps to keep us cool in the same way. When we exercise, we begin to sweat, and the sweat evaporates, taking heat from our skin. This is nature's way of cooling our engines.

Since, in nature, water is continuously changing from liquid to vapour or from vapour back to liquid, heat is continuously being absorbed from or released to the atmosphere. This has a great moderating effect on the Earth's climate. If the air temperature rises, more water evaporates from the lakes, absorbing heat and causing the temperature of the air to fall again.

ACTIVITY

We have seen that water is a most peculiar substance. Make a list of the chief properties of water and indicate the importance of each to people and to the environment.

The treatment of water

Good drinking water is odourless, tasteless, clear, and free of harmful bacteria. Seldom is such water found in nature. To provide a town with drinking water, it is usually necessary to treat water from a nearby lake or river. The steps that must be taken to treat water depend on the initial condition of the water. Generally these steps include coarse straining, fine straining (or microstraining), alum flocculation, settling, sand-filtering, and chlorination. In some places, fluorine is added to help prevent tooth decay.

Water on your hand feels cool because evaporation absorbs heat.

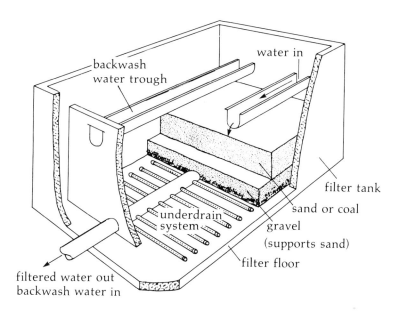

A sand and gravel filter

backwash water trough

water in

filter tank

sand or coal

gravel (supports sand)

underdrain system

filter floor

filtered water out
backwash water in

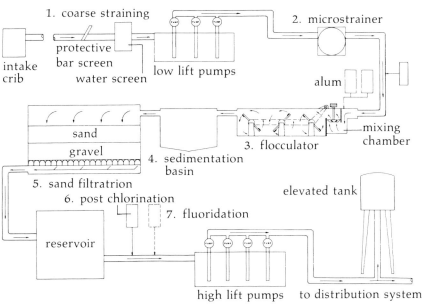

Steps in water treatment

1. coarse straining

2. microstrainer

protective bar screen

intake crib

water screen

low lift pumps

alum

mixing chamber

sand

gravel

3. flocculator

4. sedimentation basin

5. sand filtratrion

6. post chlorination

7. fluoridation

elevated tank

reservoir

high lift pumps   to distribution system

Coarse straining eliminates fish, logs, seaweed, and such unwanted objects. Microstraining screens out finer particles, such as algae. Then the water enters a flocculator, which is a large concrete tank containing some of the chemical, alum. The alum forms a jelly-like substance (floc), to which very fine particles of sediment adhere. Large paddles agitate the contents to prevent the floc from settling. The water and floc are then transferred into a settling basin, where the floc is allowed to settle on the bottom. The water then passes into a sand filter, where it goes through a bed of fine sand laid over gravel, and from there to a reservoir. Chlorine is added to the water to kill any harmful bacteria that might be present.

INVESTIGATION: To treat some muddy water

MATERIALS

kitchen strainer
alum (sodium aluminum sulphate)
nail
muddy water
fine-weave cotton cloth
3 large plastic containers
liquid chlorine or Javex

PROCEDURE

1. Coarse straining. Pour the muddy water through the kitchen strainer.
2. Fine straining. Filter the water recovered from step 1 through a fine cloth draped inside the kitchen strainer.
3. Alum flocculation. Add a small quantity of alum to the water recovered from step 2, and stir.
4. Settling. Allow the floc to settle. You may have to leave the container overnight.

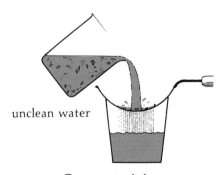

Coarse straining

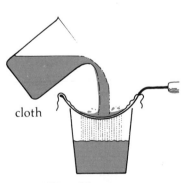

cloth

Fine filtering

alum

Alum flocculation

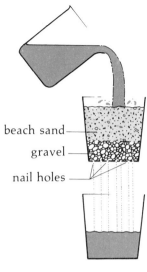

beach sand
gravel
nail holes

Sand filtering

liquid chlorine or Javex

Chlorination

5. Sand filtering. Prepare a filter by punching small holes with a nail in the bottom of a container. Add a 5 cm layer of gravel, and then a 10 cm layer of clean beach sand. Clean your filter by flushing it thoroughly with tap water. Then pour through your partly treated water.

6. Add a small spoonful of liquid chlorine or Javex to the filtered water. *Caution*: Chlorine and Javex are dangerous. Do not inhale the fumes or get these liquids on your skin. If necessary, wash your skin with plenty of water. Do not drink the water you have been treating, in case it is not perfectly pure. (Chlorine takes some time to do its work.)

OBSERVATIONS

1. Write a description of what happened when you added the alum to the water.
2. Compare the treated water with the original water and record this information in note form.

QUESTIONS

1. Write a paragraph explaining why it is necessary to treat water that will be used for domestic purposes.
2. Why were you told to use alum in step 3?
3. Sand filters have been used for centuries. Some people say it is nature's way of purifying water. Explain why this is true.

4. "Water would require less treatment if industries were more careful about dumping their waste." Write a paragraph commenting on this statement.

Distillation

Straining, flocculation, and filtering will not remove salt or other dissolved particles from water. In areas where only salt water is available, a process called distillation is sometimes used to obtain drinking water. Salt water is boiled and the vapour is captured and condensed back to a liquid. The salt remains behind, and the distilled water is pure. The main problem with distillation is the cost of the energy that is needed to boil the water. Some large desalting plants use nuclear reactors to supply the energy. Others use solar energy. On the island of Symi, near Greece, the 4000 inhabitants get all their fresh water from a solar-distillation unit which supplies more than 4 kL/d.

INVESTIGATION: To make distilled water from salt water

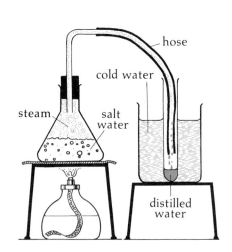

MATERIALS

salt	rubber hose
alcohol burner	beaker (250 mL)
glass elbow	one-hole stopper
flask	burner stand

PROCEDURE

1. Set up the apparatus illustrated.
2. Make a salt and water solution by stirring 3 or 4 small spoonfuls of salt into 50 mL of water. Taste the solution on your finger.
3. Distill 1-2 cm of water into the test tube. Taste the distilled water.

OBSERVATIONS

Note the taste of the water before and after distillation.

1. Why is it expensive to turn salt water into fresh water this way?
2. Explain how solar energy can be used to desalt water with the equipment illustrated. (This is a process that produces only about 4 L/d of fresh water for every square metre of salt-water surface.)
3. (a) Why do you suppose chemists use distilled water in their experiments?
   (b) Why should car batteries be filled with distilled water?
   (c) Why does distilled water have a strange flat taste?
   (d) Why is natural water better than distilled water for plants and animals?

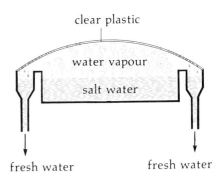

The importance of water to living things

Many scientists believe that life began in the sea. And although it eventually spread to the land and into the air, water continued to be essential for every new organism. A person can live for up to two months without food, but it is doubtful that anyone could last for more than a week without water.

All living things contain water, in varying amounts. The human body is about 65% water, but the percentage varies somewhat from person to person. A lean person with firm body tissue may be 70% water while a chubby individual may be only 55% or 60% water, since fat is low in water content.

Blood has the highest percentage of water (83%) of any part of the human body. Bone has the lowest (22%). Muscles are high in water content (75.6%) and so is the brain (74.5%).

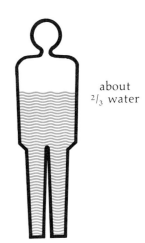

about $2/_3$ water

INVESTIGATION: To determine the percentage of water in an apple

---

MATERIALS

apple
balance
knife

PROCEDURE

1. Determine the mass of a fresh apple and then cut it into quarters.
2. Set the pieces in the sun, on a radiator, or in a warm oven.
3. Determine the mass of the apple daily for a week.

OBSERVATIONS

1. Enter your results in a suitable table.
2. Plot your data on a graph of mass against time, like this one.

QUESTIONS

1. Calculate the percentage of water in the apple, based on what happened to the apple in the seven days.
2. What evidence is there that the water content of an apple increases if it remains on the tree until it is ripe?
3. Dried sunflower seeds have a low water content (5%). Most fruits and vegetables have a higher one (corn 78%, pineapple 87%, tomatoes 95%). Can you name the fruit with the highest water content (97%)?

ACTIVITY

How much water does your body absorb in a day? To find out, prepare a list of the foods you might have for breakfast, lunch, and dinner on an average day, with the quantities. Be sure to include between-meal snacks and drinks. Estimate the percentage of water in each food and calculate your total water intake for one day. A table like the one below might help.

	FOOD	AMOUNT	ESTIMATED % WATER	AMOUNT OF WATER (mL)
Breakfast	cereal and milk	200 mL	95	190
	juice	150 mL	98	147
	2 slices toast	60 g	25	15
Lunch				
Dinner				
Snacks and drinks				

MATLOCK COLLEGE LIBRARY

Plants seem dry on the outside, but inside their cells is sap, which is mostly water. The sap rises through a plant, exerting pressure on the inside and so keeping it upright. Water is given off at the leaves and vaporizes into the air.

INVESTIGATION: To determine how much water is given off by the leaves of a plant

---

MATERIALS

healthy potted plant
balance
plastic bag

PROCEDURE

1. Water the plant and then enclose the pot in the plastic bag to prevent water from evaporating from the soil.
2. Determine the mass of the plant at the start and daily for several days. Do not water the plant during this period.

OBSERVATIONS

1. Make a table of your results, and plot them on a graph of mass against time.
2. Keep notes on any changes you observe in the appearance of the plant.

QUESTION

How much water did the leaves of the plant give off in a week?

plastic wrap

Conservation of water

You probably have plenty of water where you live, but there are places where water can be used only a few hours each day, and then the supply is shut off. Could this ever happen in your community? You can reduce the chances that it will by taking care not to waste any water. Think about the way you use water, then try to cut back. If we each save a little, we will all save a lot.

INVESTIGATION: **To determine how much water is used in your home**

MATERIALS

stopwatch
pail graduated in litres

PROCEDURE

1. Measure the water you use when you take a shower. Measure the water flow from the shower in litres per minute, using the stopwatch and pail. Then time yourself with the stopwatch as you take a shower. To calculate the water you used:

$$\text{minutes} \times \frac{\text{litres}}{\text{minutes}} = \text{litres}$$

2. Now measure the amount of water when you take a bath. Follow the same procedure as in step 1.
3. Measure the amount of water your toilet uses when flushed by counting the number of litres it takes to fill the empty tank.
4. Use the same method again, to determine how much is used in washing a car.
5. Calculate the amount of water you use when you water your lawn for 2 h.

OBSERVATIONS AND CALCULATIONS

Record your calculations in a table like this one.

	TIME (min)	FLOW (L/min)	WATER USED (L)
Showering			
Bathing			
Flushing the toilet			
Washing the car			
Watering the grass			

QUESTIONS

1. Which uses more water – the shower or the bath?
2. Suggest ways of reducing the consumption of water when your family takes showers and baths.

3. How could you use a brick to reduce the amount of water used by a toilet each time it is flushed?
4. Comment on the amount of water used to water lawns, mentioning whether you consider this practice necessary.
5. List some other ways in which water is used in your home.

Industry uses enormous quantities of water – for example, to carry heat in heating systems, to cool hot steel in steel mills, and as a coolant in air conditioning systems. Water goes into beverages, paints, chemicals, and thousands of other products. It is also used to carry away waste. To give you an idea of how much water is used, consider these estimates:

–To produce one automobile takes 120 kL of water.
–To grow one head of cabbage requires 20 L of water.
–To produce 1 t of steel requires 80 kL of water.
–To produce 1 L of gasoline requires 70 L of water.

It is estimated that every Canadian uses water at the rate of 600 L/d. What is even more alarming is the fact that the rate is increasing every year.

REVIEW QUESTIONS

1. "Water is the most important substance on earth." List five points in support of this statement.
2. Explain the part each of the following processes plays in the water cycle.
   (a) evaporation
   (b) condensation
   (c) infiltration
   (d) transpiration
3. Make a diagram showing how you could use a floodlamp, a pan of water, and a tray of ice to demonstrate part of the water cycle.
4. Describe how electricity can be used to take water apart. Include a diagram in your answer.
5. You have a test tube of a gas that you suspect to be oxygen. How can you test the gas, to make sure?
6. Describe a similar test for hydrogen.
7. Write a word equation for the making of water.

8. How many elements are there? What is a compound?
9. Draw a water molecule. Explain why water molecules stick together in clusters.
10. Why is water called "the universal solvent"?
11. Why are the oceans salty?
12. What chemical test gives the best indication of water quality? How does oxygen get into water?
13. What reduces the dissolved oxygen in a lake?
14. What adds carbon dioxide to water? What happens when the carbon dioxide level in a pond gets too high?
15. What causes water to be "hard"? Why is it easier to wash in soft water?
16. How do phosphates get into water? What can they do to a lake?
17. What does the pH reading of a sample of water tell you?
18. How can lakes become acidic? What can this do to fish?
19. Why does the pH reading for a pond usually decrease as the pond gets older?
20. How is it that a steel razor blade can stay on the surface of water? What liquid has the highest surface tension?
21. Why is the surface of the water in a test tube curved?
22. How can you demonstrate the capillary action of water? Include a diagram in your answer.
23. Why is capillary action important for plant growth?
24. What do we mean when we say that water has a great heat capacity? List three places where water is used as a coolant.
25. What happens to the volume of water when it is cooled below 4 °C?
26. What is the temperature of water at the bottom of an ice-covered lake in winter? Explain your answer.
27. What happens to the volume of water when it freezes? Why is this important in nature?
28. Why is heat energy required, for evaporation to occur?
29. What are the qualities of good drinking water?
30. List six steps that are taken to treat water from a lake or river, to make it drinkable.
31. Describe how you could remove salt from a mixture of salt and water.
32. List three uses of distilled water.

33. What percentage of the human body is water? Is the percentage the same for everyone?
34. How could you determine the percentage of water in a worm you find dead after a heavy rain?
35. Why are we using more water today than our ancestors used?
36. List three industrial uses of water.

IMPORTANT TERMS

water cycle—the continuous movement of water – evaporating from the ocean, condensing into clouds, dropping as rain or snow, and flowing in rivers back to the ocean

infiltration—water flowing within the ground to lower levels

transpiration—the process by which plants give off water through their leaves to the air

condensation—the change from a gas to a liquid

evaporation—the change from a liquid to a gas

element—a pure substance that cannot be broken down into simpler substances

compound—a substance made up of two or more elements

molecule—the smallest part of an element or compound that displays all the properties of that element or compound

surface tension—caused by the attraction of water molecules – makes water droplets curve into balls and enables pins to "float"

capillary action—caused by the attraction of water molecules for molecules of other substances – makes water rise in narrow channels

filtration—the process of straining through a fine filter

solute—a dissolved substance

solvent—a liquid that has the power to dissolve a substance, that is, to form a solution of the substance

distillation—a process by which a liquid is changed into vapour, and the vapour then condensed back into a liquid

WEATHER

The weather is always with us. It has an inescapable effect on our lives, often controlling what we eat and wear, where we go, and what we do when we get there. It affects not only our activities and our behaviour but also our mood. According to a study of a group of students, disciplinary action was necessary about five times as often in wet weather as when the sun was shining! The weather also affects our health – for better and for worse.

In this chapter you will learn about the atmosphere, where weather happens, the properties of air, the importance of water vapour in air, what causes rain and snow, how to make and use weather instruments, types of clouds, forecasting the weather, lightning, and how air pollution affects the weather.

The Earth's atmosphere

The atmosphere is a thin blanket of mixed gases that surrounds the Earth. We live at the bottom of this layer of air, and, just as a fish will not survive out of water, we could not survive without the atmosphere. Air is not one gas but many. It is a mixture composed mainly of nitrogen (78%) and oxygen

The weather affects almost all our activities.

MATLOCK COLLEGE LIBRARY

(21%), but also small amounts of argon (0.9%) and carbon dioxide (0.03%) and traces of a few other gases. In addition, the air nearest the Earth contains water vapour and dust particles.

The atmosphere does not get steadily cooler as you rise through it, as you might expect it to do. If you could take a trip in a rocket, you would find that after blast-off the air would become steadily colder until it reached $-60\,°C$ at an altitude of about 12 km. From there to about 25 km above the Earth it would remain the same, but as you ascended farther the air would get warmer, until at an altitude of about 50 km it would be almost back to $0\,°C$. The graph on page 318 shows that, in rising from 50 km to 100 km, you would pass through another drop and rise in temperature.

Scientists have given names to the different temperature layers of the atmosphere. In the *troposphere*, the layer of air nearest the Earth (0-12 km), the temperature drops as you rise. The weight of the air above compresses this layer. As a result, it contains about three-quarters of the total mass of the atmo-

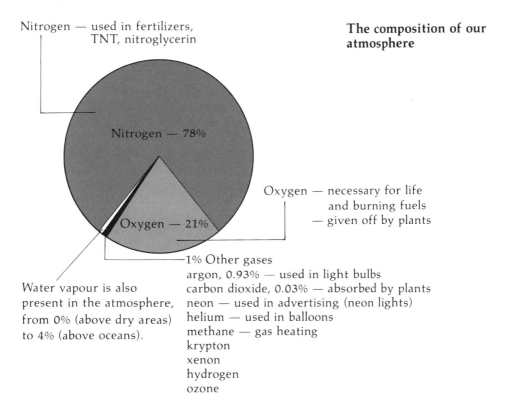

Nitrogen — used in fertilizers, TNT, nitroglycerin

Nitrogen — 78%

The composition of our atmosphere

Oxygen — 21%

Oxygen — necessary for life and burning fuels — given off by plants

Water vapour is also present in the atmosphere, from 0% (above dry areas) to 4% (above oceans).

1% Other gases
argon, 0.93% — used in light bulbs
carbon dioxide, 0.03% — absorbed by plants
neon — used in advertising (neon lights)
helium — used in balloons
methane — gas heating
krypton
xenon
hydrogen
ozone

The hot and cold layers of the Earth's atmosphere

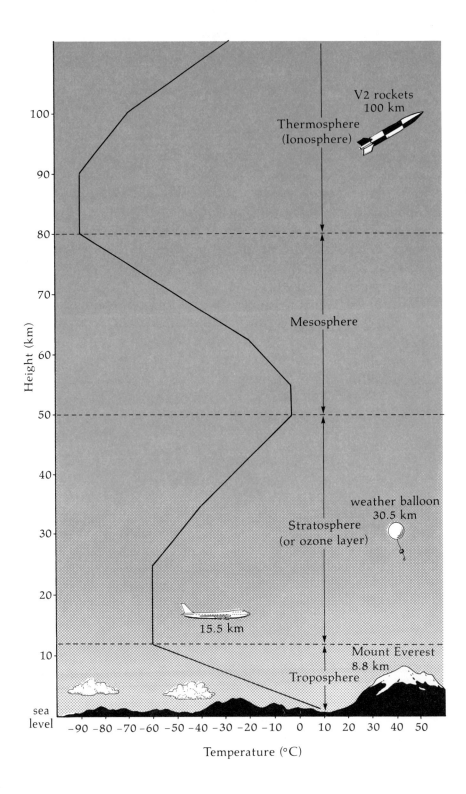

sphere and most of the water vapour and dust. This means that nearly all the clouds are found there. The air there is constantly in motion – up, down, and sideways. Airliners frequently encounter turbulence. The troposphere is a relatively thin layer of gas, extending only slightly higher than Mount Everest. To us it is the most important layer, because we live within it and all of what we call weather takes place there.

In the *stratosphere* (12-50 km), the temperature increases from bottom to top. This temperature rise is caused by the absorption of part of the sun's radiation. Here ultraviolet light is absorbed by oxygen (O_2), which is changed into ozone (O_3). For this reason, the stratosphere is sometimes called the ozone layer. But for this layer, intense ultraviolet light would reach the Earth, and this would be very harmful to us. Water vapour and dust do not penetrate far into this layer, so there are few clouds. Pilots like to fly in this calm, almost weatherless part of the atmosphere where visibility is generally excellent and the thin air offers little resistance.

Above the stratosphere is the *mesosphere* (50-80 km), where the temperature drops to about $-100\,°C$, making it the coldest part of the atmosphere. Still higher is the *thermosphere*, also called the ionosphere (80-700 km). There, temperatures again rise, this time to several hundred degrees. The air is extremely thin, but it manages to absorb the sun's X-rays and ultraviolet rays, which would be lethal to us if they reached the Earth. In the process of being filtered out of the sun's radiation, those rays form a layer of electrically charged particles called ions. This explains why the thermosphere is often called the *ionosphere*. The ionosphere is important in communications because radio waves are reflected by it.

Atmospheric pressure. When you swim under water, the deeper you go, the greater is the pressure of the water on your body. This pressure is caused by the weight of water above you. Similarly, the layers of the atmosphere above us create pressure. We call this pressure atmospheric pressure because it is due to gravity pulling the atmosphere towards the Earth. We are not aware of this enormous pressure because inside our bodies there is an equal pressure pushing outwards. If we rise above the surface of the Earth, we find that the atmospheric

Visibility is clear and flying is smooth in the stratosphere. You are above the weather.

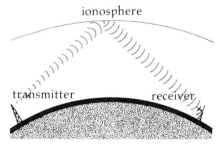

Radio waves are reflected back to Earth off the ionosphere.

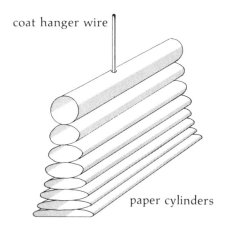

coat hanger wire

paper cylinders

Demonstrating the cause of atmospheric pressure. Make several paper cylinders. Punch holes in them and slide them on a wire. Notice that the bottom layers are under greater pressure.

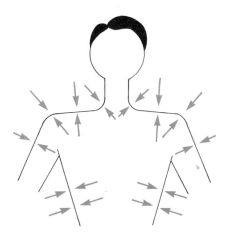

Air presses on us. The pressure inside our bodies just balances the air pressure outside.

pressure decreases. This is only to be expected, since there is now less air above us.

In an airplane flying at a great altitude, the passenger cabin is pressurized to allow the people on board to breathe normally. Athletes at the 1968 Olympic Games in Mexico City, which is 2400 m above sea level, had difficulty getting used to the low pressure at that elevation. Some even collapsed from exhaustion.

It takes more than air to make weather. It also takes the sun. The sun feeds energy into the atmosphere, causing changes in temperature, wind speed, pressure, and humidity. These are the elements of weather which, without the sun, would always be the same. The atmosphere then, is like a machine powered by the sun.

Much of the solar energy which enters our atmosphere never reaches the Earth's surface. Some is absorbed by the atmosphere and some is reflected back into space. The energy that is absorbed causes the atmosphere to heat up. Sunlight that does reach the Earth's surface is absorbed, causing the ground to warm up. The soil radiates this heat back into the atmosphere, but the atmosphere holds the heat, like a blanket. Sometimes the atmosphere is compared with a greenhouse. It lets the light in but won't let the heat out.

Imagine what it would be like to live on the moon. It has no atmosphere, so the days are extremely hot and the nights extremely cold.

The physics of air

The meteorologist must know a great deal about the properties of air if he is to make accurate predictions about the weather. The next few investigations will give you an opportunity to observe some of these properties.

INVESTIGATION: To demonstrate that air occupies space and has mass

MATERIALS

glass
aquarium or pail of water
inflated basketball
air pin
balance

PROCEDURE

1. Crumple a piece of paper and stuff it into the bottom of the glass. Invert the glass and push it straight down into the water. Pull the glass straight out of the water and examine the paper.
2. Measure the mass of the basketball. Let some air out of the ball by pushing in the air pin, and measure the ball's mass again.

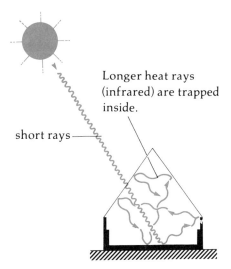

Longer heat rays (infrared) are trapped inside.

short rays

A greenhouse traps sunlight — and so does the Earth's atmosphere.

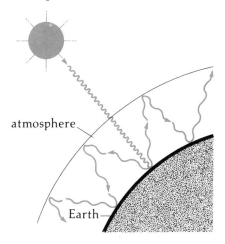

atmosphere

Earth

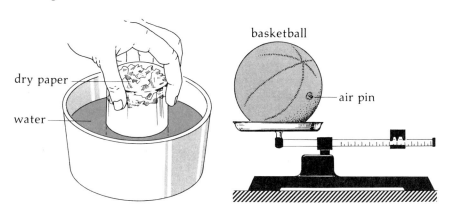

dry paper

water

basketball

air pin

OBSERVATIONS

Record all your observations from steps 1 and 2.

QUESTIONS

1. Does air take up space? Explain how you know.
2. Does air have mass? Explain how you know.
3. What was the mass of the air that escaped from the ball?

INVESTIGATION: To demonstrate what happens to air when it is heated and cooled

---

MATERIALS

balloon
large pop bottle
pail
hot water
ice cubes

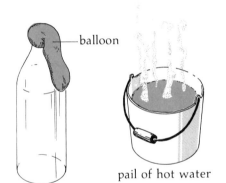

balloon

bottle of air

pail of hot water

ice

PROCEDURE

1. Fit the balloon over the mouth of the empty bottle.
2. Half-fill the pail with hot water, and stand the bottle in it. Observe what happens to the balloon.
3. Remove the bottle from the pail. Dump out the hot water. Half-fill the pail with cold water and add ice cubes. Stand the bottle back in the pail. Observe the balloon.

OBSERVATIONS

Record your observations from Steps 2 and 3.

QUESTIONS

1. What happens to air (a) when it is heated and (b) when it is cooled?
2. A child's balloon bursts when it is taken outside on a sunny day. Why would this happen?
3. A motorist checks the air pressure in his tires before setting off on a trip and again three hours later when he stops for gasoline. What change is he likely to find, and why?

INVESTIGATION: To demonstrate that air exerts pressure

MATERIALS

empty duplicating fluid can and cap
candle (or alcohol burner)
oven mitt
burner stand

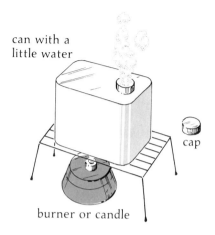

can with a little water

cap

burner or candle

PROCEDURE

1. Rinse the can two or three times with water.
2. Pour about 25 mL of water into the can, leaving it open.
3. Heat the water over the candle until it boils and you see steam coming from the opening.
4. Blow out the candle.
5. Screw the lid tightly on the can and allow the can to cool. Observe what happens to the can as it cools.

OBSERVATIONS

Write a brief description of what you observed in step 5.

QUESTIONS

1. How did the air pressure outside the can compare with the air pressure inside the can (a) when the cap was off and (b) when the cap was on and the can was cooling?
2. Why was steam used in this experiment?
3. Why was it necessary for the cap to be screwed on tightly?

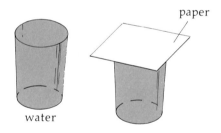

paper

water

ACTIVITY

Try this trick over a sink at home. Fill a glass to the top with water. Place a fresh sheet of paper on top of the glass. With one hand holding the glass and the other firmly pressing on the paper, turn the glass upside down. Pull away the hand that is holding the paper. Air pressure will hold the water in.

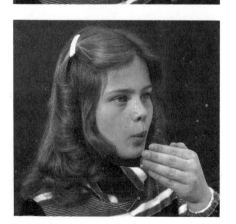

INVESTIGATION: To demonstrate what happens to the temperature of air when it is compressed and when it is allowed to expand

MATERIALS

bicycle pump
basketball
air pin

PROCEDURE

1. Connect the hose of the pump to the ball.
2. Feel the barrel of the pump with your hand. Note its temperature.
3. Pump air into the ball.
4. Again note the temperature of the barrel of the pump.
5. Hold the palm of one hand 5 cm from your face and, with your mouth wide open, breathe air onto it.
6. Repeat step 5, this time forcing air through tight lips.

OBSERVATIONS

Write brief notes on the temperature of the barrel in steps 1 to 4 and the temperature of your breath striking your palm in steps 5 and 6.

QUESTIONS

1. To pump air, you compress it into a smaller space. What happens to the temperature of air when it is compressed?
2. When you blow air through your wide-open mouth, the air does not expand much, but when you blow through tightly pressed lips the air expands considerably as it leaves your mouth. What happens to the temperature of air when it expands? How do you know?

SUMMARY: PROPERTIES OF AIR

1. Air has mass and occupies space.
2. Air expands when heated and contracts when cooled.
3. Air exerts pressure.
4. Air heats up when it is compressed and cools when it expands.

Water in the atmosphere

Our atmosphere consists mainly of nitrogen and oxygen, with traces of other gases, and up to 4% of it may be water vapour (see page 317). Meteorologists regard water vapour as the most important part of it, because it is a trap for the heat given off by the oceans and continents. But for its water vapour, our atmosphere would lose heat to outer space much faster than it does, and the Earth would grow too cold for most forms of life.

How, then, does water get into the atmosphere? This will become clear in the next investigations.

INVESTIGATION: To demonstrate evaporation

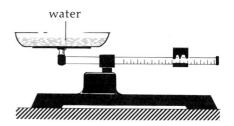
water

MATERIALS

floodlamp
2 identical pans
balance

PROCEDURE

1. Pour about 25 mL of water into each of the pans.
2. Measure the mass of each of the pans.
3. Direct the floodlamp at one of the pans, and turn it on.
4. Leave the pans for 24 h, and then measure their masses again.

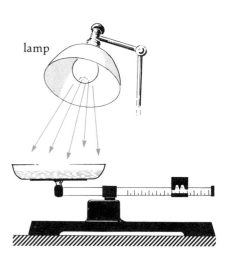
lamp

OBSERVATIONS

Record your measurements in a table like this one.

	WITH LAMP	WITHOUT LAMP
Mass of pans and water at start		
Mass of pans and water after 24 h		
Difference		

1. Which pan lost the most water by evaporation, and where did the water go?
2. Would you expect evaporation from the oceans to be more rapid near the equator or near the poles? Explain your answer.
3. What effect does wind have on the rate of evaporation of water from the surface of the ocean?

INVESTIGATION: To demonstrate evaporation from soil

MATERIALS

balance
pan of moist soil
floodlamp

PROCEDURE

1. Measure the mass of the pan of moist soil.
2. Leave the pan uncovered in the classroom for 24 h, with the floodlamp directed at it.
3. Measure the mass of the pan again.

OBSERVATIONS

Record your measurements.

QUESTIONS

1. Why do the measurements differ?
2. Where did the moisture go?

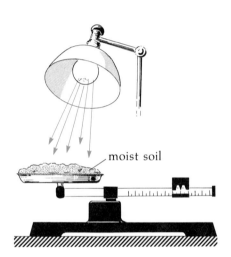

moist soil

INVESTIGATION: To demonstrate that plants emit water vapour into the atmosphere

---

MATERIALS

potted geranium
stick
clear plastic bag
string

PROCEDURE

1. Push the stick into the soil so it stands higher than the plant.
2. Cover the plant with the clear plastic bag and tie the bag with string around the base of the stem.
3. Place the plant in the sun or by a window and leave it there for a few hours.

OBSERVATIONS

Keep notes on what you observe on the inside surface of the plastic bag.

QUESTIONS

1. Write a paragraph summarizing what you conclude from this experiment.
2. Why is it often misty in forests and jungles?

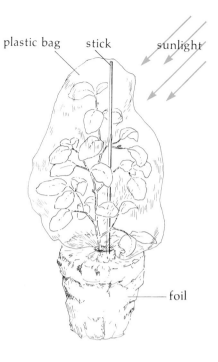

plastic bag   stick   sunlight

foil

INVESTIGATION: To demonstrate that burning produces water vapour

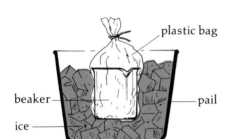

beaker

ice

plastic bag

pail

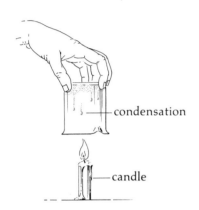

condensation

candle

MATERIALS

candle
beaker
ice
small plastic bag
pail

PROCEDURE

1. Dry the beaker and seal it in the plastic bag.
2. Chill the beaker by placing it in a pail of ice for several minutes.
3. Remove the beaker from the bag, and dry it again (make sure it is dry).
4. Hold the chilled beaker upside down over a candle flame. Observe the inner surface of the beaker.

OBSERVATIONS

Record what you saw in step 4.

QUESTIONS

1. Does burning produce water vapour? Explain how you know.
2. List five things we burn that add a great deal of moisture to the atmosphere.

SUMMARY: WATER IN THE ATMOSPHERE

In the last four investigations, you saw that water vapour is added to the atmosphere in four ways:

1. by evaporation from oceans, lakes, and rivers
2. by evaporation from soil
3. through the leaves of plants
4. by the burning of materials

Note that the sun plays a part in each of these processes.

Characteristics of precipitation

The processes that add water vapour to the atmosphere are hard to observe. But the process that brings water vapour back out of the air is well known to everyone. Meteorologists call it precipitation, and it is the process that turns water vapour into rain, dew, frost, and snow.

INVESTIGATION: To demonstrate how dew and frost
are produced

MATERIALS

empty soup can
ice cubes
salt
spoon

PROCEDURE

1. Half-fill the can with ice cubes and add a little water.
2. Let the can sit for several minutes and then examine the outside of it.
3. Add three or four small spoonfuls of salt to the ice-and-water mixture. Then stir the mixture.
4. Let the mixture sit for several minutes, then examine the outside again.

OBSERVATIONS

Record what appeared on the outside of the can in step 2 and step 4.

QUESTIONS

1. Explain why dew sometimes forms on the inside of a house window.
2. In what circumstances does frost form on the inside of a window?

In the last investigation, you saw how dew can form on a cool surface. The temperature to which moist air must be cooled for condensation to occur is called the dew point. You can measure the dew point by slowly cooling a container of water until dew just begins to form on the outside. Then take the temperature of the water. It is the dew point of the air. The dew point changes from day to day. It depends on how much water vapour there is in the air at the moment when the measurement is taken.

INVESTIGATION: To measure the dew point

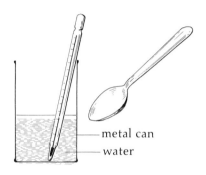

metal can
water

ice

MATERIALS
empty soup can (label removed)
ice
thermometer
spoon

PROCEDURE
1. Half-fill the can with warm tap water.
2. Take the temperature of the water.
3. Spoon in a little ice and stir until it has all melted.
4. Continue to add more ice slowly and to stir until you see the first sign of dew forming on the outside of the can.
5. Take the temperature of the water when dew first begins to form. It is the dew point.

OBSERVATIONS
Record your observations from step 2 and step 5.

QUESTIONS
1. What is the dew point of the air in your classroom?
2. Compare your result with those of your classmates.
3. Why does dew often form on the grass at night?

What causes fog? If you have ever seen a layer of fog hovering over a pond, it was probably in the morning, after a cool night and before the sun had warmed things up. The water in the pond was still warm because bodies of water hold their heat for quite a time. Warm water vapour had risen from the pond but when it met the cold layer of air it cooled to below the dew point. Millions of tiny water droplets formed in the air as the water vapour condensed into a liquid. These droplets formed the fog you saw.

INVESTIGATION: To make fog in a bottle

MATERIALS

clean empty bottle
ice cube
electric kettle
filmstrip projector

PROCEDURE

1. Boil some water in the kettle. Make sure the ice cube is big enough to cover the mouth of the bottle. If necessary, use masking tape to make the opening smaller.
2. Slowly (so the bottle won't crack) pour the hot water into the bottle to a depth of 3 or 4 cm.
3. Quickly put the ice cube over the mouth of the bottle.
4. Place the bottle in the beam of the filmstrip projector.

OBSERVATIONS

Record what you observed in the bottle, in step 4.

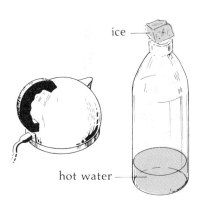

QUESTIONS

1. Explain what happened inside the bottle, mentioning the roles of the hot water and the ice.
2. Find out the difference between fog and smog.

How are clouds formed? As warm air containing water vapour rises above the Earth, it expands, or spreads out, because of the reduced pressure. When air expands, it gets colder (see page 325). If the water vapour in the air is cooled below the dew point, it condenses into tiny water droplets which form a cloud. Dust particles in the air provide the vapour with surfaces on which it readily condenses. When you are flying through a cloud in an airplane, it is like going through fog.

The shapes of clouds depend on how the clouds are formed. If the cooling air is rising, the clouds it forms will be large and puffy, like cotton. These are called cumulus (meaning "heap") clouds. Cumulus clouds are flat on the underside. They are usually associated with fair weather, but on a hot summer afternoon they may grow large and dark, and produce a storm

The three main types of clouds

cirrus (6-18 km)

cumulus (1-14 km)

stratus (below 2.5 km)

with thunder and lightning. If the cooling air is moving rapidly and almost horizontally, the clouds it forms will be stretched out and will have thin curls, like feathers. These are cirrus (meaning "curl") clouds. They are the highest clouds in the sky, and they usually consist of tiny crystals of ice.

The lowest clouds in the sky are called stratus (meaning "layer") clouds. They often cover the whole sky, keeping out the sunlight. Stratus clouds usually bring rain or snow.

INVESTIGATION: To make a cloud in a bottle

MATERIALS

large, clean glass bottle with a small mouth
match

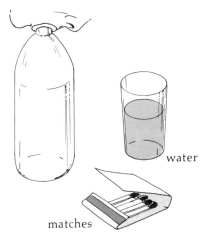
water
matches

PROCEDURE

1. Pour a cup of water into the bottle, swish it around, and pour it out.
2. Blow hard into the bottle while sealing its mouth tightly with your lips.
3. Release the pressure suddenly by removing your lips, and observe the inside of the bottle.
4. Repeat step 1. Then force a little smoke into the bottle by blowing out a match while holding the flame near the mouth of the bottle.
5. Repeat steps 2 and 3, and observe the inside of the bottle.

OBSERVATIONS

Write notes on what you saw in the bottle in steps 3 and 5.

QUESTIONS

1. Three things are necessary for clouds to form: moisture, cooling, and dust particles. Explain how you were able to create these conditions in the bottle.
2. What was the purpose of blowing into the bottle and then suddenly releasing the pressure?
3. Why are dust particles necessary, for clouds to form?
4. Name and briefly describe the three types of clouds.
5. Read the poem on the next page.

The Sky
Today
The sky is very far away,
So blue
It is; and, soft as squirrel's tails,
Float over it, like little sails,
Small clouds.

M. Bardwell

What type of cloud do you think the poet sees?

Rain. A raindrop forms within a cloud when a number of tiny water droplets join together, forming a drop that is so heavy that it falls out of the cloud. Rain is not new water, but water that was added to the atmosphere in the four ways you read about on page 328. The same water falls as rain over and over again in what is called the water cycle.

The water cycle

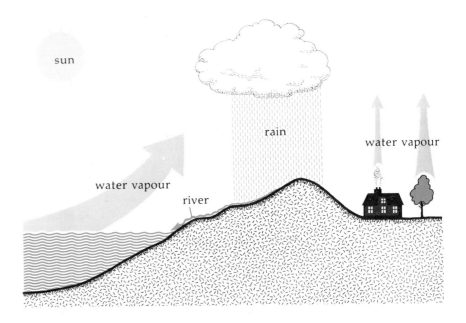

MATERIALS

hot plate or alcohol burner and stand
pyrex glass baking dish
pie plate
ice cubes

PROCEDURE

1. Heat some water in the baking dish until it almost boils. Observe the surface of the water.
2. Put ice cubes in the pie plate and hold the plate over the hot water. Observe the underside of the plate.

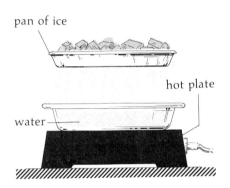

pan of ice

hot plate

water

OBSERVATIONS

Write notes on what you saw rising from the water and falling from the plate.

QUESTIONS

1. In a natural water cycle, what takes the place of (a) the hot plate, (b) the pan of ice, and (c) the dish of water?
2. Vancouver gets more rain than Winnipeg. Suggest why.
3. Look up "cloud seeding" in the library, and write an explanation of it. Why might some people consider this stealing?

Measuring atmospheric conditions

Before meteorology was developed as a science, weather was often the subject of superstitions. For example, it was believed by many people in England that a person who carried a stinging nettle was protected from lightning and that a whole house was protected if it contained a piece of mistletoe. Primitive tribes held ceremonial dances and made offerings to the gods, hoping to obtain rain.

As time went on, people relied less on superstition and began to develop rules of thumb, such as, "Red sky in the morning, sailors take warning; red sky at night, sailors' delight." Such

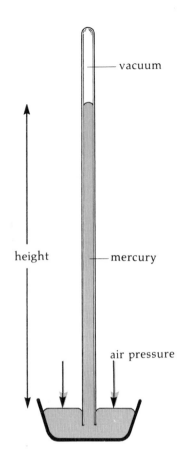

A mercury barometer

sayings were based on repeated observations by ordinary people. Though they were little more than folklore, they often worked well. Then it was realized that instruments would have to be developed to permit more precise measurements than could be made with the senses alone.

Today, weather observers throughout the world daily measure and exchange information about air pressure, air temperature, cloud cover, humidity, wind speed and direction, visibility, and precipitation (rain or snow). You will learn next about some weather instruments and how they work.

Measuring atmospheric pressure. The weight of the layers of air above us causes pressure in the air (see page 319). Instruments that measure the pressure of the atmosphere are called barometers. There are two types of barometers – mercury barometers and aneroid barometers.

The *mercury barometer* is the type used by most weather stations. It was invented in Italy in 1644. It consists of a glass tube a little less than a metre long filled with mercury and inverted into a dish of mercury. The mercury is held up in the tube by the pressure of the air outside. The greater the air pressure, the higher the mercury rises in the tube. The length of the column of mercury, then, is a measure of the air pressure. A scale beside the tube is marked off in kilopascals (kPa), which is the SI unit of pressure. Normal atmospheric pressure is about 101.3 kPa, but it is not uncommon to have pressure readings as low as 98.0 kPa or as high as 103.0 kPa.

The *aneroid barometer* is not as accurate as the mercury barometer, but it is more widely used because it is less expensive and more easily portable. You may have one at home. The aneroid (meaning "no fluid") barometer is a thin metal box from which the air has been removed. The corrugated shape of the box allows it to spring in and out with changes in the air pressure outside. Higher air pressure pushes the top of the box in, lower air pressure allows it to spring out again. Gears and levers magnify the pressure changes and transmit them to a pointer on a scale.

INVESTIGATION: To show how a barometer can help
predict the weather

MATERIALS
aneroid barometer

PROCEDURE
1. Prepare a table like the one shown under Observations.
2. Read the barometer and record the pressure reading morning and afternoon each day for 5 d. Note the sky condition at the same times.
3. Analyse your results.

OBSERVATIONS

	Monday		Tuesday		Wednesday		Thursday		Friday	
	a.m.	p.m.	a.m.	p.m.	a.m.	p.m.	a.m.	p.m.	a.m.	p.m.
Pressure (kPa)										
Sky										

An aneroid barometer with the cover removed

QUESTIONS
1. When the barometer falls substantially, this usually means that clouds are approaching, and that there may be precipitation. Comment on this statement, referring to your table.
2. An increase in pressure usually means that fair weather is approaching. Comment on this statement, referring to your table.
3. Do barometers give the same readings inside a building as outside? Explain your answer.

INVESTIGATION: To make a simple barometer

MATERIALS

balloon	scissors
drinking straw	elastic band
jar	cardboard
tape	

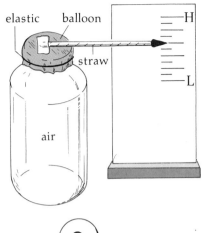

elastic balloon

straw

air

H

L

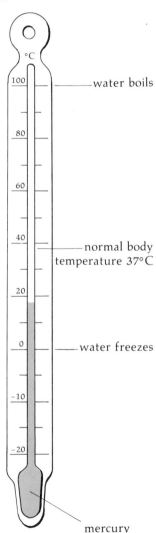

°C

100 — water boils

80

60

40 — normal body
temperature 37°C

20

0 — water freezes

-10

-20

mercury

PROCEDURE

1. Cut a circle of rubber from the balloon that is large enough to cover the mouth of the jar.
2. Stretch the rubber tightly over the mouth and secure it with the elastic.
3. Fasten one end of the straw with tape to the centre of the rubber seal, as illustrated. The other end of the straw will serve as a pointer.
4. Make a scale out of cardboard and mount it behind the pointer.
5. Take pressure readings daily for five days with your barometer and with an aneroid barometer.

OBSERVATIONS

Record your readings from step 5 in a suitable table.

QUESTIONS

1. Why would your barometer give a higher reading if it were placed in the sun?
2. What is the advantage of an aneroid barometer over the one you made?

Measuring air temperature. The most common type of thermometer for measuring air temperatures is the liquid type, using mercury or alcohol. Mercury cannot be used in extreme cold because it freezes at −39°C. Alcohol stays liquid down to −114°C. Red dye is usually added to the alcohol to make it easy to see. A liquid reservoir (thermometer bulb) is located at the bottom end of the scale. The glass is thinnest there, so that the thermometer will react quickly to small changes in temperature. For meteorological purposes, temperatures are read in the shade, so thermometers are kept in ventilated shelters that are painted white to reflect the sun's radiation.

The modern meteorologist uses an electric thermograph, which automatically reads the temperature and records it on a rotating drum. This provides a continuous graph of the temperature changes.

A thermograph

A thermometer shelter (open and closed)

A *maximum-minimum thermometer* is used to measure the lowest and highest temperatures reached during the day. It uses a combination of alcohol and mercury, as illustrated. As the alcohol in bulb A increases in temperature it expands, forcing the "index" at B to move down and the mercury (from B to C) to move up on the right side. The index at C is tight enough in the tube that it will remain at the highest level it reached, when the alcohol (from B to A) contracts. The index at B then remains at the level it reached, registering the minimum temperature. The indexes at B and C are small metal cylinders that float on top of the mercury. The thermometer is reset each day by using a magnet to pull the cylinders down until they are again floating on the mercury.

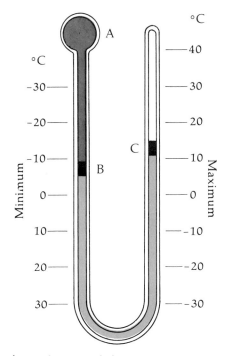

A maximum-minimum thermometer

INVESTIGATION: To measure high and low temperatures

MATERIALS

maximum-minimum thermometer
magnet

PROCEDURE

1. Put the thermometer in a safe, shady place outside the school. It must be a place that will remain shady all day.

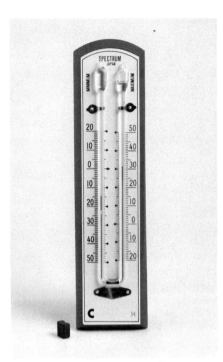

A maximum-minimum thermo-meter with magnet

2. Use the magnet to set the indexes on the mercury surfaces.
3. At the same time each morning, for a month, read the maximum and minimum temperatures that were reached in the last 24 h, and reset the indexes.

OBSERVATIONS

1. Record your results in a table like this one.

DATE	MINIMUM (°C)	MAXIMUM (°C)
Oct. 3	6	12
Oct. 4	7	14
Oct. 5	8	15
Oct. 6	5	11

2. Draw graphs of the maximum and minimum temperatures for the month.

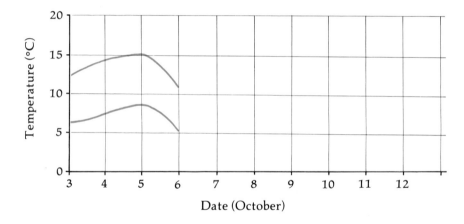

Measuring the direction and speed of the wind. The device used to determine wind direction is the wind vane, which rotates freely in such a way that an arrow always points in the direction from which the wind is coming. Directly below the pivot point of the arrow is a disc marked with the points of the compass. Wind vanes are mounted outdoors, usually near the centre of a large open space.

MATERIALS

plastic drinking straw
(milkshake size is best)
pencil with eraser
plasticine
straight pin

bristol board
protractor
plastic food container
stapler

PROCEDURE

1. Examine the illustration. Begin by cutting the tail of the arrow from bristol board; staple two thicknesses together. Flatten one end of the straw and staple the tail to it. Push enough plasticine into the opposite end of the straw to make the arrow balance in the middle.
2. Push the pin through the balance point of the straw and into the eraser.
3. Use the protractor to make the eight compass markings shown on the bottom of the container.

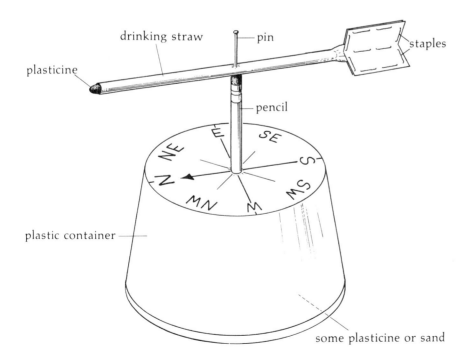

4. Cut a hole at the centre of the bottom of the container and push the pencil through. Punch a small hole at the centre of the lid of the container, to receive the point of the pencil.

5. Put some sand or plasticine in the container, so that it will provide a steady base.

INVESTIGATION: To study wind direction with your wind vane

MATERIALS

magnetic compass   wind vane

PROCEDURE

1. Choose an open spot outdoors for your wind vane. It should be at least a metre above ground and away from trees or buildings.

2. Use the compass to locate north.

3. Read the wind direction at the same time each morning and afternoon for a month.

OBSERVATIONS

1. Enter your data in a table like this one.

DATE	WIND DIRECTION a.m.	WIND DIRECTION p.m.
Feb. 1	NW	NW
Feb. 2	W	NW
Feb. 3	W	SW
Feb. 4	S	SE
Feb. 5	E	E
Feb. 6	SE	S
Feb. 7	SW	W

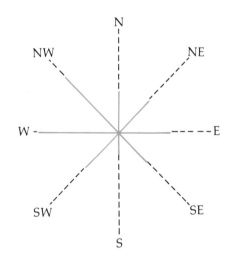

A wind rose shows the predominant wind directions over several days or a month. In this case the wind blew most often from the west. From what direction did it blow least often?

2. Observations of wind direction made over a month are often displayed on a special graph called a wind rose. A wind rose shows the percentage of the total time that the wind blew from each direction. Use your data to make a wind rose, as illustrated. From a central point, draw light guide lines representing the eight principal compass points. Record your 60 readings by adding a 0.5 cm solid line for each reading in the appropriate direction.

Every measurement is subject to possible error. Suggest some reasons why your observations of wind direction are likely to be inaccurate.

Wind speeds, usually expressed in kilometres per hour (km/h) are measured with an *anemometer*. This instrument consists of a wheel of four hollow cups fixed at the ends of two crossed rods. The wind causes the wheel of cups to rotate on an axle. The stronger the wind, the faster the wheel turns.

An anemometer and wind vane

You can make an anemometer by slicing two ping-pong balls in half and mounting them on soda drinking straws, as illustrated. Staple the straws together where they cross. Use a straight pin and a pencil with an eraser as an axle and handle.

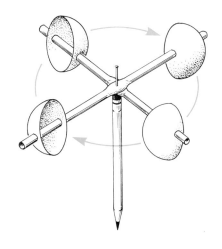

MATERIALS

commercial anemometer

PROCEDURE

1. Find an open place outdoors, away from trees and buildings.
2. Hold the anemometer at arm's length. Be careful not to shield it from the wind with your body.
3. Measure the wind speed at the same times each morning and afternoon for at least 5 d.

OBSERVATIONS

1. Enter your wind-speed measurements in a table like this one.

DATE	WIND SPEED (km/h) a.m.	WIND SPEED (km/h) p.m.	AVERAGE WIND SPEED (km/h)
Nov. 3			
Nov. 4			
Nov. 5			
Nov. 6			
Nov. 7			

2. Plot a graph showing how average wind speed changed during the period you studied.

QUESTIONS

1. How could you use a car on a calm day to check whether an anemometer reads wind speeds accurately?
2. Describe three uses of wind energy.

Measuring relative humidity

You have seen that air contains water vapour. When it contains more vapour than we are accustomed to, we say that it is humid. When it is very humid our clothes feel damp and we notice perspiration on our skin. Wet clothes take a long time to dry when hung outside in humid weather and wallpaper has been known to peel itself off walls.

When air is very dry, which is often the case inside buildings during cold winters, other undesirable things happen. Furniture dries up and warps and its joints get loose, floors squeak, carpets and clothing generate static electricity, and our noses and throats become dry. Also, because our skin moisture evaporates faster in dry air, we have to set the thermostat higher to feel comfortable.

There is a solution for each of these problems. To lower the humidity in summer time, a dehumidifier may be used. You can actually see the moisture dripping into a catch bucket. To add water vapour to the air in wintertime, a humidifier is installed in many furnaces. In electrically heated homes, it is usually necessary to use a room humidifier. Both types of humidifier should add several litres of water every day to the air in your house.

The amount of moisture in the air is expressed as a percentage of the amount of moisture the air is capable of holding. This percentage is called the relative humidity. When it is raining the relative humidity is 100% since the air is saturated and

Relative Humidity Table

DRY BULB TEMPERATURE (°C)	TEMPERATURE DIFFERENCE between dry and wet bulb (°C)																
	2	2.5	3	3.5	4	4.5	5	5.5	6	6.5	7	7.5	8	8.5	9	9.5	10
30	83	80	76	73	70	67	64	61	58	56	53	51	49	47	45	43	41
28	83	80	75	72	69	66	63	60	57	55	52	50	48	46	44	42	40
26	82	79	75	71	68	65	62	59	56	54	51	49	47	45	43	41	39
24	82	78	74	70	67	63	60	58	55	52	50	47	45	43	41	39	38
22	81	78	73	69	66	62	59	56	53	51	48	46	44	42	40	38	36
20	80	77	72	68	64	61	58	55	52	49	47	44	42	40	38	36	34
18	79	76	70	67	63	59	56	53	50	47	45	42	40	38	36	34	32
16	78	74	69	65	61	58	54	51	48	45	43	40	38	36	34	32	30
14	77	73	68	63	59	56	52	49	46	43	40	38	36	34	32	30	28
12	76	72	66	61	57	54	50	47	43	41	38	35	33	31	29	27	26
10	74	70	64	59	55	51	47	44	41	38	35	32	30	28	26	24	23
8	73	68	62	57	52	48	44	41	37	34	32	29	27	25	23	21	19
6	71	66	59	54	49	45	41	37	34	31	28	25	23	21	19	17	15
4	69	63	56	51	46	41	37	33	30	26	24	21	19	16	14	13	11
2	66	61	53	47	42	37	33	29	25	22	19	16	14	11	10	8	6
0	63	57	49	43	37	32	28	23	20	16	13	10	8	6	4	2	1

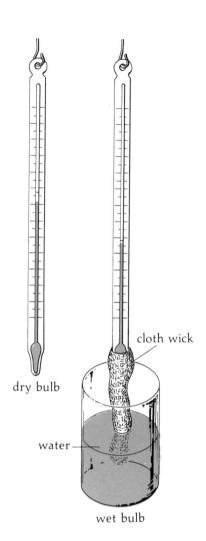

dry bulb

cloth wick

water

wet bulb

cannot hold any more vapour. In a desert, on the other hand, the relative humidity may be as low as 3%. A relative humidity of 50% to 60% is considered ideal for good health.

One instrument that is used to measure relative humidity is the wet and dry bulb hygrometer. It consists of two thermometers, one of which has a dry bulb and the other a bulb that is kept wet with a damp cloth. Evaporation of moisture cools the wet bulb, and the dryer the air is, the cooler the wet bulb becomes. The difference between the readings on the two thermometers will indicate the degree of humidity of the air. When the temperatures have been taken, a table of relative humidities for various wet and dry bulb readings is consulted to obtain the relative humidity (see table).

INVESTIGATION: To determine whether the relative humidity inside the classroom is the same as that outside

MATERIALS

2 thermometers
cotton batting
pill bottle
thread
ring stand

PROCEDURE

1. Suspend the thermometers by string or tape from the ring stand.
2. Use thread to attach a piece of cotton about 10 cm long to the bulb of one of the thermometers. Arrange a pill bottle of water under this thermometer so that the cotton dangles in the water.
3. When the cotton is soaked and has carried water up to the bulb, fan it several times with a sheet of paper.
4. When the level on the wet bulb thermometer appears to be steady, read its temperature. At the same time, read the temperature of the other thermometer.
5. Repeat steps 1 to 4 out of doors.

Enter your results in a table like this one.

	DRY BULB	WET BULB	DIFFERENCE
In the classroom			
Outdoors			

QUESTIONS

1. Using the relative humidity table and your temperature readings, determine the relative humidity inside and outside the school.
2. If the relative humidity in a house is too low, what can you do to increase it?
3. How can you decrease the relative humidity in a house if it is too high?

Forecasting the weather

The first weather measurements in Canada with instruments were made in the late 1700s. It was not until 1839 that the first permanent weather station was established – in Toronto by an army lieutenant. Five years after Confederation, the Meteorological Service of Canada was established. Today, there are more than 1600 weather-observing stations across Canada and they all feed information to the Atmospheric Environment Service Headquarters in Toronto. This centre also receives weather information that is beamed from weather satellites

A satellite antenna at the Atmospheric Environment Service Headquarters, Toronto

and information provided by the U.S. Weather Bureau. All this data is processed by computers and interpreted by meteorologists, who forecast what our weather will be in the immediate future.

Weather satellites orbit the Earth at altitudes of 700-1200 km. They have huge wings on either side that convert solar energy into electric energy. This energy powers television cameras and other equipment on board. Thus, areas of the Earth that have no organized weather service are surveyed, and storms are tracked around the globe.

ACTIVITY

You can be an amateur meteorologist and make your own forecasts. All you need is a reliable barometer, a wind vane, and some experience using weather signs. These are simple rules of thumb that will enable you to make reasonably accurate predictions:

1. *Expect rain or snow when:*
   - the barometer is falling steadily
   - cirrus clouds thicken and are followed by lower stratus clouds
   - a ring is visible around the moon

AES/SDL VISSR VIS 13/03/79 1500Z 40.0N 076.0W 4A S9 ONT-QUE

A weather satellite photograph

– dark clouds are visible in the western sky
– the wind shifts from north to west to south
– southerly winds increase and clouds come from the west

2. *Expect fair weather when:*
   – the barometer is rising or steady
   – there are gentle west or northwest breezes
   – morning fog rises, or "burns off"
   – afternoon cumulus clouds dot the sky
   – the wind shifts from east to west
   – low clouds "lift", or move higher

3. *Expect temperatures to rise or remain the same when:*
   – the wind is from the south
   – there is cloud cover at night
   – the sky is clear in the morning

4. *Expect falling temperatures when:*
   – the wind is from the north
   – there is clear sky at sunset

INVESTIGATION: To observe and forecast the weather

MATERIALS

barometer
wind vane
thermometer

PROCEDURE

1. Measure and record the atmospheric pressure, the temperature, and the wind direction at the same times each morning and afternoon for a week. Also note and record the condition of the sky (type of cloud and amount).
2. On the basis of your observations, and referring to the list of weather signs, make a forecast each day of the weather for the next 24 h.

DATE	PRESSURE	TEMPERATURE	WIND DIRECTION	TYPE AND AMOUNT OF CLOUD	FORECAST

QUESTIONS

1. Would you expect your forecasts to improve with time? Why?
2. Make a collection of sayings about the weather.
3. Discuss why some of these sayings might well be scientifically sound.
4. Is it easier to make a long-range forecast or a short-range forecast? Explain your answer.
5. With all the data that is available to meteorologists, why are their forecasts often wrong?

Lightning

In 1750, Benjamin Franklin flew a kite with a metal key on the end of the string close to his hand, to prove that lightning is caused by static electricity. An electrical spark jumped from the key to his knuckle. A very dangerous experiment indeed!

Scientists now believe that the static electricity that causes lightning originates from rising air currents within thunderclouds. Water droplets in the clouds get torn apart by these updrafts. In the process, lighter droplets of water with a positive electric charge rise high in the cloud and heavier droplets with negative charges remain at lower levels. The result is that thunderclouds are usually positively charged at the top and negatively charged at the bottom. As the charge within a cloud builds up, a positive charge is induced on the ground below the cloud. When the charges are strong enough, an electrical path, or leader, forms within the cloud. Then in less than a second there is a sudden surge of negative charge, which we call lightning.

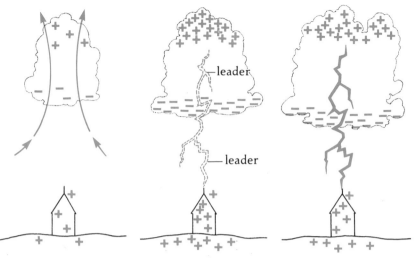

Stage 1 — updraft   Stage 2 — buildup of   Stage 3 — lightning
                        electric charge

Photographs of lightning show that each electrical discharge is made up of many strokes, each lasting less than a thousandth of a second. The discharge may occur within a cloud, or it may move from a cloud to Earth or from Earth to a cloud. In any case, air along the path of the lightning is quickly heated to about 15 000 °C. This causes the air to expand rapidly, with the noise and force of an explosion. We call the noise thunder.

Lightning tends to strike the highest objects, such as towers. To protect yourself in a thunderstorm, stay away from wide open spaces. For example, it is dangerous to go swimming or boating. Don't take shelter under an isolated tree, but you will be safe in the woods. You will be safe, too, inside a car, since the metal body acts as a shield. Large buildings have metal beams that shield the occupants in the same way.

INVESTIGATION: To make a flash similar to lightning with static electricity (This experiment works best on a dry day.)

MATERIALS

long-playing record   balloon
wool scarf, or sock   paper bag
aluminum foil

PROCEDURE

1. Crumple some paper into a ball and wrap it in aluminum foil. This represents the Earth.
2. Charge the record negatively by rubbing it with a piece of wool. This is your cloud.
3. Hold up the charged "cloud" in one hand, and hold the "earth" below it in the other hand. Let the two come closer until you hear a cracking sound.
4. To show that lightning tends to strike the highest point, unwrap the "earth" slightly so that a corner of the foil sticks out. Repeat steps 2 and 3, and note carefully what happens.
5. To find out whether expanding air causes thunder, stick a pin in an inflated balloon, or pop a bag of air.

OBSERVATIONS

Record what happened in steps 3, 4 and 5.

QUESTIONS

1. Why is a farmer in danger if he insists on ploughing his field when an electrical storm is near?
2. Is much electric energy released in a thunderstorm? Discuss.
3. What causes thunder?

The effect of air pollution

Every day thousands of tons of gases and dust particles are being added to the atmosphere. The result is that the air is being polluted at an increasing rate.

The sources of air pollution are both natural and man-made:

Some natural sources of air pollution
- sand blown from fields and deserts
- volcanoes erupting gases and solid dust particles
- salt particles from oceans blown high by the wind
- forest fires creating gases and ash particles
- plants giving off spores and pollen grains
- dust from outer space pulled into our atmosphere by gravity
- ozone and oxides of nitrogen created by lightning

Air pollution over the city of
Toronto

Some man-made sources of air pollution
- exhaust fumes from cars and trucks
- home-heating furnaces
- incinerators that burn garbage
- furnaces of industry
- power plants that burn coal, gas, or oil
- atom and hydrogen bomb tests

Natural air pollution is as old as the Earth itself, but man-made pollution has become a major problem only in this century. To understand how this has happened, we have only to look at the increasing numbers of motorized vehicles. In the last 25 years the number of cars, trucks, and buses in North America alone has increased from 50 million to well over 100 million. The pollutants produced when an average car burns 1 L of gasoline while travelling at 40 km/h are:

Air pollution from 1 L of gasoline

carbon monoxide	284.9 g
nitrogen oxide	22.2 g
hydrocarbons	15.8 g
solid particles	1.3 g
sulphur oxides	1.0 g

How many litres of gasoline does your family use in a week?

In earlier centuries, man added only slightly to the natural pollution of the atmosphere. Today, one very large industrial country may add more than 150 000 000 t of gases, smoke, and dust to the atmosphere each year. One common pollutant, sulphur dioxide from the burning of coal and oil, produces irritation of our eyes and throat. Each year more than 30 000 000 t of sulphur dioxide are released into the air over North America.

Air pollution reduces visibility and cuts down the amount of sunlight reaching the Earth. The heavily polluted air hovering over a city acts like a blanket, resulting in higher temperatures there than in rural surroundings.

Temperature Inversion

Air pollution becomes more serious when weather conditions are such that polluted air cannot be blown away. This occurs when there is a layer of cold air near the ground and warmer air above it. This condition is called a "temperature inversion".

In the London "smog" of 1952, more than 4000 people died in the combination of smoke and fog that was trapped in the city. Los Angeles, located in a valley and with one of the highest concentrations of automobiles, is also prone to smog.

To combat air pollution, governments have made regulations and are constantly monitoring pollution levels. The large automobile manufacturers have been required to reduce emis-

A temperature inversion

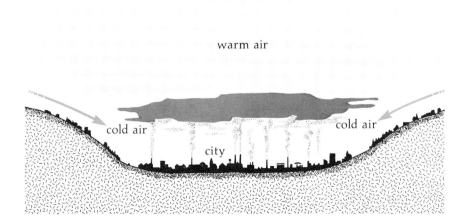

warm air

cold air

cold air

city

sions to prescribed levels by specific dates. Smoke stacks are being made higher and some are equipped with "scrubbers" to remove pollutants from the smoke before it is released. Industries are being told to switch to "cleaner" fuels, when their pollution levels are too high. There is still much more that needs to be done to preserve our atmosphere. We can't survive without it.

REVIEW QUESTIONS

1. How does the weather affect (a) our daily lives, (b) our behaviour, and (c) our health?
2. Explain what air consists of.
3. (a) Name the four layers of the Earth's atmosphere.
   (b) How did scientists establish the existence of these layers?
   (c) Which layer is the hottest?
4. Why do pilots prefer to fly in the stratosphere?
5. (a) What is another name for the thermosphere?
   (b) In what way does this layer protect us?
6. How does the ozone layer help us?
7. Explain how the ionosphere helps radio broadcasting.
8. What causes atmospheric pressure?
9. What is the normal pressure of the atmosphere at sea level?
10. What happens to the pressure as you ascend through the higher levels of the atmosphere? Explain your answer.
11. How is our atmosphere like a greenhouse?
12. Why do meteorologists regard water vapour as the most important part of our atmosphere?
13. Describe four sources of the water vapour in the atmosphere.
14. Name two forms of precipitation.
15. What is meant by "dew point"?
16. Name and make sketches of three types of clouds.
17. Describe the rain cycle.
18. What instruments are used to measure (a) atmospheric pressure, (b) temperature, (c) wind direction, (d) wind speed, and (e) relative humidity?
19. How would the reading on a barometer at ground level compare with the reading on the same barometer at the top of the CN Tower? What would happen to the reading

on a barometer if you took it up in an airplane?

20. What is a maximum-minimum thermometer used for?
21. (a) What are weather signs?
    (b) Describe two signs that indicate coming rain or snow.
    (c) Describe two signs that the weather will probably improve.
22. What causes lightning?
23. Describe three lightning safety rules.
24. When did air pollution start to be a problem?
25. Name three natural and three man-made sources of pollution.
26. What are the three major pollutants that come from automobiles?
27. How does air pollution affect human health?
28. What does air pollution do to the weather?
29. List five steps that could be taken to reduce air pollution.

IMPORTANT TERMS

troposphere—the layer of air nearest the Earth (0-12 km)

stratosphere—the layer of air from 12-50 km above the Earth's surface

mesosphere—the layer of air from 50-80 km above the Earth's surface – the coldest part of the atmosphere

thermosphere (ionosphere)—the layer of air from 80-700 km above the Earth's surface

atmospheric pressure—the pressure of the air caused by gravity

meteorologist—a person trained to make observations and predictions concerning the weather

precipitation—the process that changes water vapour into rain or snow

dew point—the temperature to which moist air must be cooled before condensation takes place

barometer—an instrument used to measure atmospheric pressure

maximum-minimum thermometer—an instrument used to measure the highest and lowest temperatures reached during a day or night

wind vane—an instrument used to measure wind speed direction

anemometer—an instrument used to measure wind speed

relative humidity—the amount of moisture in the air expressed as a percentage of the amount of moisture the air is capable of holding

temperature inversion—what happens when there is a layer of cold air near the ground and warm air above it

Index

MATLOCK COLLEGE LIBRARY

MATLOCK COLLEGE LIBRARY